T0319562

COMPETING
BY DESIGN

COMPETING BY DESIGN

Creating Value and Market Advantage in New Product Development

---

Craig Erhorn and
John Stark

omneo

An imprint of Oliver Wight Publications, Inc.
85 Allen Martin Drive
Essex Junction, VT 05452

Published by Oliver Wight Publications, Inc.

Oliver Wight Publications books may be purchased for educational, business, or sales promotional use. For information, please call or write: Special Sales Department, Oliver Wight Publications, Inc., 85 Allen Martin Drive, Essex Junction, VT 05452. Telephone: (800) 343-0625 or (802) 878-8161; FAX: (802) 878-3384.

Artwork prepared by Ron Trap.
Text design by Irving Perkins Associates.

Library of Congress Catalog Card Number: 93-060673

ISBN: 978-0-4711-3216-5

Printed on acid-free paper.

2   4   6   8   10   9   7   5   3   1

To those who understand the difference
between leading and managing, and choose to lead.

Contents

Introduction

During the writing of this book, we contacted an "expert" to ask for some examples to help illustrate key points. His background was in engineering and engineering management and we knew he had done significant work in areas that we were writing about. We discussed the content of *Competing by Design* and its intended audience with him. After some initial explanation, he commented, "but other people have written excellent books on reducing product development time using concurrent engineering and other techniques, aren't you just doing the same thing over again?" We explained that our approach was different, that *Competing by Design* is not a technical book and that we were not focusing solely on technology or techniques. Our focus was to be on management of the product development process in terms of the strategy of the firm and the emerging competitive environment of the 1990s. He replied, "but the other books include excellent chapters on management's perspective. Is yours a strategy book?" We replied that our intention was not to concentrate just on strategy, and that while there are some excellent books on the market that include advice for management, most have been unsuccessful in reaching the executive audience because they are perceived as technical in nature. The conversation continued for a little longer, with our friend attempting to fit us into any number of single-focus categories ranging from computer-aided engineering to strategy and techniques.

We think of our "expert" friend as a little like a blind man trying to describe an elephant. He "sees" potential product development improvements from his personal perspective, which is based on the parts he has touched (his experience and particular abilities). His engineering background predisposes him to think in terms of technology and techniques, not an integrated approach which combines strategy, techniques, and technology to gain market advantage. Technically oriented people such as our "expert" are certainly improving aspects of product development in industry through application of techniques and technology. But in most cases, their work has not been developed as part of the overall mission and strategy of their company, and it is therefore missing the major potential for breakthrough change that will be essential in the coming years.

As we will illustrate, technical improvements in product development are not always translated into significant competitive advantages. Techniques and technologies are being implemented in ways that do not add any improvement to the overall process and do not support the mission and strategy of the firm. Often, new techniques and technologies are merely implemented as a result of the engineer's tendency to experiment with them. Sometimes they buy new technologies or implement techniques because they have heard that their competitors are using them. This is like putting together pieces of a complex jigsaw puzzle without knowing what the completed picture is supposed to look like. More often than not, the puzzle doesn't get completed.

Meanwhile, competitive strategies continue to evolve. Executive management is trying to deal with global competitors who are continually driving down the time it takes to develop new products and get them to market. The quality of these products is excellent, and manufacturing costs are relatively low. Techniques and technology are only used as supports for strategy in these companies, not as the basis for competitive product development. Solutions which rely solely on technology, such as General Motors' attempt to completely automate an assembly plant, have been dismal failures. Similar applications which rely solely on technology in the engineering and R&D departments have not made any serious dent in catching up to the leading competitors.

To be fair to the engineers, the reality is that no single function in the company can provide the leadership and broad outlook necessary to meet the competitive challenges facing companies in the 1990s and beyond. Those who intend to survive and prosper will recognize that the leadership and vision must come from an active, informed, and involved executive management team which understands that the bases of competition are shifting. Quality is no longer a differentiating factor, it is the price of admission to the game. Time-to-market is increasing in importance, as are accurate assessment and satisfaction of customer needs. Product development and introduction capabilities are becoming more critical competitive factors with major impact on long-term success. World-class manufacturing is no longer sufficient to remain competitive. World-class product development is emerging as the next major competitive frontier.

A few companies we know are already engaged in world-class product development. Some of their stories are in *Competing by Design*. Unfortunately, in the vast majority of companies we visit, the departments responsible for new product development are not performing well. In fact, we think most of them are out of control. They continually spend sums that are difficult to justify based on the results they achieve, they are overstaffed for the amount of real development activity that is required, they regularly fail to take full advantage of technical advances, implementing islands of automation that ignore the potential for integration, and they do a dismal job of project management— missing deadlines with predictability. Senior management is often unhappy with their performance, but is at a loss as to how to correct the situation.

Just as there was a clear movement to world-class manufacturing in the 1980s, there is a clear direction toward world-class product development in the 1990s. World-class product development will require a basic level of technical understanding and active leadership on the part of management, much the same as world-class manufacturing initiatives such as Total Quality Management (TQM) and Just-in-Time (JIT) did. What is needed is a resource for executive management that provides the information necessary to understand how to bring the product development process under control and to use it to compete effectively. This requires an understanding of how to apply the techniques and technologies that are available, as well as a familiarity with the philosophical, organizational, and strategic changes necessary to achieve success. We hope to help establish and enhance this complex level of understanding in the following pages.

COMPETING
BY DESIGN

CHAPTER 1

Don't Worry: You're Not So Different

SETTING THE SCENE

One advantage of being a consultant is having the opportunity to work with a wide range of companies of different sizes and in different industries—some good, some not-so-good. Based on our experiences, we have concluded that "all good companies are similar but all not-so-good companies are different." This book looks at the characteristics of the best companies to help you make your company, good or not-so-good, into a better one.

In this chapter we will examine the similarities and differences among companies by looking at four different companies—a medium-sized electronics manufacturer, a large company with broad interests in mechanical and process engineering, a major automotive manufacturer, and a company in the aerospace sector.

Managers often feel that their company is unique. Because the product it makes is different from other companies' products, they feel that they cannot take advantage of improvements made in other companies. Of course the products are different, but many of the processes, systems, and techniques are the same in most companies, and perhaps most important, employees are human beings. In today's world cultural and organizational issues are as important as technological and product-specific issues.

3

As you read about the four companies highlighted in this chapter, you'll notice that although their products are different, they share many similarities. All four companies are under pressure to adapt to a fast-changing environment, all have been trying to respond to change, and all are less than happy with their results thus far. Their lack of success is provoking internal tensions, and executives are asking themselves, "What should we do next?"

These companies, like most others, are already trying to make major improvements. Many companies have a long shopping list of initiatives they wish to be implemented. These initiatives will be described in detail later in the book. They include activity-based costing (ABC), benchmarking, business-process reengineering (BPR), concurrent engineering, companywide quality control (CWQC), continuous improvement, teamwork, and Total Quality Management (TQM). There are information system (IS) initiatives such as client/server computing, computer-aided design (CAD), computer-aided design/computer-aided manufacture (CAD/CAM), computer-aided engineering (CAE), computer-aided manufacturing (CAM), computer-aided process planning (CAPP), computer-aided software engineering (CASE), computer-aided test (CAT), computer-integrated manufacturing (CIM), electronic data interchange (EDI), electronic mail, engineering data management (EDM), frameworks, object-oriented technology, simulation, and virtual reality (VR).

Some initiatives address engineering practices. They include Design for Assembly/Design for Manufacture (DFA/DFM), Early Manufacturing Involvement (EMI), Failure Modes and Effects Analysis (FMEA), Fault-Tree Analysis, Just-in-Time (JIT), Life-Cycle Design, Plan-Do-Check-Act (PDCA), Quality Function Deployment (QFD), Value Analysis (VA), and Value Engineering (VE). Some of the activities address standards and standardization. They include computer-aided acquisition and logistic support (CALS), Group Technology (GT), ISO 9001, and Standard Generalized Markup Language (SGML).

Before looking at these improvement initiatives in detail, let's look at some typical companies that are trying to implement them.

TYPICAL COMPANY SITUATIONS

Company A: A Medium-Sized Electronics Manufacturer

Company A, a medium-sized electronics manufacturer, is facing issues such as the globalization of its markets, global competition, and rapidly advancing technology. One of its major problems is how to keep its many multinational customers happy. It has had problems recently with multinational companies because it produces different-quality products in different countries. It also has had problems ensuring that the various companies and their divisions are given the correct discounts even when they order across national boundaries. The multinationals want the same product and service from Company A wherever they are operating. They also expect Company A to respond to local market conditions, which implies that Company A may have to engineer special products anywhere in the world—quite a challenge when its engineers are located on only three sites.

In the electronics sector the pace of change is rapid. Leading companies that offered five new versions of a product each year in the mid-1980s were producing ten new versions of a product each year by the end of the 1980s. Some were able to reduce the cost of a product by 30 to 50 percent over a three-year lifespan.

Motorola reduced order-to-manufactured-product time for one basic consumer electronics product from four weeks to two hours. Apple Computer reduced product development cycles from eighteen to twenty-four months in 1990 to nine months in 1993. Intel's 586, for which volume shipments began in 1993, had a four-year product-development cycle, whereas it took five years to get the 486 to market in 1990. The 586 has 3 million transistors compared to the 486's 1.2 million. Many electronics companies, such as Hewlett-Packard, now derive more than half of their revenues from products less than three years old.

In this environment, Company A's prime objectives are to increase its ability to develop new products and services and to find new ways to make and deliver them to the customer faster than competitors. Time, not cost, is becoming the key parameter. High quality is no longer optional.

The life cycle of some new electronic products, from conception to obsolescence, is already down to less than two years. As product lives continue to fall, being three months late with a product, even a product that is cheaper than the competition's, becomes disastrous. Most customers will already have bought the competitor's product, and those who have not will be waiting for the next generation of product. Similarly, producing a product that does not meet customer requirements will lead to disaster for Company A. There will be no time for trial and error; the product will have to be right the first time.

Company A has made tremendous efforts to adapt to this new environment. It has the latest computer-aided design (CAD), computer-aided engineering (CAE), and computer-aided testing (CAT) systems and has invested in new manufacturing facilities. Performance has improved, but nowhere near as much as it must if Company A is to remain competitive.

In analyzing some of its recent initiatives, the company noticed that in the 1980s and early 1990s attempts to make changes tended to be uncoordinated, project-oriented, noninterrelated, and nonsustaining. For example, one vice president would push the idea of strategic IS, while another tried to do TQM, and someone else did fuzzy logic.

These initiatives were not integrated, and in practice the resulting activities sometimes conflicted. By the time these initiatives filtered down the hierarchy to practicing engineers, they often had already been diluted, the next initiative was known to be on its way, and no one could be motivated to change their behavior.

A great deal of effort and money has been invested in the attempt to change, but the result has met no one's expectations and has left some people very unhappy. Top management has concluded that the engineering department is an unmanageable black box, a black hole that sucks up dollars that are never seen again. It now believes that engineering doesn't understand the business environment—that it lives in an ivory tower. Not only is engineering habitually late with new products, but the software that it develops to go in the products is 90 percent of the time more than three months late and always full of errors. Forty percent of engineering's efforts go into fixing the bugs.

Top management has been devastated by engineering's refusal to come out of its ivory tower and talk to people in other departments in the company. The engineering department has refused to talk to the corporate management information system (MIS) department and mocked the performance of the research department and the shop floor. The only good thing the engineers ever said about the sales people was to compliment them on the speed with which they got coffee served in customer meetings. They have had little respect for marketing since the marketing VP was seen polishing his shoes on the backs of his trouser legs when an important customer turned up unexpectedly.

At times engineering has admitted it isn't perfect. Engineering management admitted it sometimes wasted a lot of time putting too much effort into the wrong project and then not receiving the expected payback for their investment. However, engineering management believe the real problem lies with top management. Top management responsibilities change frequently. Because managers are moved around before initiatives and projects are finished, they try for easy short-term success and leave the long-term problems to the next guy. After starting something with a bang, a few months later it would disappear without even a whimper.

Engineering feels that top management is dominated by bean counters—namely, the financial controller who runs the business and puts together plans and budgets. Although he does this very well, he lives far from reality in a world of figures on paper. Engineering claims he doesn't understand the customers or the products and thinks they don't really matter: to him everything's just another financial management problem to be resolved by a spreadsheet. Top managers are generally so busy looking at these figures that they don't have time for the customers and products. Engineers claim that top managers use the wrong measurement systems to judge performance. The main indicator for engineering performance is engineering headcount and not productivity or customer satisfaction. Engineers complain they rarely are involved in decision making and, moreover, that top managers have a macho style—that they want to make all the decisions, even when they clearly are not competent to do so. They feel there's no attempt to get a consensus—that the big cheeses just lay down the rules and everyone is expected to obey.

Company B: A Large Mechanical Engineering Corporation

Company B, a large mechanical engineering corporation, operates in many countries and has found currency instability and inflation to be major problems. Many of the projects it develops take several years to implement, and only a few percentage points change each year in the value of the dollar is enough for them to lose all their expected profit. The sales VP talks fondly of being able to go into the best restaurants in Paris a few years ago and pay the same price as he would have in a restaurant back home. Now, he says, on that basis he can eat only fast food in Paris. In addition to currency problems, there's been increasing competition from Japanese companies that seem to be impervious to the rising yen and are still able to make cheaper yet higher-quality products.

Customers are increasingly looking for customized solutions to their problems that offer more function, higher precision, and more reliability, and yet are at the same time cheaper, resource-saving, and "new." Company B has to respond quicker to market needs with a greater variety of solutions. In this environment, Company B's primary objective is to increase the quality of today's products and the productivity of today's processes, while simultaneously preparing for more adaptable products and more flexible processes in the future.

By increasing quality, Company B can reduce the customer's cost of ownership, improve customer relationships, and increase profits. Increasing productivity will reduce the cost of products. Shorter development cycles resulting from increased adaptability will lead to more products getting to market faster. Without increased flexibility, Company B will not be able to produce a wider range of products in small batches. Together, the improvements in quality and productivity should lead the company to a position as a highly competitive low-cost producer. The improvements in adaptability and flexibility bring products to market faster and increase market share. With reduced costs and increased sales, profitability can rise significantly.

To meet these objectives, Company B has instituted several improvement programs. It's a world leader in CAD, especially solid modeling, and has developed some very effective interfaces to stress-analysis programs. It has connected its sites with an electronic mail system. Every engineer has a personal computer and many also have workstations. It has a highly regarded make-to-order MRP 2 system, and its flexible manufacturing system (FMS) is regularly featured in press reports and business school case studies. In recent years, Just-in-Time (JIT) techniques have been introduced in most of its plants, and cycle-time-reduction teams have been set up to bring lead times down. In the late 1980s, Company B started benchmarking its engineering performance against that of other companies. From this exercise it determined that concurrent engineering would be big in the 1990s and set up a corporate concurrent engineering program.

Despite all these improvement programs, Company B is not satisfied. The many problems it has encountered with its basic technology have not been alleviated by the availability of the electronic mail system to communicate error reports rapidly. Recently, new product introductions over a range of product areas have been delayed for apparently random and minor, but cumulatively significant, reasons. Despite vast investments in engineering and manufacturing technology, product quality is erratic, and lead times seem to remain the same. Overall, the costs associated with engineering and development rise rather than fall. Competitors don't seem to have these problems. They just go on cutting engineering labor hours and reducing design cycles. One Japanese rival slashed its time to market in a particularly competitive market segment from four years down to two.

Looking back, Company B realizes that in the 1980s its corporate focus wasn't on long-term issues like engineering and new product development. Instead, much of top management's attention was spent on attaining the right quarterly financial results. The 1980s were years of expansion, and it was easier for top management to improve quarterly results by buying companies in faraway parts of the world rather than by improving the core business.

Many of the improvement programs have developed a life of their own and instead of helping to reduce costs have only increased them. For example, the benchmarking program set up in the late 1980s followed the trend of many other companies that benchmarked their engineering performance against that of other companies. However, most of the company's effort and investment went into the benchmarking exercise itself and not into interpreting the results and finding ways to improve performance.

From its benchmarking program, Company B learned that increasing the speed of new product introduction usually requires stripping out unnecessary levels of middle management and bureaucratic control, taking a new look at the entire development-to-finished-goods process, and promoting multifunction teams. Instead of letting engineering do its job alone, then handing over the product to manufacturing, which does its job alone, and then handing the product over to sales, Company B brought individuals from marketing, design engineering, manufacturing engineering, production, and logistics into a product team with total authority for product functionality, build, and cost. This concurrent engineering concept soon ran into problems, however, because many people either didn't want to work with people from other departments or didn't know how to.

In spite of the effort that top management was putting into the improvement process, engineering managers felt that no clear direction was being set. Instead, there were countless exhortations to work harder, to schedule better, and to "do your best." One manager even spread the message that people weren't expected to work the forty hours specified in their job contracts but to do sixty hours a week. This was received badly by teams trying to reduce cycle times. They felt that wasted effort causes most problems in business processes and that if it could be removed things would get done faster and with less effort. The sixty-hour work week was seen by engineering as confirmation that top management had lost control by setting yet another unrealistic target that would distort the process. Unrealistic targets proposed by top management or the sales force gave the impression that engineering was always late, when it was actually on time according to its own target.

Far too many projects were being handled at the same time, and time was lost switching from one project to another. Top management came up with the idea of using a scheduling system on a PC to enable engineers to do more work. Engineering management explained that scheduling wasn't the problem but was forced to implement this brilliant idea from above, even while top management held up projects by forcing everyone to wait for management decisions that were made only at monthly management meetings.

Engineering management was aware that product-development performance could be better but wasn't quite sure what to do about it. It was known, for example, that 80 percent of a new product usually already existed in other products, but no one knew how to access the information or how to reuse it.

Top management was exhausted by the appalling performance of the engineering organization and its unquenchable desire for high-risk, high-development-cost projects. The culture of the engineering organization didn't seem to harmonize with that of the rest of the company. The engineers were individualistic and didn't seem to want to work with each other. They never seemed to talk to their colleagues in manufacturing. The manufacturing engineers were treated as inferior to the design engineers, and anyone in a staff position was treated with contempt. Top management tried for a long time to communicate with the engineers but gave up since the engineers never said anything in meetings. At times top management discussed outsourcing the entire new product development process and focusing on production and marketing. As far as they could see the engineers didn't even track the cost of developing a product. Invariably the first prototypes were garbage and then had to be changed at great expense. The whole process seemed a waste of time and money.

Company C: A Major Automotive Manufacturer

Company C, a major automotive manufacturer, is faced by issues such as the globalization of its markets, global competition, the quality revolution, environmental issues, and rapidly advancing technology. In the automotive sector change has been continuous since the early 1970s.

Company C once led a cozy existence and was a dominant player in the domestic market. It even had significant sales in overseas markets. Then its world seemed to collapse around it. Environmental groups and product liability attorneys were a continual menace and interfered with many new developments that would have enabled it to enter a fair fight with the competition. Competitors from newly industrialized countries appeared from nowhere to compete against its models. Customers started expecting cars to run more than a few thousand miles without a costly service visit. Although it invited all the quality gurus to visit and spread the gospel, Company C always had the impression that it trailed behind its competitors. At times, its management wondered if its competitors' television ads were more than hype. Perhaps they were really true.

The real problem, of course, was the competition. If competitors would only go away, Company C could return to producing cars the way it always had—its traditional way. But the competitors kept improving. Somehow, a team of only eighty-five people had designed Chrysler's Dodge Viper in thirty-six months instead of the traditional fifty-four months. GM's Corsa, launched in early 1993, had 30 percent fewer parts than its predecessor and cost 25 percent less to assemble. Thirty percent of Honda's 1992 Civic came from the previous model compared with traditional reuse of less than 10 percent. Another Japanese manufacturer did an entire new vehicle project for less money than it took Company C to do a midlife redesign of one of its aging models. Ford had saved millions by using a new technique called stereo lithography.

Many competitors seemed to have mastered the apparently contradictory challenge of being at the same time both a low-cost producer and a provider of high value added. Top management at Company C still could not understand how this could be done. Apparently some of these companies could even use existing manufacturing capacity for new models. They seemed to have mastered techniques for rapid development and introduction of new products and technologies with short life cycles and minimal lead times. As a result they were capable of efficient make-to-order and low-volume development and production and could apparently manufacture anywhere in the world. It was a frightening prospect.

Company C reacted to these changes with the aggressive actions to be expected from a company that had long ruled the roost. It invested heavily in robots and computers. It closed plants and squeezed its suppliers. It followed the path taken by its main competitors and ordered the introduction of Japanese techniques such as Kaizen, Poka Yoke, and Hoshin Kanri. Even so it found that it did not immediately increase market share. Soon its primary objective was to hold on to market share, to cut costs, and to improve quality.

Company C made tremendous efforts to improve engineering performance and regain its position as a world leader. It developed its own CAD system so that it could make the best designs, built its own robots to ensure the best quality, and supported all the improvement initiatives being launched.

Nevertheless, market share continued to decline. More and more problems occurred with new technology. As more and more computer systems were used in the development process, the cycle time actually became longer rather than shorter. Increasing customization of models made it more difficult to verify all the design parameters, and the only way quality could be maintained was by employing more and more inspectors at the end of the line. Many of the computer systems were incompatible, and it seemed the more advanced the functions they offered, the more unlikely they were to fit in with other systems. A lot of money was spent on developing a system to support customized styling, but because the mathematical algorithms were so obtuse, when the prototype got to the shop floor the hood wouldn't close because the system apparently hadn't accepted some data about a new, bigger engine.

Company C eventually decided to stop firefighting and instant decision making and took a look at the way it was running the new-product-development process. It found that it never really had a strategy for new product development. There had been a corporate strategy—highly paid consultants had been brought in to dream about a vision of the company ten years forward—but no one had developed an engineering strategy. All the initiatives had just happened. Managers who wanted to do something went ahead and did it. How was it that top management had not noticed what was happening? Company C came to the conclusion that in the 1980s the corporate focus wasn't on engineering but elsewhere—for example, on getting trade barriers erected and maintained, diversifying into other industry sectors, and getting JIT and MRP 2 introduced into the plants.

In the 1980s, there was publicity about major changes and progress in Company C, but much of it was generated to impress its customers. Little real progress was made, and when a particular project did succeed, the lessons that should have been learned from it often were forgotten and not institutionalized.

Few corporate managers understood the new environment for new product development. They were happy to leave the engineering function alone and let it do what it liked—provided it didn't spend lots of money. The main criticism top management had of engineering was that the products appeared to represent the engineers' dreams and not the customers' requirements. New designs were for rugged pickup trucks and gas-guzzling sports cars or luxury models, whereas most customers wanted a low-cost reliable car to get to and from work, the mall, and the football stadium.

Top management couldn't understand why engineers always started their designs with a blank sheet of paper. Couldn't they reuse existing parts or use purchased parts? Why did they always try to do it all themselves? Couldn't they try to see what customer needs really were? Couldn't they listen to the marketing specialists and use the specifications that came from the market? Couldn't they make themselves clear when they communicated with the plants? Couldn't engineering understand the difference between lowest initial cost and lowest lifetime cost? Couldn't engineering see that competitors' designs were fresher, had more variety, and were technically more sophisticated? Wasn't it obvious that it's better to take only three years on a design rather than seven years? Couldn't engineering understand that when a midlife replacement was late, customers didn't wait for it to arrive but bought a competitor's product?

Engineering management recognized it had problems, but it also knew it had a lot of solutions. Approval for the development, over the next five years, of its proposed new product realization process would guarantee quality improvement by an order of magnitude. If top management would only provide the funding for its ten-year computer-integrated engineering (CIE) project, it would be able to slash lead times. The company could always source components from competitors while waiting for these megaprojects to come on line. Joint ventures with companies in other countries would provide knowhow about the way competitors were doing things.

For engineering management, the main problem was top management's attitudes and behavior. Top management seemed to have no understanding of the underlying engineering processes and seemed to run the business on the basis of a simplistic, top-down, cost-centered view. In this picture the business runs itself, and top management fine tunes through annual "flavor of the year" adjustments. One year this would be Total Quality Management (TQM), then it would be customer focus, and then logistics management, or cycle-time reduction. They all knew that by next year it would have disappeared.

When things looked bad, top management would "downsize." Downsizing by 10 percent meant reducing headcount by 10 percent, so a certain number of people, regardless of their skills, knowledge, or their role in the engineering process, would have to go. Middle management decided who would go and who would stay, so middle management stayed and the people who were good enough to face the outside world left. Generally they were then hired back as temps to do the work while those who had stayed spent their time in endless meetings.

Company D: An Aerospace Company

Company D, an aerospace company, is faced by issues such as global competition, a rapidly increasing electronics component in its product, the end of the cold war, and the resulting peace dividend. The recent recession has had a devastating effect as the government becomes more bureaucratic and the airlines cancel orders and hold on to their old planes. The general slowdown in business has led to downsizing and corporate reorganization. The continuous demands for improved information access by the government have led to the DOD-inspired computer-aided acquisition and logistics support (CALS) initiative.

In this environment, Company D's prime short-term objective is to ensure survival over the next few years, which it expects to be very difficult. Long-term objectives are to increase its ability to develop new products and services—possibly by increased joint venturing with companies on other continents—and to find new ways to make and deliver products and services to customers faster than competitors. In the short term, cost reduction is all important, but in the long term, time, not cost, will be the key competitive parameter.

Company D has made tremendous changes. It has tried many new strategies and is torn between the benefits of focused-factory, low-cost, niche, agile, and high-velocity manufacturing. As a leading company in its sector it is generally one of the first to develop and use new techniques. It has all the latest and greatest CAD, CAE, CAM, aerodynamic, and structural analysis systems. It has invested a lot in new plants, introducing new techniques wherever possible. It has invested heavily in TQM, computer-integrated manufacturing (CIM), and time-based management.

Unfortunately, in spite of all this investment, performance has improved but nowhere near as much as expected. Competitors are known to be making much faster progress. Boeing aims to cut the production cycle of the 737 from thirteen months to six months. It's in the process of reducing the development cycle of a major 767 derivative from the traditional forty months to thirty months. On the RAH 66 project, Sikorsky is accomplishing things with computer technology that were previously impossible.

Recently, Company D has been evaluating its efforts and trying to pinpoint where it went wrong. It recognizes that in the 1980s the company focus strayed too far away from engineering. With business conditions favorable, top management attention was elsewhere—for example, on mergers and acquisitions. Without attention from top management, engineering, like other functions, felt no pressure to significantly improve performance. It overengineered many of its products. In the early 1990s, with the recession and the peace dividend, top management has been so worried about not getting enough work that there's been no time to think about productivity improvement.

In the 1980s, engineering functions in the aerospace industry were heavily influenced by computer vendors and by vendors of systems such as CAD. These systems were sold with the promise of productivity improvement, but when the bottom line showed no improvement, the feeling was that systems can't be trusted. Although system performance has increased greatly, the distrust continues.

Without an overall focus, many of the improvement programs have developed a life of their own and instead of reducing costs have only increased them. For example, too much money was spent on customizing the CAD system and developing an engineering data management

(EDM) system. Both of these programs should have been left to the vendor community. The company's mission is to develop aerospace products and services, not to develop software.

Top management is concerned that engineering still seems to be unable to agree on and keep to a plan. Invariably no sooner is a plan in place than engineering wants to change it. The different engineering departments seem unable to work together; reports from different departments are often inconsistent; and even when they address the same subject, different departments come up with different answers. There appears to be continual interdepartmental strife: instead of working together to solve problems, each has to solve problems from its own viewpoint. They don't share important data between departments (such as customer requirements and competitors) and don't share reasons for engineering choices with manufacturing engineers.

The engineering function has become extremely expensive to run and a major customer for capital investment. In view of its cost, top management is pursuing options to spin it off as a separate company or to sell it to a competitor. Any increase in its internal efficiency will have a positive effect on its chances of survival. However, much of the engineering process remains apparently uncontrollable, and engineering management is finding it difficult to achieve noticeable improvements in productivity.

Engineering managers recognize that they frequently have missed important deadlines and that some big projects have taken too long—for example, the one that came in nine years late. They realize that marketing, engineering, and manufacturing processes are changing rapidly under the influence of new techniques, and they know that management processes and organizational structures must change correspondingly. They read about other companies using new approaches to reduce product-development time, to reduce batch sizes, to increase quality, and to improve overall productivity of the workforce. When they look at the way their own company is behaving, they see nothing is likely to help the company gain or maintain a competitive advantage. They feel instinctively that they are missing out on something—but they do not know what to do about it.

Engineering managers feel that the real problems lie at the top-management level: there are too many corporate staffers in headquarters and far too many levels of middle managers, and countless horror stories highlight top management's failure to understand the specifics of the business. Although theirs is essentially a long-term business, they say that management is primarily oriented to the short-term and unable to define or stick with a long-term view. They are wary of the attempt to introduce activity-based costing, and because they can't trust top management, they say they always add 15 percent to cost estimates, so that when management makes across-the-board cuts, their programs won't suffer.

MOVING ON

Although these four companies are in very different circumstances, there is a lot of similarity among them. Companies like these are being squeezed by rapidly evolving technology, demanding customers, and aggressive competitors.

They all face several major issues—the effect of the increasing amount of electronics in products, the possibilities offered by widespread communication networks, and the rapidly decreasing cost of computer power. These imply more frequent design and volume changes, smaller volumes, and much more responsive management. Other corporate requirements will be influenced by issues such as the rapidly changing world business environment, increasing globalization and global competition, new technologies, deregulation, privatization, environmental requirements, and consumer resistance to price increases.

Reduced product development and overall product costs, reduced product development cycle times, and improving performance are impressive targets that, for the most part, can be achieved only by the engineering function.

The requirements are fairly clear, but how does a company reduce product-development lead times? How can costs be reduced while quality is increased? There already seems to be too much to do, so how can we work faster with fewer people? What options are available? How can I make it happen? What methodologies work?

The existence of successful, world-class companies shows that it is possible to make progress. Many technologies and techniques are available. Those that have succeeded in making techniques and technologies work have discovered that the best results occur when technology is used to support a more efficient process. Although there are potential pitfalls, there are also many opportunities for improvement. In the following chapters you will see how traditional product-development processes can be greatly improved, and how technology and techniques can be used to support new ways of making your company, good or not-so-good, into a better one.

CHAPTER 2

The Link to the
Business Strategy

COMPETITION IS ACCELERATING

For most companies, getting product to market on time has already become a dominant factor in determining product profitability. And ultimately, profitability (and therefore time to market) will affect company survival. The equation of profits and survival should come as no great surprise to anyone, but basing the focus of competition on time to market is relatively new and growing in importance.

Competition is increasingly global, and markets that were once "owned" by dominant firms are eroding due to increasing challenges from competitors with excellent quality and quick response times to customer demands. Quality and service have become "givens" in the global competitive arena, and time-based competition has become the new battleground. The product design process is becoming a key component of business strategy.

RESEARCH AND DEVELOPMENT IN STRATEGY

In many consumer-oriented industries, product life cycles have dropped below one year and continue to shrink. Consumer electronics producers like Sony are replacing products in less than a year to take advantage of new features and functions as soon as they are developed. Research and development is an essential part of their strategy and a primary factor in their continuing success at holding a major share of their markets.

Cannondale bicycles, a U.S.-based producer of high-end cycles, has pioneered the concept of a model year in the bicycle business, introducing new models every year and eliminating others. Customers have come to expect the introduction of enhanced features and capabilities each model year. Cannondale annually sells their entire production capacity and is expanding its market in Europe and Japan.

In the automobile business, where product development cycles are longer and model-year changes are often just enhancements to the same basic product, great strides are being made in reducing time to market for completely new models. Chrysler Corporation has showcased its new design center in television advertising, touting the new capabilities it has developed to produce exciting new models in far less time than was previously possible.

What is happening here? A shift in the competitive model is occurring, and it will accelerate as other companies recognize what is happening. The price of admission to the global manufacturing game, the baselines for competition, were defined in the 1980s as quality and service. Companies have already recognized that these are essential. Those that aim for leadership know they must go beyond these baselines, and they are competing with time-based strategies. Much has already been accomplished in the manufacturing facilities to reduce production cycle times and inventories. Now leading companies are reengineering their white-collar processes to reduce business cycle times. Some have already recognized that tremendous potential exists for reducing product-development time, thereby reducing time to market and improving the ability to respond to the "voice of the customer."

MARKETPLACE CONSIDERATIONS

One computer company executive determined that in his industry, a 50 percent overrun in the development budget for a new product decreased the product's lifetime profit contribution by 10 percent. Certainly, 10 percent of lifetime profits is a significant amount. But his research showed that a six-month *delay* in the introduction of a new product decreases product contribution 50 percent. Ten percent reduction in profit potential can be painful, but 50 percent can mean the difference between a successful product and one that puts you out of business. Here is a powerful example of the competitive potential to be exploited through time-based competition. Not only can companies be more profitable by being first to market, but the increased margin gives a firm the strength to exploit other opportunities—to take risks, make investments in technology that will enable even faster development and manufacturing times, and dedicate additional funds for research and development of more new products. But knowing this, management cannot afford to merely reduce development cycle times. Linking this capability to the direction and strategy of the business is essential. Shorter time to market is worthless if you cannot exploit this advantage to compete more effectively. Technology and improved processes are not ends in themselves. New technologies and improved business processes must be part of a solution to meet valid customer needs.

A "Technology" Lesson

One lesson that was learned during the 1980s was that investing in technology as a panacea or "magic" solution or to duplicate what others were doing (however ill-advised) often only automated and perpetuated practices that should have been eliminated. There seems to be a form of management disease that affects the judgment of otherwise level-headed executives and causes them to invest in technology "solutions" as soon as they discover that other companies are investing in the same technology. An apt acronym for this management disease is WEED, or "what everyone else is doing." These magic solutions frequently divert attention from addressing the real problems of the marketplace and often make situations worse by disrupting operations and using up funds that could be better spent elsewhere. Nowhere was this pattern more evident than in manufacturing. Real-world examples of this experience lend perspective to the picture that is taking shape.

Ice Cream

At a major U.S. ice cream producer in the mid-1980s, competition was intense, and a major rival was aggressively competing against this producer's label, making significant inroads in market share. Ownership of this company had transferred from private owners to a large food conglomerate, and there was significant pressure to maintain margins in spite of the aggressive competition. Management felt that one part of the solution to their problems would be to implement an MRP II system, as they had heard of the experiences of other companies that used this system to reduce inventories and gain better control of their production and distribution functions. Their major competitors and their corporate parent were all using this technology, so they felt they had to have it too. In truth, their inventories were not out of control, and the production and distribution systems, while not entirely modern, were sufficient. Ice cream manufacturing is relatively simple, and this company already had short production cycle times and Just-in-Time deliveries of major ingredients. Actually, they had quality and market-image problems that were the primary areas that should have been addressed in terms of responding to their competition.

Management had to do something that would demonstrate to the parent company that it was taking action to improve the competitive situation, and it accepted without question the experiences of other companies that had reduced inventory and improved customer service through MRP II. Very little effort was expended to quantify and validate the expected benefits versus the implementation costs, and even less effort was invested in looking beyond the symptoms of lost market share to find the root cause. Management believed that MRP II would improve its bottom line and without doing any in-depth analysis decided that their hodge-podge of manual and personal computer–based systems would be replaced by an integrated manufacturing control system. Computer hardware and software were purchased, and an implementation project was inaugurated. If these managers had not been afflicted by WEED, they would have discovered that such activity would not yield the level of benefits they expected from this "technology" solution.

Management, at first heavily involved in the definition of functional requirements and selection of the system, now moved on to other concerns. It assumed that once the technology had been identified and purchased, the system would eventually provide the intended benefits so management's role could be reduced. As long as the implementation appeared to be moving forward, management believed that the technology itself would reduce inventory costs and improve the company's ability to price aggressively and compete for market share. The quality and market-image problems were being addressed, but only by lower-level employees who were unable to prove that their problems merited closer attention and more resources. Management placed more importance on the system project as the biggest potential contributor to improvement. All available funds and human resources were being used to implement the system. The technology project consumed vast amounts of money for hardware, software, and consulting and delivered only a middling result. Management didn't realize until it was too late that the system would never provide the kind of results it was expecting. Unhappy with performance, the corporate parent later sold the company.

A similar situation was experienced by a technically oriented company. This firm produces highly engineered, custom-built products that are major capital expenditures for its customers. A big competitive advantage is the ability to design and manufacture in less time than other firms. The sales cycle can be quite long, and the process of designing and producing the products can take more than a year. Management is proud of the company's computer-aided design capabilities, which automated the drafting function. It spent millions of dollars and nearly two years to implement this technology. These systems allowed the firm to reduce the number of draftsmen in engineering but did little to improve the product development time through reusable designs. CAD workstations are distributed throughout the engineering department, but none are integrated with each other or into the company business systems, despite having the capability to do so.

Designs for each order are often very similar, but no provision has been made to document and catalog existing designs. These still reside in paper blueprint files. Engineering and manufacturing are adversaries, and they do not communicate well. Products are de-signed by an engineering group that is isolated from manufacturing (engineering and manufacturing are in different states). Manufacturing receives designs from engineering on paper, when engineering "releases" the product to manufacturing. Often, manufacturing returns a new product design to engineering, refusing to produce it until design changes they deem critical have been incorporated. Designs frequently reinvent products that were produced many years ago because engineers were unaware of the preexisting design and have no ability to look up older designs on their CAD systems.

Once again, management invested in technology and failed to recognize its potential to address strategic business issues. Large sums were invested in information systems and computer-aided design systems, with no attempt made to use these technologies to reduce time to market, even though time-to-market can make the difference between winning and losing a contract in this business. Integration capabilities inherent in the systems have been ignored. Management at this company has made a choice to follow rather than lead. An alternative view might hold that the choice is really due to a lack of vision and is therefore not deliberate. But the fact remains that there is tremendous competitive potential here that no one in this particular industry has yet exploited. When others in this market achieve a real advantage in time-based competition, this company will be at a distinct disadvantage.

These are only two examples of many similar situations that are occurring repeatedly across industry. Technology by itself will not deliver the needed competitive benefits if it is not linked to a strategic business objective that suggests how it should be used. Even then, technology may not be the answer. As General Motors found out in the 1980s, inappropriate use of technology can be a disadvantage. GM "went wild" in automating their Hamtramck plant in Michigan and discovered it was virtually impossible to run. Simplifying the process, as the Japanese had done, worked better. Automation should be used to support processes that can benefit from technology after they have been simplified and not simply to reduce the labor costs necessary to produce the product.

Leaders Versus Followers

The example of the firm making highly engineered custom products suggests that companies will be divided into leaders and followers. Some will consciously choose to follow; others will follow by default as a result of a lack of vision or misdirected focus. Given the emerging global economy and the increasing emphasis on time, a strategy of following the leaders is possible if it is chosen consciously. But it will get progressively harder to execute a follower strategy as the leaders compress their reaction time. Eventually, such a strategy will require more effort than the leaders are expending.

Reengineering the process of product development to support a strategy of reducing time to market will simplify designs and the manufacturing process, giving the leaders a greater measure of flexibility. This flexibility will make the company a very nimble competitor, able to change direction quickly. It will also greatly reduce the risks and costs formerly associated with a strategy of constant new product innovation. Meanwhile, the followers will have to spend more resources to be able to keep up with the leaders. If a company has built strong time-based capabilities to support a follower strategy, it could just as well aim for market leadership without incurring significantly more risk. And realistically, if a company fails to develop time-based competency, it will risk market erosion and a lower product-success rate.

INCREASING COMPETITIVE PRESSURE

Important competitive factors have changed dramatically in the latter half of the twentieth century. Traditionally, functionality and cost were keys to product success. Recently, the success factors were cost, quality, and innovation. Now, and for the near future, these factors have become the price of admission to the game. Flexibility and time to market have become the new keys to product competition. Stated in simple terms, the marketplace has become a lot more competitive. The computer industry is a good example of where this competition is taking us.

At Hewlett-Packard in the 1980s, management recognized that time to market was a growing source of competition, as progress in technology provided real gains in capability at a rapid pace. It took action that has paid off. For its personal computers and Laserjet printers, the life cycles are now down to eighteen months. When your window of opportunity is this narrow, if you are months late to market, your product may never be profitable. HP developed a concept they called "break even time" or BET. This measures the time between the start of product development until the product has shipped and enough revenue has been received to equal the funds spent to get to market. HP has begun measuring BET and has set a goal to cut it in half. They have made progress but have not yet reached the goal of reducing BET by 50 percent. But just by identifying this critical factor and measuring it, they are continuing to stay ahead of their competition. Judging by HP's dominant position in the market, the process is bearing fruit and will continue to serve them well as they move toward their goal.

HP identified key trends in its marketplace and saw what had to be done to compete. This is an important factor. HP management has taken the time to focus on events in the marketplace and what their strategy should be. Technology has been developed concurrently, and it is an integral part of the strategy. HP has recognized that it must go beyond the cost and quality factors and must compete on flexibility and time to market.

A CHANGING MARKETPLACE DEMANDS FLEXIBILITY AND SPEED

In the computer marketplace, the advent of industry standards for hardware and software has made competition even more difficult. One significant by-product of standards is that more companies can easily enter the market. The number of competitors in this industry has increased significantly over the last ten years, creating pressure to do everything as well as possible to maintain market share.

A related example of competition due to standards can be found in the recent history of the telecommunications industry. Before the government dissolved the AT&T monopoly, if you wanted a telephone, you got it from the phone company. Colors and styles were limited. You paid whatever the phone company charged, and a service man came out and wired it in place. All the equipment and wiring belonged to the phone company.

Now telephone systems are required to have a standard plug-in termination, and there are hundreds of styles of telephones that you can buy and install wherever you want them. Due to the creation of simple termination standards, a whole set of unstandardized products has been created, and a new group of businesses produces these products.

In the computer industry, open systems and standard interfaces are creating the same sort of situation. There is more opportunity to innovate and differentiate, while all are moving toward conformance to the same basic standards. This opens up opportunities for new companies to enter the market, and competition increases.

Partnering is also increasing, fostered by the growing need for innovation and the limited time available to produce new designs. As baseline standards have become more common, as in the computer and telecommunications industries, the need to cooperate with other companies that offer complementary products has grown. Partnerships between companies allow greater value and more features to be offered to customers, while allowing companies to concentrate their efforts on things they do well. This is a positive situation for everyone, and it illustrates the kinds of changes taking place in the marketplace that should be driving company strategy.

These are the market forces that are propelling time-based competition. To compete effectively, more and more companies are going to have to develop tools and techniques that allow them to innovate quickly and with flexibility. The pace of competition is accelerating, and time to market is a major factor in the equation.

MANUFACTURING AND ENGINEERING VERSUS MARKETING AND FINANCE

In this new competitive environment, manufacturing and engineering capabilities figure heavily in the formulation of business strategy. Innovation and flexibility must come from the product-development and production functions. This contrasts with traditional methods of determining strategies, which assumed that technical capabilities would be able to support business goals and that the marketplace would not be influenced by engineering and manufacturing disciplines. The traditional approach focused on how to compete in a given segment, what the company's goal should be in the segment, and what actions are necessary to achieve the goal.

The traditional process ignored the possibility that engineering and manufacturing could provide something that would influence the marketplace. Once a strategy was formulated, it was expected that engineering and manufacturing would be flexible enough to respond to the need. Marketing and finance played major roles in the analysis of the markets and the development of strategy. The abilities of engineering and manufacturing were not considered to be major inputs to the process. In fact, in many corporations today manufacturing management positions are still filled with persons who have less academic preparation than their peers in marketing and finance, reflecting top management's bias against manufacturing.

Compare this traditional method with business practices in some Asian countries, which compete based on the astute use of manufacturing excellence. The Asian producers of consumer electronics are a good example. They have reduced manufacturing times to the minimum, continuously pump out new and innovative products, and have developed the flexibility to take new concepts into production in a very short time. Manufacturing and engineering are equals with marketing and finance in the eyes of top management and considered essential to the process of developing strategy. The success of these companies speaks volumes about the effectiveness of their strategy development process and proves that significant marketplace benefits can result from improving product development and manufacturing capabilities.

Competition is increasing globally, the focus of competition is shifting, technology in and of itself has not proven to be a panacea, and new strategies are called for to cope with changing conditions. Where should a company begin to address these key developments?

STRATEGY FORMULATION

To develop a strategy that gives the appropriate emphasis to manufacturing and engineering and seeks to address the important time and flexibility issues, all of the functions of the firm must be included in the strategy development process. Those responsible for strategy development will need to take sufficient time to understand their own internal capabilities. The following points should be considered in determining or reformulating a strategy:

- What is the current position of the firm in terms of how it perceives itself: what does it do and how well does it do it?

- What factors in the marketplace will have the most effect on the firm?

- Which products earn the most revenue, by percentage contribution to overall revenue?

- Who are the main competitors, and how do they compare in terms of manufacturing capability, flexibility, and quality?

- What is the position of the firm, based on how the marketplace perceives it, in relation to the competition?

- Who are the customers, and who are the most important customers?

- What products do the most important customers buy?

- Is competition price sensitive?

- What is the firm's financial condition versus that of its competitors?

- What capabilities in engineering and manufacturing can be exploited?

- What is the current strategy of major competitors?

In the past, attempts have been made to identify strategic classifications. These were essentially of three types:

- *Leader*: A company that is constantly innovating and aims to lead the market. This requires excellent engineering and manufacturing capabilities and has traditionally been thought to require huge amounts of engineering, marketing, manufacturing, and distribution resources.

- *Follower*: A company that entered the market when the innovator moved on to newer products or when the innovator could be attacked through cost or quality advantages. This strategy assumed that the innovator would not be most cost effective, due to the supposedly huge amounts of resource required to execute the innovator strategy.

- *Opportunist*: A company that is basically a combination of the first two types, innovating on some product lines and attacking an established innovator on other lines through cost and quality advantages.

These categories are rapidly becoming obsolete. Cost, quality, and flexibility are the new price of admission to the game, and companies that are not at least on a par with their competition in these critical capabilities will probably not survive. The flexibility and process simplification required to innovate and drastically reduce time to market are significantly reducing the costs and risks previously associated with a market leader or innovator strategy. Large resource capabilities are not absolutely necessary if the process is flexible and greatly simplified (therefore less costly). If the innovator has excellent quality and low manufacturing costs, there is no advantage for another firm to try to compete on these factors. This situation actually makes obsolete the follower category and likewise the opportunist category because it depends partly on the follower category for its definition.

The shift to a new competitive model reduces the strategic categories to only two—leaders and followers. The level of flexibility and time-based capabilities will distinguish the leaders from the followers. Followers will struggle to achieve the cost and quality levels necessary to stay in the game and will survive primarily on any remaining weaknesses of the leaders, such as a lack of capacity to meet market demand.

How should companies develop strategies?

- There is a price of admission: cost, quality, and flexibility are prerequisites.

- Partnering, innovation, and time to market will be major determining factors for success.

- Engineering and manufacturing capabilities must be developed to achieve the full potential of competition on a time-to-market basis.

Since much has already been written about and accomplished in manufacturing, engineering's role deserves further illumination.

COMPETITIVE CAPABILITIES AND THE DESIGN PROCESS

Rapid response to the marketplace is becoming more important. Product development has some of the best potential to provide time advantages but has been one of the least understood areas by executives who must develop strategy. Some technology-oriented firms have begun to exploit the potential in engineering, but others are still trying to address the strategic issue of time to market with technology alone. They buy new machinery and new computers, invest in the latest fad in software, and change management styles to make decisions faster. Without an understanding of what really happens in engineering, they do not see the opportunity there.

In the United States and many other countries, the traditional method of developing new products has been linear or sequential. A concept or technology is invented, a need in the marketplace is identified, and a product is developed (not necessarily in the order listed). Prototypes are created and tested in the engineering department. Sometimes prototypes are also test marketed or reviewed by major customers. Modifications are made based on the product tests, the design is refined and finalized, and the product is turned over to manufacturing. Manufacturing has to develop the process for producing the product, and may have to buy machinery or other technology. Meanwhile, materials have to be acquired and workers have to be trained. Storage space and distribution facilities may have to be added or modified. Once the product is produced in manufacturing, it is usually tested again to make certain that it meets specifications.

Meanwhile, due to the time lag from identification of the need for the product to the actual production of the product, the customer may have changed its requirements. One of the best examples of this was during the 1970s, when U.S. automakers could not react fast enough to changing market conditions. The Arab oil embargo created a gasoline shortage that quickly caused consumers to buy small, energy-efficient cars. The automakers were building large, gas-guzzling vehicles. Due to the long design lead time required under the traditional linear process, customers moved quickly to other manufacturers that already had more fuel-efficient models. Although it is not true that the foreign car makers had anticipated this turn of events, the situation illustrates what would happen in similar circumstances if a firm was able to identify a new market need and respond to it quickly. Consumers who bought Japanese cars noticed that they were of high quality. The reputation for quality became well known among consumers, and the Japanese automakers made large gains in market share.

Today, high quality is expected by automobile consumers, and reliability ratings are published for all major models. The Japanese and other automakers are essentially equal in quality now, and the differentiation factors have moved to innovation, flexibility, and time to market. The Japanese have held on to their market share by learning how to do concurrent development: involving marketing, engineering, and manufacturing from the beginning of the process. They can create new products and deliver them faster than many of their U.S. and European competitors. Only recently have Chrysler and Ford made advances that seem to be giving U.S. automakers parity.

Another company that has spent considerable time and effort to reengineer its design process is Hewlett-Packard. Its leaders recognized the coming changes earlier than most companies, and then took action. They initiated a project to develop concurrency in their product-development processes, as part of an overall strategy to exploit time-to-market advantages. It is important to note what they did right:

- They first identified a need.

- They developed a strategy for meeting the need.

- They redesigned the process to meet the need.

- They invested in technology where it appropriately supported their new process.

In this particular case, HP analyzed and categorized over 100 different designs for reusability. They reengineered their design processes to incorporate concurrency and to increase efficiency. They trained hundreds of people at more than twenty-five locations in the United States and Europe. As part of the development of concurrent engineering processes, they established teams that included engineers and manufacturing staff. They chose design automation tools to support reusability and their redesigned engineering processes. And they built prototyping and testing capability in the *manufacturing* organization, breaking the traditional barriers that separated the design and manufacturing processes.

The result of this effort is an incomparable flexibility and time-to-market capability. Hewlett-Packard's gains in market share are well known now, and their ascendancy was under way well before IBM and Digital Equipment ran into the trouble they are experiencing. It is important to note that HP had already established itself as a quality supplier. Being the first to market with an inferior product will not win any market share. One of the ways HP helps ensure that it develops a quality product is inherent in the new concurrent design process. No longer do engineering and manufacturing departments work on producing a new product independently. This eliminates the "throw it over the wall" syndrome that was so common in the days of the sequential design process. Manufacturing and engineering work together as a team, and there are far fewer opportunities for someone to add something to the design that will cause problems further along down the process and that might make the product hard to produce. Concurrent development incorporates problem solving across functions, which greatly reduces (and usually eliminates) redesign later when the prototypes are being tested. Reliability and quality are natural by-products of the process. Manufacturability is greatly improved and is expected as a matter of course.

Up to 80 percent of the cost, quality, and manufacturing characteristics are usually solidified by the time a product design is complete. This is a commanding realization, and it confirms the potential in reengineering the design process to include active participation from every major company function. Unfortunately, most efforts at process redesign in product development have been assigned to engineers, due to a lack of understanding in the executive suite. As a result, engineers have implemented technology solutions for the most part, without the necessary link to the business strategy. In company after company, we visit the engineering department to find islands of design automation such as CAD and largely traditional sequential product development processes. The problem cannot be attacked from a single functional perspective, and we have learned that we cannot automate our way out of trouble.

A major shift in competitive strategy is occurring, and much of the competition is worldwide. Where markets have been lost, we have heard politicians try to place blame on lazy American workers and product dumping across borders. Equal access to markets is the new rallying cry. NAFTA and GATT may open doors, but equal access will not create market demand for inferior products. The ability to compete in world markets depends on the intellectual and creative abilities of leaders to innovate and the ability to get their ideas to market first. Leaders will need a strategy that considers market forces and their own strengths and one that elevates the role of engineering and manufacturing in the strategic process. Some companies have already done this. Honda used to take five years to develop a new car. Now it takes three, and that time continues to shrink. AT&T now creates a new telephone design in one year, compared to two years previously. Hewlett-Packard has cut printer development time from four and one-half years to less than two years.

Stories like these were extremely rare only a few years ago. As time goes on, those who realize this shift is occurring and implement changes in their management processes will increase their competitive advantage and make it more difficult for latecomers to catch up. The warning is clear: integrate product development into the business strategy and redesign the management process for R&D, or you risk falling far behind competitively.

CHAPTER 3

Design Interfaces with Other Company Functions

IT'S NOT JUST ENGINEERING ANYMORE

The face of competition is changing and propelling companies in new organizational and management directions. Leading companies have rethought relationships among the functions involved in new product development. Teamwork and the breaking down of functional barriers are necessary for companies to be effective in this new environment of increasing global competition and shrinking product life cycles. Functional lines are blurring, and organizations must become more process oriented to facilitate the kind of performance required by a changing competitive environment. Functions outside of engineering are becoming heavily involved in new product development, and the roles they play in supporting the product design process are important.

In the 1980s the term "world-class manufacturing" commonly described the changes being implemented in factories to meet competitive challenges from around the world. Manufacturers made great strides in reducing manufacturing cycle times, inventories, and costs, and they substantially increased quality and customer service. These components of world-class manufacturing are now considered minimum requirements for competing in the world marketplace. As more companies achieve comparable levels of performance in these areas, and the leaders continue to refine their flexibility, innovation, and time-to-market strategies, the pace of change will continue to accelerate. Clearly, if a firm is to be a leader and have a major share of markets, every company function must be world class. A look at the roles played by functional departments in product development and the requirements needed for achieving world-class status will help to identify what needs to change.

MARKETING AND SALES

Marketing plays a major role in new product development through the process of identifying customer and marketplace requirements. Its job is to know what products are selling and why. A world-class marketing function should follow trends and technological developments to better predict what enhancements and new products should be developed to meet emerging needs. Because new products usually reflect either new technology or a new market, the engineering, sales, and marketing departments have traditionally been the source for new product ideas.

At leading companies new product ideas are solicited from employees throughout the company, and customer needs are met through Quality Function Deployment (QFD). But it is still marketing's job to analyze the potential of new product ideas in most companies. It is interesting to note that this analysis excludes direct customer input in many cases. Test marketing does occur, but only selectively. This could be characterized as a traditional method of product development.

Toshiba America, the manufacturer of personal computers, has instituted a different method for determining which new products it will send to market. From 1989 through 1992, Toshiba introduced between forty and fifty new models of laptop computers. Due to their flexibility, innovation, and speed-to-market capabilities, marketing plays a different role in determining which product ideas have merit. Instead of making product go/no-go decisions based on internal analysis or limited test marketing, Toshiba quickly produces new models and enhancements based on expressed customer needs and wants. Then Toshiba lets the market itself identify which products will be successful by launching *every* product. This strategy of experimenting in the marketplace to find out whether product ideas will sell is very effective and leaves little doubt as to which products to continue to produce. It also gives immediate feedback, letting Toshiba adjust its product offerings to more closely fit what the market is responding to. As a world-class business it has high levels of part interchangeability between models, low inventory, short production cycles, and high quality. With a product development process integrated across all functions, it is flexible and quick to bring out new models. Discontinued models are not difficult to phase out, due to interchangeable parts, the short production cycle, and low inventory.

The cost of operating this way may prove to be less expensive than the methods employed by other manufacturers in the personal computer business. Most other personal computer manufacturers determine what they think will sell, produce it, and then hope that it sells well. They have less flexibility than Toshiba and have not developed the capability to quickly adjust to consumer demand. By pinning their hopes on one or two new models, these companies risk significant financial and market-share loss due to misjudged consumer needs or long development lead times.

An illustrative case is that of Next, Inc., the computer company Steve Jobs founded after exiting Apple Computer. As reported in *The New York Times,* Next used up $200 million in capital from Canon Ltd., Ross Perot, and Mr. Jobs himself only to find that the intended market for the Next computer did not materialize. The Next machine incorporated state-of-the-art technology when it was introduced, and the company itself received a significant amount of publicity in the press concerning the world-class techniques employed in producing it.

This is not at all an unusual story, and many more lesser-known companies fall into the same set of circumstances. Next tied its fortunes to a single product, which was excellent in terms of the technology incorporated. But the target market for the machine was never focused, and the company continually announced new intentions for the machine as each successive target market failed to produce success. When Next finally did hit upon a use for the machine that brought the company its first profit, the machine was already becoming obsolete.

Next had not built sufficient innovation, flexibility, and time-to-market capabilities in product development, and Mr. Jobs realized that Next was too late to capture a leadership position. So Next has sold the product design to an investor and has withdrawn from manufacturing to produce software.

In contrast, Toshiba America provides a good example of how marketing can contribute significantly in reducing time to market and in achieving success in the marketplace. By eliminating the more traditional processes that rely on internal analysis of market needs and test marketing before full-scale production of a new model or feature, it has cut months from time to market and greatly increased the chances of meeting consumer needs with one or more products before their competitors can react.

A major enabler and support for the development of the necessary flexibility and time-to-market capabilities is the information system. While systems are not the "solution," they can make a major contribution through the integration and communication of critical information throughout the enterprise.

INFORMATION TECHNOLOGY

One of the most underutilized resources available to product developers is the information systems (IS) staff. It may be dangerous to apply technology to the automation of processes that should be redesigned, but there is still substantial potential for systems to provide integration across functional boundaries and improve communication. Unfortunately, technology has more often been misdirected to piecemeal design automation. Nevertheless, some companies have demonstrated that information systems can be applied to support a teamwork approach.

At Harley-Davidson motorcycles, the information systems group has become part of the product development team and has provided technology that is helping to integrate engineering efforts and reduce design time. Once IS staff members became part of the team and gained an understanding of the process, they were able to suggest ways to improve it.

Product designers and manufacturing engineers are physically separated and located at three different geographical sites. IS provided the design teams with videoconference facilities that are used nearly every day of the week. In the past, the designers sent paper drawings and documentation to the manufacturing engineers, and manufacturing engineers reviewed and revised the design as they saw fit. Next, they sent their revision requests back to the designers. Many iterations occurred before a design went into production. Now the two groups work together as a team via video, eliminating the time-consuming paper shuffling between locations. Technology allows teams to work together, even when they are not physically located in the same facility.

Another technology solution was applied to the correction of problems reported by Harley-Davidson dealers. In the past, engineers had no efficient way to analyze warranty data to help with their analysis of technical problems and had to do significant amounts of testing to resolve reported failures. Now, engineers have been provided with easy-to-use query facilities to analyze warranty data already resident on the company database. Analysis of failure data helps them to focus quickly on likely causes of problems. The time to identify a probable cause, and the amount of testing necessary to resolve reported problems is expected to be reduced substantially, giving Harley the quick response capability necessary to maintain its customer-service level. Technology can also be used in a more strategic sense, going beyond the tactical applications that are being implemented at companies like Harley-Davidson.

At a machine tool division of a very large diversified industrial company, information technology was used to foster communication and institutionalize teamwork between engineering and manufacturing. In this particular case, the company builds large, complex computer-controlled milling machines. Each machine is built to order and, prior to creation of an integrated design environment supported by information technology, required as much as two years to design and build.

The company integrated its computer-aided design system with its manufacturing system. This technology has existed for quite some time, and it is not especially difficult to implement. What is noteworthy about this particular company is that it recognized the competitive drivers in its business (time to market) and used technology appropriately. Graphic displays are available throughout the company to enable all members of product design teams (and even production workers) to access technical data on line. Data redundancy between the CAD system and the manufacturing system has been eliminated. Essentially, all barriers between engineering and manufacturing have been eliminated. To users, there appears to be only one system that includes applications for product design, process design, scheduling, and manufacturing. Teams working on development of a product share design data and product information whether they are physically located in the same location or not. Manufacturing personnel building a machine can access drawings and process data on line, in the factory. Anyone concerned with the progress of a particular machine can access scheduling data. The integration of the entire design and manufacturing process, supported by the integrated systems, has helped the company achieve shorter time to market, lower inventory investment, lower purchased material costs, and improved quality.

Eastman Kodak has achieved similar results through integrated design and manufacturing, supported by integration of software applications. Kodak's IS department first became involved in integrated design during the creation of a disposable camera that was introduced to the market only nine months after initial concept. The product was developed on a CAD system and utilized a single integrated information system for storage of all data required by the project. Everyone involved in the design efforts for this camera used the system to design the product and manage the introduction to the market. Kodak claims 40 percent reductions in product development times through exploitation of the integration techniques employed in that first product development project.

Most companies have used information technology in other business areas, such as accounting and manufacturing, to support efficiency in their internal processes. But comparatively little has been accomplished in the product design function, in terms of use of information technology to support integrated product development. Kodak is one company that is taking a leadership position in supporting integrated development and has since built on its capabilities to quickly produce flash, underwater, and panoramic versions of the original disposable camera. The Kodak IS function has been given a major role in supporting the product innovation process. One of its main missions is to get deeply involved in the product life cycle to help reduce product development cycle time. It already is accomplishing this as it works to synchronize the flow of information between product development teams.

Application of Technology

Although technology is indispensible in speeding up manual functions and fostering team communication by providing a single point of reference, technology by itself is clearly not the answer. Information systems can be critical to making significant progress in time-to-market reduction, but they must be part of a larger strategy that seeks to simplify processes and eliminate unnecessary steps. It is interesting to note that Japanese automakers use less technology than their U.S. counterparts and have more integrated product-development processes. Until very recently, they have enjoyed a time-to-market advantage over the U.S. car companies that was measured in years, not months.

Information systems professionals must be part of the product development teams, and they must consciously avoid the temptation to use the technology resources at their disposal in ways that contribute only to their parochial interests. All too frequently, IS has undertaken large development projects that are justified on the basis of relatively minor benefits and that really serve to maintain full utilization of the information systems technical staff. One of the most common complaints about information systems departments is that the return on investment in technology is poor. To gain real advantages from information technology, the IS people need to be indoctrinated into the company strategy. Then they need to gain experience in the product development process itself, understanding problems that technology can help to solve. This is a better way to apply their talents than building applications that perpetuate obsolete ways of doing business.

Frameworks

One recent example of the potential available in information technology is the use of "frameworks." Frameworks offer all design team users a common screen interface and control the flow of the product development process on a common database. Framework software is now being offered by major players in the hardware and software industries, and framework standards are being developed by the top technology-driven companies in the United States. As is typical of integration and automation initiatives begun by engineers, frameworks do not yet incorporate links to business functions outside the product design process. A standards group known as the CAD framework initiative (CFI) has begun to define what frameworks should include and has covered all processes within the technical product development process, including overall management of the design process. What is missing is integration with the rest of the business systems of the firm. There is no reason given current technology why all the functions of the company cannot be linked and redundant data consolidated through the common interface of the framework. An example of such an effort was described in the machine tool company anecdote mentioned earlier, and companies are looking forward to standards groups and vendors eventually providing off-the-shelf technology to make more comprehensive frameworks a reality.

MANUFACTURING'S KEY ROLE

Manufacturing must be an integral part of the design process, probably more so than any other function outside of engineering. The relationships between manufacturing and engineering receive considerable coverage in other chapters, but it is useful at this point to briefly outline the relationship with engineering that is necessary for an integrated design process.

First, it is very important for design teams to understand existing and planned production technologies, and this requires a considerable amount of communication between technical people in manufacturing and engineering. Close cooperation and communication are also required for engineers to effectively design products for ease of manufacture, lowest cost, and highest quality. Engineers on the design team can provide valuable assistance to the manufacturing people to help reduce tooling costs and to add their technical expertise to the make-versus-buy decisions.

Regarding time to market, engineering and manufacturing should test new technologies together to help ensure that no redesign or major modification will be needed once the design has gone into production. There must be a point in the design process where new technologies are proven to the satisfaction of both functions, before any further development of the product can be undertaken. If this doesn't occur, it is virtually certain that unacceptable levels of design change will occur after the product is in production, and design change means delay in getting to market.

On the people side, manufacturing will need to be trained in the use of modern tools and techniques that are necessary to create new designs. If this does not occur, it is likely that the design process will revert back to the old process of performing development tasks in sequence, instead of simultaneously across functions. Manufacturing's role in the design process is to be a full partner with engineering and the other functions represented. Manufacturing people can influence the product development team with their more pragmatic viewpoint, which is something frequently lacking in engineering departments. Manufacturing's role is to challenge design decisions, to participate fully in moving the design toward maximum producibility, and to keep the cost of tooling and test equipment as low as possible. Manufacturing often does a significant amount of product-function testing before units are shipped, and it must be heavily involved in producing designs that simplify and reduce testing as much as possible. The remaining testing should be standardized, including the type of equipment used for testing. All of these actions will serve to support concurrency in product development and dramatically shorten time to market for products.

ENGINEERING'S CHANGING ROLE

Multifunction teams are an essential part of the integrated product design process. Marketing and sales, information systems, and manufacturing must be members of the design team, along with engineering. Financial and human resource functions can be included on the team too. They function to address specific issues and tasks, such as product cost estimates and employee training programs. One of the greatest challenges for the engineering organization in this new model of the design process is simply to learn how to cooperate and function as part of a team. Engineering can no longer retreat into what some pundits have termed the R&D "country club," produce a design, and release it to the rest of the company without regard for its impact. Competition, and the focus on quality, are forcing greater interdependency between company functions.

To achieve the necessary integration, there will be organizational change among all of the functions involved in product development to align people with processes, not functional departments. This will require cross-training of many people who may consider themselves specialists. Expertise in specific functions is not to be discarded, but it is also not to be hoarded. Team members with specialties and in-depth experience in particular areas are necessary for continued innovation and creativity. Without them, many product ideas would never see daylight. But in a team environment, they must make the effort to cross-train others and share their experience.

The synergistic effect of this integration and collaboration is difficult to measure but almost always results in new advances as members of the team adapt knowledge of another's specialty to their own experience. Engineers will work in close cooperation with their team members from production to test manufacturability of designs as they are created. When designs are approved by teams, tooling and manufacturing processes are tested with prototype runs on production facilities. Engineers and manufacturing staff on the team will work together during these tests, to evaluate designs and make necessary adjustments concurrently in both process and design. Management of design activity in this manner will minimize the risk of disruptive product changes after production has started.

Engineering will acquire design automation tools, learn how to use them, and integrate them into the framework of company information systems where appropriate. Rapid prototyping technology may be adopted to create solid models of new designs using stereo lithography. Although rapid prototyping speeds design work and helps to prevent costly changes to designs at later stages of development, engineering will again have to invest time and resources to learn to use the technology.

Engineers have traditionally designed with the objective of producing a required level of product functionality and features. Cost and quality were always considered but were issues revisited after achieving functionality. To support the requirements of the new model of product development, including flexibility and time to market, engineers must:

- Give cost, quality, and simplicity factors consideration equal to functionality.

- Have manufacturing process information to understand the effect of their design on process capability.

- Have cost data on purchased material, processes, and the product life cycle to develop products that meet cost and pricing needs of the market.

- Have technical data and analysis capabilities that allow them to ensure that their designs meet reliability requirements and prevent tolerance build-up that will cause changes further along in the process.

Overall, designs need to be as simple as possible. This is accomplished through modularity and use of common parts, including the reuse of existing designs where possible. It also allows for simpler tooling and production processes. Simplicity allows greater flexibility in reacting to market forces and therefore shortens time to market. But simplicity is not always easy to achieve in parallel with the technical demands for product performance, and this places considerable pressure on the engineers.

ADDRESSING PRESSURE

A major part of what must occur to support engineering's new role involves the redesign of the product development process. In the past, product development was performed primarily by engineering in a series of sequential steps. A product need was identified, and a plan for the development of products to meet the need was formulated. Engineering then began development of a product concept. Once the concept took form, a review was held to evaluate the design concept. Based on the outcome of this review, work began on development of a preliminary design. When the preliminary design was ready, another review took place to evaluate it. In all of the evaluation steps, problems that arose caused a return to the previous step to make revisions to either the concept or the preliminary design. Then another review was required before continuing the process. Once a preliminary design received approval, work began on a detailed design. Upon completion of a detailed design, engineers could then work on making models and proving the design concepts. Based on this work, further changes would be identified and incorporated into the product until the engineers were satisfied that they had met the functional requirements for the product. Now prototypes could be created and tested. Based on fabrication and testing of prototypes, additional refinements would be identified and incorporated. At some point, the engineers would determine that the design was ready for production and release drawings to manufacturing. Now tooling could be designed, production facilities readied, and material purchased. The business of producing the product could begin.

In the 1980s, companies began to automate the design activities as computer-aided design (CAD) capabilities became available. Unfortunately, the result had little effect on time to market and efficiency in the product design process. The improvements gained through CAD resulted in offsetting increases in manual efforts to translate design information into business systems. Inventory planning, manufacturing engineering, and costing functions received printouts from the CAD system and other data from engineering documentation systems, which had to be reformatted and entered into the business systems.

Later, more engineering data management systems and technology support became available, providing even greater automation of the design process. The ability to reuse existing designs stored electronically, to do modeling and simulation on line, and to produce scale or even full-size solid models directly from CAD data began to reduce engineering design time. Links between CAD, other engineering data-management systems, and the company business systems became more common, automating the manual translation effort previously required. While these advances have increased the efficiency of the product development process to new levels, the process is still too sequential and there is even more potential available. This level of automation is common today at many companies. Only leaders have taken the next step to a more integrated model of product development.

Integrated development has eliminated sequential processing wherever possible. It requires the use of multifunctional, cross-trained teams. Development and evaluation of a new product concept overlap the design activities leading to creation of prototypes. Modeling and proving of design concepts are a continuous process throughout the development time frame, as is release of parts to production. The concept of a product design being completed in engineering and released as a whole to manufacturing is obsolete. Manufacturing and others on the team participate in the development and testing of designs. Once tested and approved by the team, the design is ready for manufacture. Tooling and production facilities have been prepared as an integral part of the design process and are usually ready by the time the design is finalized. Formal design reviews are unnecessary, documentation and communication are either face to face or electronic (not paper), and manufacturing processes are defined by the time the design is completed. Pressures on engineering are actually reduced when this type of environment is achieved, as cross-functional teams shoulder more of the development responsibilities once carried solely by engineering.

Getting to an integrated environment is not necessarily easy. Change exerts great stress on any organization, and engineering will feel considerable pressure as the design process moves from a serial product development orientation to an integrated, simultaneous orientation.

Engineers will adopt the technology tools that give them the design support they need, integrate their systems into the company business systems, and work cooperatively with a design team assembled from all the company functions.

TOTAL QUALITY DESIGN

The guiding concept of integrated product development is truly quality. What has been described here could be called Total Quality Design. Total quality can be thought of as a process itself, and the result of the process is performance to the standards set by customers. Quality is defined in terms of customer expectations, and there are internal and external customers.

Internal customers are the people within the company who are the recipients of the work we perform and pass along to them in the process. An engineer delivers a design to his customers, who are the members of the product development team. All the team members uses his work product to perform their assigned functions, and their output is passed along to their customers until the product is shipped to external customers. Of course, external customers are clients of the company who buy the product.

Everyone in the company must be trained to understand total quality concepts and their role in an integrated product development process. Without a companywide understanding of Quality Function Deployment and an understanding of the objectives for an integrated product design process, employees will not be able to achieve the desired results. Employees have to be committed to the integrated design process, and this requires changes in thought, the focus of team efforts, what is managed, how incentives are used, and the culture of the firm. Top management has to establish a positive work environment, employ a participative style, encourage employee involvement, and build teams. This is not trivial stuff.

Without a quality-driven design process, product development is most often carried on in a problem-driven atmosphere where individual fiefdoms react to events. Results-at-any-cost thinking pervades the process, while waste and rework are everyday occurrences. The focus is on management of individuals, and firefighting is necessary and rewarded.

Contrast the previous all-too-familiar scenario with the following description of a total quality environment:

- Product development is customer driven and is focused on preventing problems rather than reacting to them.

- Teams are process oriented and interact with their internal customers to deliver the required results.

- Management's focus is on controlling the overall process and rewarding teamwork.

The customer-driven process helps to prevent errors and comes much closer to production of defect-free output. When problems do occur within the product development process, they are generally discovered and resolved before they can get to the next internal customer. The main benefit of customer-driven and process-oriented product development is the simplicity and efficiency that greatly reduce the time involved. Simplicity is gained through the concurrent efforts of design teams, and efficiencies are realized from the elimination of non–value-added effort such as redesign work. The result of the equation is a dramatic improvement in the elapsed time from product concept until first shipment.

Dramatic improvement is what must be achieved to beat the competition to market with products that will be successful. Moving from a traditional, sequential, or semi-automated product development process to one that is integrated and simultaneous is the type of dramatic improvement that can bring a firm into a dominant market position. Many firms have become interested in achieving world-class status, and there is much discussion and promotion of the concept of continuous improvement as a solution. Continuous improvement is not a bad method of operation, and it may have helped some companies to reach parity with their competitors in the 1980s. But in the 1990s, if companies are not already in a leadership position, continuous improvement is too incremental a technique to allow them to catch up with leading firms that have already achieved speed and flexibility. The breakthrough change to integrated product development is a necessity to achieve competitive success in the 1990s.

In one company that had been steadily losing market share, management determined that it had to take action to prevent eventual business failure. Believing that achievement of world-class manufacturing status was a possible solution, it appointed a manager to oversee corporate productivity, and he subsequently established productivity committees. The productivity committees decided that the company could not compete due to its cost structure and increased the manufacturing engineering staff. The manufacturing engineers analyzed manufacturing processes to eliminate waste and simplify operations. Workflow was redesigned, and new equipment was purchased. New systems were installed, and employees received additional training. After considerable expense and effort, the increase in productivity only kept the company from falling further behind in terms of productivity. Achievement of the kind of speed, flexibility, and cost structure exhibited by the leading competitor was elusive. The company is continuing to lose market share, and the leaders in their industry are continuing to widen the gap. Incremental improvements are not wrong in themselves, but they will not bring about improvement fast enough to win. In addition, this company focused solely on manufacturing and ignored product development and time to market, where there was a wealth of untapped potential.

External customers are demanding (and receiving from the leading companies) zero defects in supplied goods, statistical data on in-process quality, and ISO 9000 compliance. Product quality is part of the price of admission to the competitive game. A company can no longer wait to react to customer dissatisfaction; products must be designed to meet all major customer requirements and prevent dissatisfaction. Innovation and the effectiveness of the product design process in recognizing and meeting customer needs are now the values that cause the market to respond. Function, product quality, and cost are all necessary, but they no longer are factors that can influence the market in a positive direction. A total quality philosophy that incorporates all major customer requirements, coupled with dramatic improvement in the product development process, is the formula for successful competition in the 1990s. All functions of the enterprise must play a role in supporting product development in an integrated way. As time to market affects product success, so too will adoption of an integrated product development process affect company success.

CHAPTER 4

Today's Product Development Process

Many companies are finding that their product development process is too slow and expensive and does not result in products that satisfy potential customers. The main barriers to a more effective product development process are the functional islands encouraged and perpetuated by the traditional departmental organization model.

A FEW WORDS ON COMPANY STRUCTURE

Before the Industrial Revolution, most manufacturing companies were small, and craftsmen handled all the operations that took a product from concept to sale. With the Industrial Revolution and mass production came economies of scale, large companies, and specialization. Operations were divided up, and responsibility for a particular set of activities was given to a specific department. Each department was expected to be independent and focused on its own activities. In most manufacturing companies, the main departments are marketing and sales, engineering, manufacturing, field service, finance, and personnel. Each is expected to concentrate on doing its particular activity as well as possible. There are good reasons for organizing the company in departments. When each department works on a limited number of activities, it becomes very good at those activities. It can train people in the skills needed in that department and give particular individuals the time needed to learn those specific skills. With this type of company structure, however, the product gets to market late, is too expensive, and doesn't meet customer requirements.

It takes a long time for a new product to go through the marketing-engineering-manufacturing chain in a departmentally organized company. Typically, what happens first is that marketing defines the product. This doesn't take long because the people in marketing want to get the product to the market before the competitors. However, because engineering is already overburdened with too many projects, it can't start work immediately on the new product, and when it does get the time, it can't meet the requirements from marketing. When the engineers bring their suggestions to marketing, they find that marketing has also thought of some changes. The engineers see if they can develop something from the new ideas, and when they have defined the product down to the last detail, they pass it over to manufacturing. But manufacturing can't produce the product the way it has been designed and asks engineering to change it. The changes will have such an effect that the engineers decide to check with marketing. When they do, they find that marketing has realized that some additional functions are needed, and the engineers go away to see if they can develop the new idea. This process continues until the departments eventually accept that the product can be released to the market.

One reason the time to market is so long is that the departments work serially. Marketing takes two weeks to do its job, then engineering takes seven weeks, then back to marketing for one week, then on to engineering for three weeks, then on to manufacturing for two weeks, then back to engineering for two weeks, then back to marketing for one week, then on to engineering for one week, then on to manufacturing for three weeks, then back to engineering for one week, then on to manufacturing for two weeks: $2 + 7 + 1 + 3 + 2 + 2 + 1 + 1 + 3 + 1 + 2 = 25$ weeks. Marketing uses only four weeks, engineering fourteen, and manufacturing seven, yet the whole process is stretched out over twenty-five weeks.

The product is too expensive because too much time is used in the development process. In addition, with so many false starts, the objective becomes murky. If an error is found in the design, it's often not clear who is responsible for getting it out. Working serially increases costs. During the eleven weeks out of the twenty-five weeks that the product is in marketing and manufacturing, engineering isn't working on it. Assuming that the engineers aren't working on another product, what happens to their wage costs during these weeks? They are added to the product cost. The product cost (and price) is increased to include many weeks of non–value-adding engineering time. Clearly, the longer a product stays in the product development phase, the more costs it picks up.

The product often doesn't meet customer requirements because too many decisions are made inside the departments without any consideration of the customer. Errors creep in as the product description is sent to and fro between departments. Because each department uses the vocabulary best suited to its activities, it has difficulty communicating and understanding the other departments' languages, and more errors are made.

As time goes on, departments develop perverse personalities based on their activity focus. Marketing departments are well known for selling products that can't be engineered and manufactured: their job is to sell, not to get involved in engineering and manufacturing details. Engineering departments are known for working on products that interest engineers and not on products that interest customers and for developing products that can't be manufactured: their job is to be innovative and come up with new products—not to involve themselves in the details of manufacturing. The manufacturing department is full of people who are dirty and not very intelligent and who spend most of their time trying to clean up the problems caused by marketing and engineering: they've been told to produce whatever marketing has sold and engineering has dreamt up. The finance department is the enemy of the other departments because it tries to prevent them from investing in projects they deem to be essential: it has been told to minimize costs.

Entrenched attitudes like these can be found in most companies, not due to the biases of individual managers but due to the way the company is structured. When each department is expected to focus on only its own activity, it neglects overall performance. Departments have been told to focus on their specific activity and to expect that their performance will be measured only on their activity. As a result, departments don't work together and often see other departments as barriers to their success or as competitors rather than colleagues.

Adversarial relationships are encouraged by the company structure. In practice, when each department is expected to be fully responsible for its activities, engineering feels it has to design every last detail of a product before passing it on to manufacturing or risk being accused of not doing its job. Yet in many cases, manufacturing is actually better equipped at doing the job than engineering. The fine details worked out by engineering often get removed by manufacturing because they are impractical to manufacture.

Looking Up the Corporate Pyramid

Look up at the corporate pyramid from the level of the working departments in a large corporation and you see multiple layers of management—business managers, top managers, corporate managers. The distinguishing characteristic of these managers is that they add no value to the product. At the very top of the corporate pyramid are the corporate pharaohs with million-dollar salaries who spend most of their time fighting off lower-level managers who want to climb higher up the pyramid. Because they can't trust their colleagues and live in fear of an uprising, they follow the strategy of divide and rule. Playing one department off against another is a guaranteed way of maintaining power.

To create an illusion that work is being done at the top, the pharaohs usually surround themselves with a mixture of green and gray staffers. The fresh-faced, bright young greens from business school work hard, show respect, keep to the rules, and still believe that the corporation revolves around plans, procedures, meetings, and agendas. They support the pharaohs by developing concepts and strategies and leading task forces. In return, the pharaohs offer the inexperienced greens very high salaries.

A few experienced but neutered old dogs also support the pharaohs in positions of confidence. These grays have shown no wish to get to the top, but they provide the pharaohs with whatever knowledge of reality may be needed. Sometimes they are sent on plant tours to keep the pharaohs informed of events in the field and to keep plant managers on their toes. But these visits are not necessary because the printouts produced by management information systems allow corporate managers to run a global manufacturing company from their desks.

From the fiftieth floor of their downtown tower, the pharaohs look down on their city and feel good about their multimillion-dollar organization and their ascent to its heights. Yet those outside the corporate hierarchy see that this company structure has resulted in a very slow product development cycle, poor quality, and overpriced products. They are appalled by the complacency and poor performance of the pharaohs and their inability to provide vision and leadership.

What most outside observers don't realize is that the pharaohs' hands are tied. They can't provide leadership because they might have to take responsibility for something that doesn't work. They can't provide a vision of the company's future because they are overly involved with internal politics. They can't participate in the everyday operations of the company because they don't want to be identified with difficult problems. They can't visit the plants because doing so will expose their lack of familiarity with operations. They bunker down in their plush corporate quarters, spending much time with public relations advisors and crafting statements for publication such as, "Yes it was bad last year, but now we've changed so much, you wouldn't recognize us." Unable to understand the reasons for their corporation's declining market share, they blame it on unfair market practices—such as competition.

Their recipe for improving results is staggeringly simplistic: close plants, lay off workers, and sue. Closing plants and laying off workers reduces costs. Suing can result in big payoffs—and also shows that corporate management is virile and active. The main reason for the pharaohs' behavior is the corporate pyramid, and the bigger the business unit, the more difficult it is to avoid a pyramid. A business unit with 5,000 employees can't have all employees directed on a minute-by-minute basis by one person. Assuming the span of control is fifteen—that one person can supervise fifteen employees—then about 400 supervisors would be needed. Assuming that one person can supervise eight supervisors, then about fifty people would be needed to supervise the supervisors. In practice, supervisors working on different sites (or living in different countries or working on different product lines) can't be supervised by the same person, so about sixty-five people would be needed to supervise the supervisors. As you go up the hierarchy (or so the story goes), responsibility increases, and one person can no longer supervise fifteen or even eight people. The span of control decreases. Assuming that one person can supervise five of each of the people supervising eight supervisors, then about ten people would be needed to supervise the people supervising the supervisors. Again, because of geographical and functional difficulties, a few more would be needed—perhaps fourteen people would be needed to supervise the people supervising the supervisors. What about supervising these people? At this level the span of control is down to three, so we'll need five people to supervise the people supervising the people supervising the supervisors. The person at the top doesn't want as many as five direct reports, so another level is added. We'll need two people to supervise the five people supervising the people supervising the people supervising the supervisors. These two people report to the top dog. So we've already got seven levels, and we haven't even started to create levels among the 400 supervisors and the 4,500 workers. With a little imagination, it's easy to get fifteen levels in a big company.

Moreover, the people in each level of the hierarchy have more responsibility than the ones in the levels below them, so they are paid more. If the workers earn $15,000 a year, someone fifteen levels up the hierarchy should get at least $15 million a year—irrespective of whether the financial results are good or bad. If the results are good, the pharaohs should be rewarded with a little bonus—say, $5 million. Anything smaller wouldn't provide sufficient motivation.

The product development cycle is long because decisions can be taken only by people at the top of the hierarchy. A simple difference of opinion between engineering and manufacturing may pass through ten levels of decision makers before a decision is reached. At each level, time is wasted, and the message rephrased. After several weeks, the reply drips down the hierarchy, being modified at each level. There are no sideways links to handle differences of opinion between departments because if they existed the need for the hierarchy would decrease.

The result of the corporate pyramid is that the product gets to market late, is too expensive, and doesn't meet customer requirements.

The corporate pyramid wastes time, and wasted time converts into increased product cost. The corporate pyramid adds no value to the product, but the product has to absorb all overhead costs.

Another result of the corporate pyramid is that the product doesn't meet customer requirements. When the CEO—or in some cases, the CEO's wife—decides on product specifications, the product usually does not reflect the requirements of the average customer. Communications up and down the pyramid lead to errors being introduced, customer requirements getting misunderstood, and problems getting resolved slowly.

Looking Outside the Department—and the Company

Looking outside the boundaries of a department or the company is not done very often since specialized departments focus on their own activity and don't look at what other people are doing. Specialists generally look no further than the neighboring department—at the people who cause all their problems.

Department managers are continually at war with other departments and with the corporate hierarchy. In fighting this war on several fronts, they avoid trouble on the home front by ruling their own departments with an iron fist. They don't want other people looking at their department, and they don't want their people looking out, getting potentially revolutionary ideas, or getting friendly with people in other departments, which could lead to espionage and even treason.

The department manager sees no need to communicate with the outside world. Being an engineer, for example, is a pretty cerebral life, and surely once you've finished your studies, there's not much else to learn. You sit at your desk and try to invent something new on your workstation. Provided you have enough MIPs and a color screen, you're happy. There's nothing to learn from the outside world, and there's always the danger someone might steal your ideas.

Similarly, workers in manufacturing are paid to make product so it can be shipped and the customer invoiced. When you spend eight hours a day on the shop floor, there's no time for pleasure trips. The supervisors and the managers tell everyone what to do and when to do it. All they have to do is make sure the product is shipped. OK, sometimes it's shipped late, but you don't need to go wandering around the world to find that out.

The marketing people and sales people *are* outside most of the time, and they have to be restrained from overspending their budgets. If the probability of getting a sale from a visit is not very high, they shouldn't be outside. From their expense claims, the salespeople seem to arrange all their meetings in bars, and marketing must really believe there are new markets for heating equipment on Caribbean beaches.

From the point of view of departmental managers, the outside environment is irrelevant and a nuisance and should be ignored. Unfortunately, sometimes the outside world intrudes, in the form of a partner or supplier, but most companies know how to handle them: set up the contract, wait till they've invested money and started working, then go back and change the terms of the contract. It works every time. Tell them that if they don't accept the changes in the contract, you'll pull out. They don't have much choice, so they can really be ripped off. Another good technique is to take delivery from the supplier, then don't pay. Generally, suppliers don't sue because they think they might get some more business later on. Of course, if they do sue, just pay up and apologize for the mix-up with the paperwork.

Some departments have to see customers because that's where the profit comes from. They estimate the product cost, add the profit margin, and quote that price to the customer. Once the customer has signed up, the price of raw materials usually goes up, or one of the suppliers raises prices, so the price has to be increased. If the customers look for another supplier, they lose time, so if the price hike isn't too drastic, there's no problem. If they catch on to that trick, ship on time and at the quoted price, but ship faulty product. When they ask for it to be fixed, whack them with a huge service charge. There's no way they can win.

Occasionally, the regulatory authorities will check out a company. Usually everyone knows when they're coming, so there's time to prepare for their visit. A lot of inspectors will be looking for jobs in industry one day so they are not too vigilant. To think companies pay taxes for government agencies to harass them! The manufacturing industry could put the country back on its feet, but the labor laws are a disincentive to employing people, and no one can understand the environmental protection regulations. Why can't we just dump the stuff like we used to?

Another bunch of snoopers is the auditors. Each year they show up and try to stop you from running the company. It's FASB this and FASB that. Even if you watch what they allow one year, and then the next year make the same allowable adjustments—modify some transfer prices, lease some foreign assets or transfer them between countries with different tax regimes, capitalize some foreign R&D, fund the pension scheme differently—they always come back and say you can't do this or that. Why can't they let us run the business?

Another unwanted intrusion from the outside world is the annual visit from the people at the state university. Aren't education organizations too academic? Boy, the kind of things they want to talk about are out of this world. They just love talking about what's happening in far-off places about which we know little. What's the relevance of telling us what's happening thousands of miles away when we're here on their doorstep? Don't they realize you don't want to change a good business? Once it's going, you just want to keep it going on a day-to-day basis.

Another problem in the outside world is the stockholders. They're mostly investment funds these days with a short-term interest in the product. Our top management dines with them in the best New York restaurants and spins them some good lines every year, and that seems to keep them happy. Invariably, the stock rises a few points in the days after the dinner, so all the managers make some money and everyone is happy. Once or twice they've made the mistake of sending someone out to see us, but a visit to our plant washrooms is a good way to ruin a $1,000 suit.

Basically, the outside world doesn't offer much to the departmental organization. On the other hand, the internal focus has many advantages. It may lead to a bit of not-invented-here behavior now and again and may make companies a little slow at times because they have to reinvent techniques that are already used elsewhere. The government may make them pay some fines, but generally people are doing their job as well as they can and run into some regulation no one's ever heard of. The auditors may threaten to qualify the accounts, but a few consultancy contracts will put things right. Of course, the biggest nuisance is the customers, who are never happy and always want something else. Fortunately, once they are hooked, they've got to pay. Once they've paid, forget them. Most companies don't want repeat business because the customers behave even worse once they think they know you.

When the outside world looks at the departmental organization, the view is somewhat different. Regulators are about to close them down for repeated violations. Business journals mock them, and education organizations treat them as case studies of dinosaurs unable to change and succeed in a new business environment. Customers dislike them, don't make repeat purchases, and switch to competitors. Suppliers don't like their bullying techniques and eventually get even.

Departmental organizations weren't meant to be like this. Departments were supposed to focus on and excel at their own activities. In theory, excellent marketing, engineering, and manufacturing departments should make an excellent company. In practice, however, departmental organizations seem to focus on fighting each other and on internal squabbles. They don't realize that the world is changing and they have to change with it if they want to survive.

The Inhabitants of the Departments

Within the departments are the workers, and from their behavior it seems they are not happy.

On the shop floor, when the whistle blows, it's tools down and get out as quickly as possible. If a part is being worked on, it waits until tomorrow. In most cases, a watchful eye on the clock ensures that no work is done for several minutes before the whistle blows, so it's easier to pick up your things and get out.

In the engineering department, there are no physical parts or products to be seen because work is done on the computer screen or on pieces of paper. Most workstations have a clock function, so as the time comes to go home, it's easy to put away the job in hand and bring up some obtuse model that looks good on the screen. If anyone asks, "I was thinking about reusing part of this design"; they can't get you on that. Once the big hand gets up to the line penciled on the screen, it only takes a second to switch off the machine and walk out the door. That way no one can hit you with the old joke about "anyone sitting at their desk after five o'clock will be assumed to be dead."

Marketing and sales people behave much more responsibly than those in engineering and manufacturing—when they are in the office. They stay late working on new strategies and plans until the boss goes home. Their behavior is slightly different when they are not in the office. Marketing professionals have to travel first class because that is where they may meet top managers of other corporations who may want to discuss business opportunities—for the company or for themselves. When salespeople are on the road, they will stop working at 3:30 P.M. Have you ever fixed a meeting with a salesperson after 4:00 P.M.? So they head for the bar and then off to a top-class restaurant with a "prospective customer"—probably of the opposite sex.

Back on site, the finance department has to process all the expense claims from "the people who bring in the money." They don't appreciate the way money is being wasted (because they don't have these opportunities) and daily invent new rules and regulations: "Your frequent flyer miles must be credited to the company"; "Your hotel booking must be made by the corporate travel department and must be for a single room at the corporate rate"; "Hotel courtesy buses must be used at the airport. Claims for taxis and rental cars to the hotel will not be accepted"; "You must fly coach unless you are traveling with a customer or with a corporate manager or this is the last flight of the day and all coach seats are taken, and the difference between the coach and first-class fares is less than a single room at corporate rate in the nearest hotel and a continental breakfast and taxi if the hotel courtesy bus service is not operational due to the late hour, or if fog prevents travel by an alternative route."

Of course, we shouldn't forget the people in the administration department. Everybody forgets them, and they don't like it, so if you call them urgently needing important information to close a deal with a customer, the phone will ring ten times before a voice mail message comes on: "Hi. This is the administration department. I'm here today but just had to step away from my desk. I'll be back in a few minutes. If you'll just leave your name after the beep, the time you called, a number I can reach you at, and the subject of your call, I'll get back to you just as soon as I get back to my desk." As soon as you hear the beep, another voice says, "You have five seconds to leave your message." Before you can say anything, the line goes dead. You decide to call back and leave your name and number. After ringing fifteen times, the voice mail message comes on again, "Hi. This is the administration department. . . ." Then another voice says, "We're sorry, but the mailbox is full. Please call back later." What can you say to your customer now?

The result of the behavior of the people working in these departments is that the product gets to market late, is too expensive, and doesn't meet customer requirements.

The shop floor workers are hired to do y hours work at \$$x$ per hour. They do it, but they won't do a minute more unless they are paid for it. Pay them overtime and they'll be happy to work more hours.

In engineering the hourly paid workers have the same attitude. Why should they stay and work for nothing when they could be enjoying themselves at home?

Engineering and marketing managers receive a fixed salary and won't get paid for overtime. They look for other benefits—travel to a conference in Florida, talk to a customer in Thailand, have a corporate meeting in Paris, with lunch and dinner in the best restaurants. Take a little vacation at the same time. Drive all the way so you can take someone along without having to pay for a plane ticket.

This may not seem very responsible behavior, but workers only work to get money. It's not like it was their company. Management runs the company, thinks it's pretty good, and makes whatever decisions it likes. The workers just do what they're told to do. Workers are not expected to be interested in the job. You can't trust them. They just milk the system, leave decisions for managers, work on their hobbies, and joke about poor performance.

Once they join the company, they're doing a life sentence. They're a cog in the system for life—perhaps doing the same thing for the next forty years. They fit into those low-level boxes on the organization chart devised by top management and are not trained to do anything else. They are hired to do a job, and they do the job. They don't learn how to do it better or how to do other tasks. They don't want to do another job.

Can you see someone in marketing doing detailed engineering work or getting dirty on the shop floor? No one in engineering would want to exist in dreamland like those guys in marketing.

From the department's point of view it doesn't matter if workers are overspecialized and waste their skills doing a job that doesn't need them. The whole idea of the departmental organization is to put workers in a specialty department, tell them what to do, and then let them get on with it. Working procedures are defined by corporate staff or by management. They may be overspecified, but they need to be. Some workers are not too bright.

The departmental organization wasn't intended to be like this. Departments were supposed to train their staffs to become excellent in their sphere—so that excellent marketing, engineering, and manufacturing departments could make an excellent company.

FOCUS

Is this really how it is? This isn't what we were taught at business school.

Is engineering really so focused on itself that it doesn't listen to what marketing is saying about the type of products that are needed? Does manufacturing really run around in circles turning out low-quality product just to meet the shipping date? Does sales really propose products to customers without checking first to see if they can be engineered and manufactured? Does marketing dream up new product ranges without checking on whether the company has the facilities to make them? Would finance really stop a department from investing in an important project? Does corporate management really spend all its time on internal dogfights?

Aren't corporate managers really inspirational leaders? Aren't engineers really great innovators? Doesn't marketing do a great job identifying future product lines?

People generally fulfill the expectations of those around them. Corporate managers are handsomely rewarded if they produce good financial results. Should they work on the figures or on a product being manufactured in a plant hundreds of miles away? At least they can influence what happens with the figures, whereas the plant is a law unto itself.

The salespeople have been set a quota, so they'll sell anything to reach it and get their bonus. Why should they turn away from a sale because the guys in engineering might not be able to design it? All they ever hear from engineering is how brilliant the engineers are, what great products are engineered, and how incapable the salesforce is of selling them. OK, thinks the sales rep; let's see what they can do with this one.

Why should engineering start thinking about anything other than designing new products? Why should manufacturing get involved in designing products and be held responsible for not shipping on time? Why should workers start working overtime for free? Why should those who manage to get outside the company walls stop trying to squeeze an extra buck here and there? Or why should those up the hierarchy cut their own salaries or stop scrambling to get up to the top or stop repulsing those underneath them?

They are all doing their job, just like the theory taught in business school says they should. The only problem is that in practice the theory taught at BS doesn't work out: it's BS.

In practice, the departmental organization translates to defending what you've got and trying to grab a bigger slice from others. It's just like the Wild West: you stake out your territory (corporate, department, or personal) and draw the boundaries. You gain control of your territory, fight off the neighbors, start expanding an empire, put down anyone who tries to rise too far up the pyramid, and when you're strong enough, you try to grab some more and repeat the process.

You try to move up the departmental hierarchy. The pharaohs are at the top, and the departmental managers are at the bottom. Among the departments, finance is top because it controls the money, then marketing and sales because they bring in the money, then manufacturing because if it doesn't ship on time the customer might not hand over the money, then engineering (of little importance because it deals with future products, and we're only interested in money today), field service (of little importance because it's physically too far from where the corporate game is being played), and finally personnel.

Once you've got to the top of the departmental hierarchy, you can move on to the next ladder—owners, directors, pharaohs, workers. Here it's a different game: you have to try to grab as much stock as possible, so that you get to be an owner. A management buyout is one strategy, but before doing it, you have to drive your stock down with poor results and then ask for options linked to apparently impossible financial targets. Once you've got them, you get performance moving again. As you get near the peak, you sell out. You let the stock drop, maybe to 30 percent of its peak, and ask for more options. While the stock's low, you buy back what you sold. Because the price is low, you get three times the number of shares you had before. Before long you advance to be an owner.

You can also become an outside director at another corporation. Then you invite someone from the other corporation to become an outside director for your corporation. Each of you gets on the compensation committee—and away you go. You support every raise asked for and then claim you deserve the same thing. Unbeatable.

The result of such a highly motivated departmental organization is an expensive product, a poor response to market, and poor product quality.

But who cares? Everyone in the organization is doing a great job and having a great time, so why worry? If things go really badly, the banks or even the government will pick up the bill.

MEASURING PERFORMANCE

The beauty of the departmental organization is that individuals can applaud themselves for doing a great job, even if useless garbage is being turned out. The marketing department measures its performance on the number of proposals it makes, so if it looks as if it might not reach target, it makes some more proposals—and *voilà*, it is on target. Some of the proposals might be for products the company can't produce at a profit, but the important thing is that the proposals are made and counted.

Engineers measure their performance by the number of engineering drawings they produce or the number of designs passed to manufacturing. If it seems that they will miss their target, they pass designs to

manufacturing without checking them. The designs will fail in manufacturing and come back to engineering for correction, but the score
won't be reduced, so it will still look as if the work has been done.

A manufacturing target might be to increase the number of times a
machine can be used without changing the operating parameters. To
meet the target scheduled maintenance checks will be missed or parameters won't be adjusted when some slightly different parts are to be
produced, with the result that slightly defective parts are produced.
Since no one's counting the breakdown rate of the machine or the
number of imperfect parts, it looks as if they are doing a great job.

So each department is doing a great job—but the customer received
the product late, paid more for it than expected, and found it stopped
working after two months. The product was late because the engineers
rushed the drawings up to manufacturing because they had to meet
their target and then manufacturing tried to produce an impossible
design. The product was much more expensive than expected because
marketing rushed the proposal to boost their number of proposals and
hadn't looked too closely at the costing. It turned out to be much more
expensive than expected to produce the product, and although the
company had taken a loss, the customer also paid more than expected
and wouldn't be making repeat purchases. The product failed after two
months because it contained a slightly imperfect part. It had been
obvious to the machinist that the part was going to be borderline, but
he had been told to produce as many parts as possible without changing
the set-up, and he did what he was told.

In a departmental organization, performance measures are at the
department level and carried out by the departments themselves. The
departments do different tasks that cannot be measured on a single
scale: comparing drawings and parts would be like comparing apples
and oranges. No department would want outsiders coming in and
taking the measures, so they create their own scales and then measure
their own performance. Not surprisingly, they find they are doing
well.

Marketing people measure the number of proposals because they
know from past experience that there is a positive relationship between
number of proposals and annual revenues. Engineers measure number
of engineering drawings because they know that the amount of engi-

neering work and the number of engineering drawings are related. They even apply coefficients based on the size of the drawing: a large drawing takes longer to produce than a small one, so it counts as two small ones. Manufacturing measures number of times a machine is used without modifying the set-up because it knows that long set-up times reduce the number of parts a machine will produce.

In practice, these measures make little sense when applied out of context. On average, given revenues probably result from a certain volume of proposals, but the opposite can't be expected to be true under all circumstances. Producing proposals won't create the revenues. On average, a given amount of engineering work probably produces a certain volume of engineering drawings, but the opposite can't be expected. Producing drawings doesn't result in salable products. A machine that is being set up is not producing parts, but it doesn't follow that avoiding set-ups makes sense.

The departmental company structure encourages departments to set internal performance measures that have no relationship to the real world and can easily be manipulated. They are not alone in doing this, since all the way up the corporate pyramid the same approach is taken. At the highest levels, the rewards for hitting the target are counted in millions of dollars, so why would anyone set himself or herself a difficult target? In this self-justifying environment, can any improvement be expected?

TRYING TO IMPROVE PERFORMANCE

It's difficult to improve performance in the departmental organization. The departments are presumed to be excellent at doing a limited number of activities. They are doing things the way they've always done them. If things were good enough for their predecessors, who started the company, there can't be any reason to change them. If they are excellent, how can they improve?

It would be wrong to say that departmental managers are complacent. Surveys show that some managers are aware that all is not well and that they should try to improve performance. Typical figures show that 65 percent of departmental managers consider their department's performance as above average, 30 percent admit to being only average, and as many as 5 percent consider they are below average.

When performance improvements are called for, they are implemented on a departmental basis. In the marketing department, bigger databases and more powerful computers are brought in to provide better segmentation of customer profiles. In the engineering department, old-generation CAD systems are replaced by the latest technology. The manufacturing department upgrades the controllers on its Numerically Controlled (NC) machines, and more modules are bought for the material requirements planning (MRP) system, which is moved off the old mainframe computer to a powerful new client/server environment.

Each department is responsible for its own performance, so it does what it can to improve itself. There would be no point in trying to improve performance in another department: people there don't want your advice, and you wouldn't be rewarded for it, anyway. Each department's "piecemeal implementation" must not affect the other departments, must involve computers because they improve everything, and must be a megaproject, a huge project that by its magnitude alone will attract management attention and demonstrate the quality of the department.

The result of the improvement project is generally invisible. The company continues to produce products that are late to market, overpriced, and of poor quality.

Even if marketing could identify exactly which potential customers were going to buy which products on a given day, it wouldn't make much difference. By the time that engineering has deformed the product specifications and manufacturing has made whatever adjustments it deems necessary, the potential customer will already have bought the competitor's product.

Even if engineering buys the most modern CAD technology, it's not going to make much difference. Designing products that customers don't want with a modern CAD system isn't any better than designing products that customers don't want with an old CAD system. More unwanted designs will be produced, creating even more pressure on manufacturing and distorting the production plans.

Manufacturing's new MRP system would probably be able to handle all the new designs, if only someone knew how it worked with the engineering department's new CAD system. It was probably needed because the only person who understood how the previous system worked had been laid off. Why hadn't engineering announced they were going to buy a new CAD system? Those engineers are so secretive and superior, and yet they're always screwing things up. We try to improve performance, and they stop us.

During piecemeal implementation, the departments see no reason to involve people from other departments because no one else understands their activities. Departments are unlikely to question their usual techniques, even if these have not changed for fifty years.

Activities involving more than one department are not considered candidates for improvement because it would be impossible for all participants to reach an agreement. So activities like engineering change—which in some companies involve sixteen departments, more than fifty documents, and many months' work—are not considered candidates for improvement.

Computer Systems

Departmental organizations have taken two approaches to the use of computers: having each department be responsible for its own computers or creating a new department that specializes in computers.

Many companies have allowed departments to choose the computer systems most appropriate to their needs, but unfortunately, the system one department chooses may not be compatible with that chosen by other departments. This is known as the productivity paradox: a great deal of money is spent on computers to increase productivity, but the result is that there is little, or no, productivity increase. The company continues to produce products that are late to market, overpriced, and of poor quality.

In theory, each department's investment plan shows where the money will be spent and where the resulting benefits will occur. When the money is spent, and the benefits don't occur, what happens in practice is generally somthing like the following.

Marketing buys a PC that runs a new application software, and marketing specialists develop the specifications for a new product and try to pass them to engineering. When it can't transfer all the information to engineering's CAD system, the files have to be modified, and some information is sent on a disk and some on paper. This takes time, and errors are introduced during data manipulation.

The engineers are probably using CAD systems from different vendors because different systems have different functions and are applicable to particular tasks. Also, some customers may demand that their suppliers use a particular system. The information from marketing is transferred to one of the CAD systems, and as the data are being keyed in off paper, more mistakes are made. The data are then transferred to the other CAD system, and because this uses a different mathematical representation for part geometry, additional errors are introduced. The company's main supplier uses a CAD system from another vendor, so once initial design work has been done, paper drawings are made and mailed to the supplier. Engineering also wants to transfer some information to manufacturing, which uses computer systems from yet other vendors, so engineering has to send paper lists. By now marketing has made a slight modification to the original specification, and this also has to go through the above chain.

Engineering now receives an apparently firm order for the new product from the sales force. The salespeople have been equipped with laptop PCs to take with them on client calls, but they are oriented to sales applications, not engineering applications, so the sales force usually prints out data to fax back to the main site. Engineering gets the fax, scans it into the CAD system, and creates a parts list. This is printed out on paper, transferred to the purchasing department, and put in another computer. The next activity hasn't been computerized yet, so the results are printed out, . . .

Only in some organizations, however, is each department responsible for its own computers. Many companies took what they saw as the logical step of creating an information systems department, reasoning that if a marketing department looks after marketing, an engineering department looks after engineering, and a manufacturing department looks after manufacturing, then they should have an information systems department look after information systems.

As we've seen, though, the departmental approach generally slows down the product development process, creates quality problems, and increases product costs—and the same effects can be seen in the IS department.

It can take a long time for the IS department to produce the applications the rest of the company needs, leading users of the computer systems to complain about the service they get from the IS department. The IS department also can be an incredibly expensive overhead. Customers of an IS department—referred to as "end-users"—can be made to wait, can be overcharged, and can be given poor service. Once again, the theory of the specialized department's doing a great job focusing on its own activities doesn't work out.

Added to the usual problems of specialized departments is the pecking-order hierarchy among the departments: finance is top because it controls the money, then sales because it brings in the money, then manufacturing because if they don't ship on time the customer might not hand over the money, then engineering, field service, and personnel.

In many companies, the information systems department reports directly to the finance department—at the top of the hierarchy—and works on producing results for the finance department and for people higher up the hierarchy. Its performance is measured by these people, so it works hard to support them. There is no reason to work with people down at the bottom of the hierarchy—like engineers and field service representatives.

When departments choose the computer systems they believe to be most appropriate to their needs, they may not choose a system that is compatible with those in other departments. The result is that a great deal of money is spent on computers to increase productivity yet little, or no, productivity increases are seen.

The result is that time is wasted as information is transferred between computers, converted, printed, reinput, waited for, and now and again used. Errors are introduced each time data are converted and transferred from one system to the next. The activity is needlessly costly. There is great duplication of resources—both in computers and in human activity. It's often difficult to transfer information from one computer to another. It can be physically difficult to transfer information between two computers, and even more difficult to get programs in different computers to communicate. The company continues to produce products that are late to market, overpriced, and of poor quality.

Information

For most of the product development process, information is all that people can work with since the product doesn't physically exist. Yet information is not valued and managed the way other company assets are. In most companies, there is no high-level manager responsible for the information describing the product and the processes that are used to develop, manufacture, and support it.

Some of the information is under the control of the Engineering Document Control Function—a department often located in a basement doing painstaking work of vital importance and yet enjoying relatively low status in the organization.

The rest of the information is theoretically under the control of the people who use it or maybe the people who create it: it's not always clear. The ownership of and procedures for handling each piece of information are difficult to resolve, and as a result, people do their own thing. Those who are to be held responsible for a task using certain information wants to feel that the information is under their control. As most information is used by people in several departments, it is controlled by several people—each of whom invents rules on how the information is managed, structured, stored, and used.

Marketing writes specifications for engineering and believes it is responsible for them, but engineering can't use them in the form it gets them from marketing so converts them to something else. Marketing certainly can't be held responsible for modifications made in another department. Sometimes engineering doesn't understand exactly what is required, takes a best guess, and then finds that it has to modify its guess because marketing wants to modify the original specification. Making interpretations of interpretations really gets difficult.

In the departmental organization, everyone is responsible for their own work, which means that each department structures information the way that is most suitable for its own needs, uses the terminology that is most appropriate for its discipline, stores information on the medium that it finds to be most effective, and defines the information elements as a function of its own needs. This helps the department work effectively for its own needs but creates problems when the information is transferred to another department.

Eventually manufacturing gets to build to the specifications given by engineering—but engineering doesn't repeat things that are obvious or include information for which it is not responsible. When a change is made to one of these details, the fun begins. The original specification isn't known to manufacturing, so it can't know about the change. It produces to the original specification and then is asked why it hasn't produced the required product.

Field service representatives often work with many different versions of a product, and the product structures they use are different from those used in engineering and manufacturing. Out on a customer site they may have to change a small part in an assembly but may find no detail on the components in the documentation because the part was purchased and not built in-house. The customer is unlikely to be happy if a major assembly is changed when only a small part is defective. The field service rep will probably only change the part but keep his own documentation on the assembly structures. Isn't that the job of the engineers, and shouldn't they at least get a copy of the documentation?

The result of the departmental approach to using and managing information is a product development process that is slow and expensive and riddled with errors. All along the process, people's time is wasted, unnecessary overhead cost is added, and a lot of non–value-adding translation of information occurs. Problems occur as paper is shuffled from one desk to another and from one department to another. On the shop floor, the result is expensive rework and scrap as the wrong parts are produced. Any transfer of information to a customer is unimaginable: who knows what might happen?

The departmental approach leads to time being wasted as information is converted and transferred. Access to information is slow, and there is always the chance that data will be lost. Copies of the same information differ, and time is lost in discussions trying to reconcile differences. When time is lost with information problems, projects overrun. People can't find existing information, so there is little reuse of information. Instead, money and time are wasted as people continually reinvent the wheel. As the departments use different formats and structures of information, it is often simplest for them to put the information on paper before transferring it to another department. Once on paper it can be destroyed, lost, or mislaid.

CHAPTER 5

The Future Product Development Process

SO WHAT'S NEW?

The product development process has changed little over the last few decades, but the forces of change are building. Product development organizations are under intense cost, quality, and time-to-market pressure as they are squeezed by rapidly advancing technology, demanding customers, and aggressive competitors.

Product development organizations face an increasingly competitive business environment characterized by rapid change, deregulation, privatization, environmental pressures, globalization, and fierce global competition as new players from Asia and the former Soviet bloc enter the marketplace.

Among the key technological forces at play are the steadily increasing electronics component of many products, the possibilities offered by widespread communication networks, and the rapidly decreasing cost of computer power. Many companies that previously have been involved primarily with mechanical engineering will find that their competitive advantage will have to be derived from electronics and software. Advances in communications will allow services to be provided in new ways, and the availability of computers at prices twenty or thirty times lower than in the early 1990s will open up new applications. See Figure 5.1.

FIGURE 5.1. The Effect of Technology

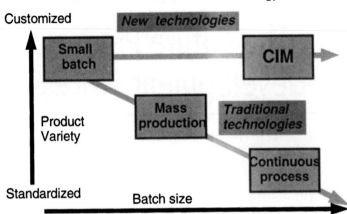

Customers will demand better products, a wider choice of products, and excellent service throughout the lifetime of the product. Their demands imply more designs, better designs, frequent design changes, and smaller batches.

Customers will expect defect-free products. By the end of the 1990s, some manufacturers will be able to guarantee product quality. Competitors who are unable to offer similar performance will go out of business as customers avoid their products.

The cost cutting that started in the 1990s will continue as companies are forced to bring their costs down so that they are in line with those of international competitors and as customers refuse to pay the price of ineffective product development processes. A major task for corporate management in the 1990s will be to cut costs wherever it is not obvious that the costs are balanced by added value. On average, companies will be looking to cut product costs and product development costs by 10 percent each year.

Product development cycles will drop on average, in the 1990s, by a factor of 5. The exact factor will depend on the industry sector and the type of product. In some cases, cycle times may be reduced by only 50 percent; in other cases, the reduction may be by a factor of 10.

Responding to customers' requirements and competitive pressures, companies will decrease product development costs and overall product costs, reduce product development cycle time, and improve quality.

This will have a major effect on business. Corporations will be forced to organize themselves so that high-quality products can be developed quickly in response to customer requirements.

The targets—reduced costs and cycle time and increased quality—can be achieved only by that part of the organization that is responsible for the product development process. In the past, the responsibility for this activity has not been assigned to a specific organizational entity but, instead, has been split between several functional groups. In the future, organizational structures will ensure that responsibility for the product development process is given to a more clearly defined and focused organizational entity.

BUSINESS UNIT STRUCTURE

To reduce costs and cycle time and improve quality, corporations need to implement organizational structures based on small, independent product-line-oriented business units (BU).

Many companies are already taking this approach. Timex now has separate business units for sport, fashion, and core Timex watches and developed a new line of watches in six months instead of twenty-four months. Black & Decker Household Products Group restructured into four self-contained business units to address major product categories. IBM's PC company has restructured into five product-focused organizations—ValuePoints, PS/1, PS/2, portable products, and Ambra.

Whereas BUs in the early 1990s were usually functional organizations departmentalized by specialization—such as marketing, engineering, and manufacturing—the future business unit will be organized by product family team.

Chrysler already has implemented a similar approach. Its platform concept brings together designers, engineers, and buyers from the beginning of a new project. Chrysler engineering is divided into platform teams—large trucks, small automobiles, minivans, and trucks and Jeeps.

Under the new organization, each BU will be made up of a lean BU staff unit and one or more product family teams, each of which will be focused on a particular product family. The organization has to be like this to get the appropriate focus on the customer.

Each product family team will be relatively independent and will focus on its customers and its product family. It will have responsibility for the complete life cycle of its products from concept to obsolescence. Product family teams will be multifunctional. Their members will have marketing, design engineering, software engineering, sales, service, finance, purchasing, quality assurance, human resource, and shop floor skills, knowledge, and experience. All the resources required throughout the life cycle will be dedicated to achieving the cost, quality, and time-to-market objectives of the product family. The product family team leader will be responsible for everything to do with the product family and have profit and loss responsibility.

Product family teams will be self-sufficient and contain all necessary expertise. These requirements will help determine their size, but corporate, geographical and business unit considerations will also be a major influence. Due to the need to be near customers and make use of the skills of engineers resident throughout the world, many product family teams will be distributed across several geographical locations. In most industries, BUs will not exceed 2,000 people, with product family team sizes of 50 to 500 people.

The BU and the product family team will have to master performance along five dimensions. Traditionally, organizations have targeted and measured performance by restricting themselves to one-dimensional targets—sales in a region or headcount in a functional department. Product family teams will target five dimensions:

- Product performance (as measured by customer satisfaction),

- Process performance (measured by cycle time),

- Regional performance (measured by sales in each country),

- Functional performance (measured by rework), and

- Cultural performance (measured by team and individual behavior).

In each dimension, a group of targets, often related to cost, quality, and cycle time, will be set.

Each product family team will be charged with getting the next few generations of its products to market in the next few years. It will need to develop a long-term product plan and decide when it should introduce new and upgraded products and when it should withdraw products.

Each team will be responsible for its business processes and for meeting continuous improvement targets. At one end of the business process is the customer (and advanced technology and innovation); at the other end is use of the product and eventual obsolescence and recycling. For environmental reasons, the product family team will have to take increasing account at the development stage of environment-friendly manufacture, use, and disposal of the product.

Product development process steps will include:

- Defining customer and performance requirements,

- Planning the position and evolution of the product within its family,

- Planning for the life cycle of the product,

- Concurrently designing the product and the processes to manufacture, support, and recycle it, and

- Production of the product.

The team will be responsible for implementing and adhering to best practices. As the product development process becomes more rigorous, team members will be expected to follow the rules and processes that have been developed. The best available techniques (such as QFD) and tools (such as CAE) will be used, where appropriate, and systematically incorporated into the process.

Within each product family team, the major engineering effort will occur at the very beginning of the product development process— close to customers and at the system level. Many detailed and downstream engineering activities will be outsourced. Quality has to be designed into a product as a prerequisite for effective manufacturing. It cannot be achieved by shop floor testing or by applying pressure on suppliers to reduce the cost of their parts. See Figure 5.2.

FIGURE 5.2.   From Invention to the Customers—a Taguchi View

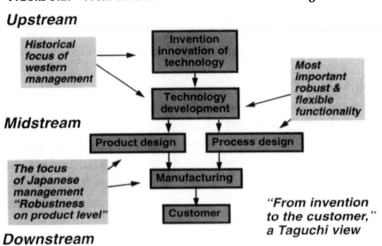

The BU staff will develop strategic plans and tactical objectives to support the overall goals of the corporation. It will work with product family team leaders to develop product family team objectives and to initiate, monitor, and support cross–product family team initiatives associated with product quality and introduction frequency, process improvement, resource development and utilization, and financing. A key role for the BU staff will be to analyze the workings of the BU and identify better ways of organizing activities. Non–value-added activities will be removed or outsourced.

To maintain functional skills, BU staff members will be given responsibility for particular areas. For example, the BU staff member given the responsibility for engineering skills would understand the corporate objectives and the way that engineering is carried out in the BU. This person would have many responsibilities, including

- Ensuring engineering process consistency throughout product family teams,

- Helping to identify and develop engineering talent,

- Creating ways to make best use of scarce, geographically distributed, engineering resources,

- Helping identify and cross-pollinate leading-edge knowledge and practices, and

- Assisting in identifying and developing new technologies, techniques, and markets.

Looking Up

Corporations will be made up of a lean corporate staff unit and multiple, small, independent, product-family-oriented business units, each of which will be focused on a particular product family. Within the overall corporate structure, there will also be some service units (such as treasury, finance, and human resources) that sell their services to the BUs on a competitive basis.

Many companies are already taking this approach. For example, ABB, with over 200,000 employees worldwide, now has a headquarters staff of about 300 people—down from several thousand.

The main role of the corporate staff unit will be to develop the corporate *vision and strategic plans* (see Figure 5.3) corresponding to corporate targets and to support BU management in their efforts to develop their own plans and objectives. The corporate staff unit members will also play an important role in initiating, monitoring, and supporting important cross-BU initiatives in areas such as product quality improvement, product introduction frequency, process improvement, and resource development and utilization.

The corporate staff unit, working with senior corporate management, will define the business philosophy and practices to be adopted throughout the corporation. It will define the reward and recognition systems to be set up to encourage people to work in the direction of corporate success.

Among the most important business philosophies and practices to be adopted in the 1990s will be TQM and top-down planning. The TQM philosophy will be applied throughout the corporation. Top-to-bottom planning techniques such as Hoshin Kanri will be used. TQM has already been adopted by leading companies such as AlliedSignal, Corning, Hewlett-Packard, IBM, and Xerox.

Figure 5.3. Deployment of the Corporate Vision

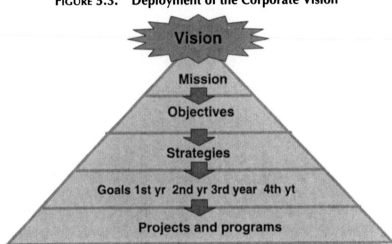

Quality has become an imperative for competitive performance for world-class companies. When people look back at the 1960s and 1970s, they will be appalled by the low quality of products, the general indifference shown to customers, and early resistance to the introduction of TQM.

Hoshin Kanri (or Policy Deployment as shown in Figure 5.4) provides a step-by-step planning, implementation, and review process for managed change. It cascades, or deploys, top management policies and targets down the management hierarchy. At each level, the policy is translated into agreed policies, targets, and actions for the next level down. The aim of Hoshin Kanri is to translate top management vision into a set of coherent, consistent, understandable, and attainable policies and actions that can be applied at all levels of the company and in all functions of the company. When these actions and policies are applied, they should result in the vision becoming reality.

Individual members of the corporate staff unit will have responsibility for specific activities. For example, one member of the corporate staff unit will have responsibility for engineering initiatives, such as developing a vision for engineering in line with the overall corporate vision, helping BUs work together, developing engineering talent, consolidating scarce engineering resources, cross-pollinating leading-edge

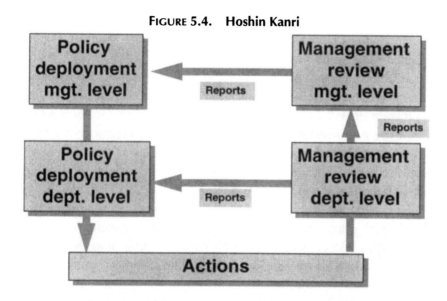

FIGURE 5.4.   Hoshin Kanri

knowledge, systems, and practices across the corporation, championing innovation, identifying and developing new technologies, increasing the ability of the organization to learn new techniques, and benchmarking the performance of other organizations.

Reward and recognition systems will be set up by the corporate staff unit to motivate people to perform both as individuals and as team members along the five dimensions of product, process, region, function, and behavior.

Looking Out

To meet the targets resulting from customers' requirements and competitive pressures, companies will need to improve their relationships with customers, suppliers, and academia. Customers are the prime source of product and service requirements, and companies will need to get closer to them. Some product family team members may work temporarily or even permanently on customer sites to find out what customers really want in terms of product, service, quality, price, and timeliness.

As companies, BUs and product family teams increasingly will focus on the part of the product development process they do best; they will outsource parts and activities that add little value, that are not cost-effective, that other companies can do better.

At the corporate level, some of the research, treasury, finance, and human resources activities that can be better carried out by other organizations will be outsourced. BUs and product family teams will retain the engineering activities that provide competitive advantage, have high added value, have a high impact on the customer, or are the core competence of the organization. They will outsource the activities where suppliers are cheaper or perform better.

Companies will improve their relationships with suppliers and work closely with a smaller number of suppliers. Relationships will become longer-term, closer, and quality-oriented, tending more toward part-nership and away from the short-term, dollar-oriented, conflictual rela-tionships common in the 1970s. Companies will see their chosen suppliers as assets and help them improve performance by providing training and process-improvement assistance. Companies will look to suppliers to offer major components rather than minor parts. Individ-ual engineers or small teams of engineers may work on supplier sites, and engineers from suppliers will be hosted by main contractors.

Chrysler used to work with 600 to 700 suppliers on a new car program but now works with far fewer. About 200 suppliers were selected for the LH project and fewer than 300 for the new Neon, for which suppliers provide 70 percent of the value. Seagate Technology engineers work at Sun Microsystems' sites to develop disk drives that meet Sun's requirements.

A company may partner with one supplier on a particular product line but with the supplier's competitor on another product family. Similarly, a supplier may find itself working with one company for one component and with that company's competitor for another com-ponent.

Companies will focus on a few academic institutions and help build them into centers of excellence that provide suitably educated future employees who have the skills and knowledge the company needs.

The trend toward outsourcing, and the focus on the activities where a company provides competitive advantage, will lead to new companies being established to perform the outsourced work. In some cases, companies will develop long-term relationships with local suppliers of product development services—some of whom may be made up of people whose work has been outsourced. Small, highly specialized engineering companies will be set up to meet outsourcing needs. Staffed by a few highly skilled individuals with low-cost, high-performance computing resources, they will offer an attractive alternative to large companies. Other suppliers may be companies set up with state support to retain jobs in the area.

In other cases, the globalization of business and the availability of telecommunications will allow companies to outsource low value-added engineering work to low-wage countries. Telecommunications will play a major enabling role in the new world of supplier relationships. Electronic data interchange (EDI) will enable fast exchange of engineering data between a company and its suppliers, wherever they are.

Workers

By the end of the 1990s, the culture within effective product development organizations will be one of responsible adults working together for mutual success. Workers will be expected to use their brains more than their muscles.

This type of culture makes sense for highly skilled members of a team aiming to reduce product development costs and cycles, improve product quality, and meet customer requirements. Unlike traditional organizations, where people were told exactly what to do and then watched over to make sure they did it, the new organization will be more open and trusting. It will train, coach, and give people an overall objective, but then rely on them to get on with the job and perform well. The workers in this type of organization will have to be highly skilled, mastering not only their own particular function but also understanding the customer and the company. Workers are key to the success of the business. They, not corporate managers, have the skills to develop, produce, and sell their products. They are close enough to the action to know where time and money are being lost. Sensible corporate managers will empower their workers to make decisions instead of waiting for orders from out-of-touch managers. See Figure 5.5.

As the culture and shape of organizations change, the roles of engineers will change. They will have an increasingly important role to play in developing new products that customers like, in reducing product costs, and in reducing development times. Corporations will be looking for engineers who understand the customer and the business and want to become more competent and useful for the company.

New career paths will open up for engineers. Companies will still need engineers who want to focus on one specialized area of the product development process for the rest of their working lives. They will also require generalist engineers who want to lead teams responsible for parts of the product, for all the product, or for the product family. They will need engineers who want to have engineering roles in many different areas of engineering—in other countries, in research, in liaison with customers and suppliers, in training other engineers, or in improving the product development process. New roles will be created to manage

FIGURE 5.5. **Traditional vs. "Empowered" Organization**

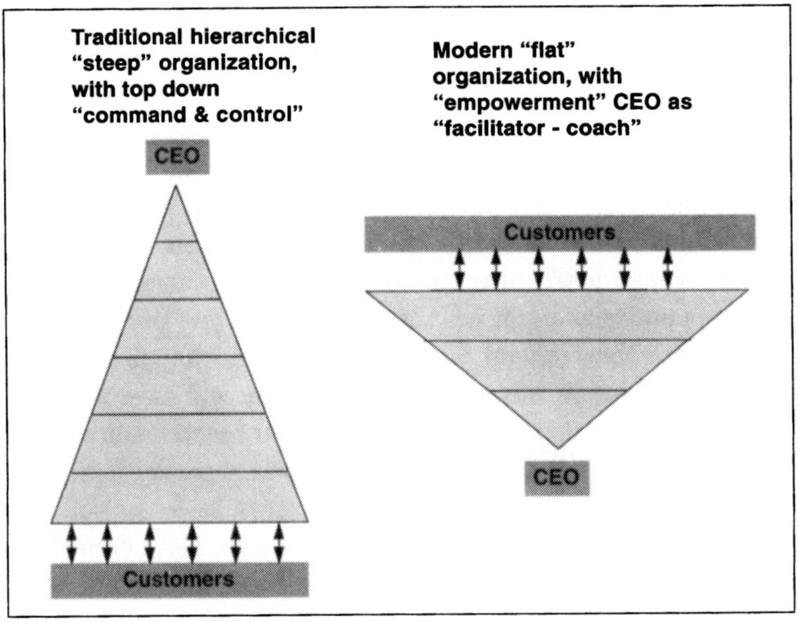

the new relationships that result from increased outsourcing. Experienced technical staff no longer needed to carry out the work in-house will take up liaison roles with outside organizations. For all these engineers the career path will include continuous learning about all areas of engineering and about the company and its products.

Highly talented, highly trained engineers will be in short supply. If a BU does not reward them well, they can easily move to another organization. BUs will reward their best engineers well to retain them. On the other hand, companies will not want engineers who add little value and who don't want to progress through continual challenge. The global forces on world-class corporations will lead them to expect high performance and good team behavior from highly talented engineers. In return they will offer appropriate rewards, training, and recognition. Engineers' remuneration will not be based solely on individual performance but also on that of their product family team and their BU.

Engineers will be nearer the front line. They will participate in product family team meetings with customers. Their colleagues in the team will not just be fellow engineers but people with other functional skills, such as marketing and manufacturing. Engineers will move from a monoculture, monogender world to multicultural, multilingual, multigender environments.

When engineers are hired, they will be given training to help them understand the organization. They will start life on the shop floor and interact with customers in order to understand how and why the product is made. Each year, engineers will receive several weeks' training, particularly in team behavior and in broadening their horizons beyond their engineering specialty. Apart from off-the-job training, engineers will be expected to learn continuously while on the job. Facilities will need to be redesigned because in the team environment engineers will spend more time in groups and less time alone.

FOCUS

To meet customers' requirements and competitive pressures, companies will organize themselves in a way that decreases product development costs and overall product costs, reduces product development cycle time, and improves quality. A lean corporate staff unit and multiple, small, independent, product-family-oriented BUs will focus on a particular product family. All the product family life-cycle resources, such as personnel, technologies, and techniques, will be dedicated to achieving the cost, quality, and time-to-market objectives of the product family.

Within each product family team, the major development effort will be at the very beginning of the product development process—close to customers and at the system level. Detailed and downstream engineering activities that add little value will be outsourced. Effective upstream performance is mandatory for effective manufacturing. Quality and cost performance have to be designed into a product; they cannot be added later by slick sales pitches, rework on the shop floor, or by delaying payment to suppliers in an attempt to get them to reduce the cost of their parts.

To carry out the highly skilled upstream work, the product family team will be built around a core of highly skilled, long-serving individuals.

Engineering's function as a separate organizational entity will disappear. It will be absorbed into a more product-oriented organization, where engineers do what it takes to make the business succeed. In this environment, the product family team (including its engineers) will ask, "Are engineering skills key to our business?" and "Which bits of engineering should we keep and grow and which should we outsource?" They will retain the engineering activities that provide competitive advantage, are the core competence, have high added value, and have a high impact on the customer. They will outsource the bits where suppliers are better, cheaper, or give better performance. The engineering work that remains in-house will be high value adding and will call for highly trained engineers using the best techniques and systems.

As product family teams move their in-house engineering activities upstream, they will need a well-defined overall product architecture. They will do more engineering at the system level and less at the component level. There will be more reuse of parts and more building on existing designs. There will be far fewer megaprojects—huge projects to develop radically new products from scratch. This trend is already apparent in companies like Polaroid. Their Captive camera megaproject cost $100 million and took five years of development time. Abandoning the megaproject approach, 75 percent of the parts of the ProCam camera were derived from parts that had already been developed for other cameras, and development costs were reduced by 65 percent.

The product development organization will need new skills to identify and avoid potential problems, know what not to engineer in-house, control outsourcing, and *continuously improve the product development process.* New jobs will appear. For example, someone will have to understand and improve engineering activities in the process. Someone will have to define the rules for continuously improving engineering skills in a team environment. Someone will have to understand how engineering information can be used most effectively. See Figure 5.6.

The focus of engineering support functions will change. They will face new requirements as organizations need to better understand the flow and steps of the engineering process and the way engineering information is used and reused.

The focus of engineering computer systems organizations will change. Instead of focusing only on the engineering function, they will address the life-cycle process. Sometimes they will operate at the

FIGURE 5.6.   Product Family Team Interactions

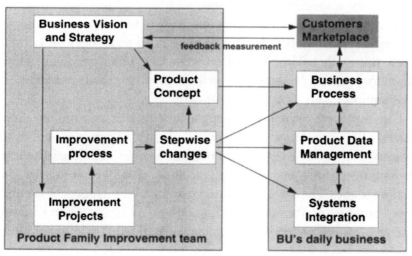

BU level or even across BUs. If so, they will be expected to be competitive and in some cases may be allowed to sell services on the outside market. In other cases, where there is no strategic or cost justification for keeping this function within the corporation, they will be outsourced.

MEASURING PERFORMANCE

The BU will have to simultaneously master its performance along five dimensions. Traditionally, organizations have taken a simplistic view of performance measurement—often restricting themselves to one-dimensional targets, such as sales, headcount, or number of drawings produced. In the future, organizations will develop metrics to allow them to target simultaneously product, process, regional, functional, and cultural performance.

A metric is a measurement that characterizes some aspect of a product or process. Metrics are needed to measure all aspects of a company's performance—to set targets, monitor progress, track results, and fix problems. They help identify, analyze, and report behavior. Without the ability to measure performance, it is not possible to ensure performance improvement. Some metrics apply to financial performance, many to operating performance. Most companies need some metrics specific to their own operations but use widely accepted metrics so that they can compare themselves with benchmarked competitors. Typical metrics include ROA (return on assets), BET (breakeven time—the elapsed time between the initial spending on the development of a product and the moment when product sales exceed that amount), and COQ (cost of quality).

The metrics by which the performance of BUs and product family teams will be measured will include a mixture of external metrics and internal metrics. The external metrics used could include sales volume, profitability, profit per engineer, product cost, time-to-market, and market share. The internal metrics used could include development cost, number of iterations of the design cycle, number of design changes, number of engineering changes in the first year of a product's life, correctness of simulation results, conformance to specifications, engineering rework, first-time yield on designs, and reuse of designs.

Performance measures for individuals will be related to those for the BU and the corporation. Reward and recognition systems will be set up by the corporate staff unit and BU management to motivate people to perform as individuals and to contribute to team performance along the five dimensions. Performance will be judged by superiors, peers, and subordinates.

Different people will be measured in different ways and be set different targets. A product team leader might have a mix of targets, including

$X revenues in Year 1,

$Y revenues in Year 2 of which x percent from new products,

$Z revenues in Year 3 of which y percent from new products,

Revenues of over $U in n countries,

V% reduction per year in new product development time and cost, and

W% improvement in team behavior and customer satisfaction,

with rewards being conditional on all targets being met over a three-year period.

A product team engineer might have a mix of targets, including

x% increase in the team's profit per engineer,

y% decrease in the number of design changes,

z% improvement in conformance to plan,

u% acceptance when coaching,

v% reduction in software errors, and

w% improvement in team behavior.

TRYING TO IMPROVE PERFORMANCE

All companies try to improve performance and set themselves various targets and rules to do so. Texas Instruments' Defense Systems and Electronics Group aims to achieve six-sigma quality by 1995 and reduce product development time by 25 percent each year. Emerson Electric aims to remove about 7 percent of costs each year. 3M has a rule that products five years old or less must account for 25 to 35 percent of annual sales.

Improved performance can be brought about in many ways. In some companies, change occurs because the company is taken over by another company with better practices. Sometimes, outsiders are brought in and introduce a new culture, or external consultants are brought in to help change occur. In the best companies, the organization learns *how to adapt itself.* See Figure 5.7.

To achieve the major performance improvements required if costs and time cycles are to be reduced sufficiently for it to be possible to meet customer requirements, top management has to take the lead and set the improvement targets. Corporate staff and BU staff will support initiatives taken to attain these targets, but the real work has to be done at product family team level.

FIGURE 5.7.   Key to Performance Improvement

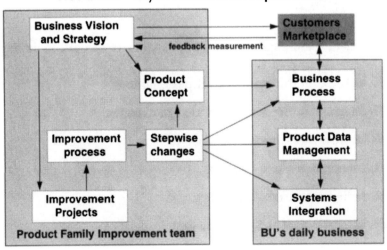

To obtain significant ongoing performance improvement requires extensive training programs, willingness to learn from the outside, identification of the right targets, and a reassessment of activities. Short-term and long-term training helps people reach a suitable level of performance and then helps them maintain that level.

Much can be derived from other organizations but only if there is a willingness to accept that they have something to offer. Suppliers, academia, and competitors are all good sources of information about improving performance. Technology watch activities and product development process watch activities can be set up on an ongoing basis to ensure that the organization stays abreast of advances in technology, systems, and practices.

Benchmarking is an ideal way of learning how other organizations perform activities, whether these companies are in the same industry sector or another. Small groups within BUs can carry out benchmarking. Group membership should change regularly to provide opportunity and experience for all and to ensure that no one becomes a benchmarking expert and forgets that the real objective is customer satisfaction.

As product family teams strive to improve performance, they will focus their activities on that part of the product development process where they add most value. Increasingly, this will be in the early parts of the design process, where it takes product-specific skill to understand customer requirements, to relate them to overall product architecture, to translate them to the language of system parameters, subsystem performance specifications, and component specifications, and to understand the many interfaces. To develop and maintain the critical mass of skills necessary for these activities, centers of expertise will be set up to make the best use of limited resources.

TOOLS AND TECHNIQUES

To achieve corporate targets aimed at reducing product costs and cycle time and improving quality, product development organizations will go far beyond the traditional techniques of literature survey, prototype building, and ineffective design reviews. In recent years, many new techniques have been introduced to support the product development process.

There are techniques to support the life-cycle process and to support parts of the process. Both types of technique will be needed in the late 1990s, and they will be closely supported by computer systems to improve product development performance.

Techniques that address and support the life cycle, such as QFD, ABC, and EMI, will be widely used. Once companies are organized along the life-cycle process, process-mapping and process-improvement techniques will increase rapidly in importance. Also, techniques to link information to the process will be needed.

Quality Function Deployment (QFD) is a step-by-step technique for ensuring that the voice of the customer is heard throughout the product development process so that the final product fully meets customer requirements. The first step of QFD is to identify and capture customer requirements, wishes, and expectations. In the following steps, these are accurately translated by multifunctional product teams into the corresponding technical specifications. QFD uses a series of simple matrices and tables as the tool for translating the voice of the customer first to design specifications, then to more detailed part characteristics, then to show the necessary process and technology characteristics, and finally to show the specific operational conditions for the production phase. The result is that before the design phase is complete, the complete product development and production process has been defined and the voice of the customer can be followed through the different steps. In doing this the team members develop a shared and documented view of the key information describing the product and the overall process.

As companies move to product-line-oriented, process-oriented organizations, they will need to change their accounting methods. Activity-based costing (ABC) will be used. The activity costing paradigm is based on the principle that it is not the products that a company produces that generate costs but rather the activities that are performed in planning, procuring, and producing the products. The resources that are necessary to support the activities performed during the course of business result in costs being incurred. Product costs, in turn, are calculated by determining how each product is supported by the activities being performed.

Product life-cycle accounting will be widely used. It recognizes that the distribution of costs changes over the life of the product, as does the potential profitability of a product. The most critical time for controlling a product's cost is in the development stage, even though most of the product's costs are not incurred until much later. See Figure 5.8.

Benchmarking is the continuous process of measuring products, services, and practices against the company's toughest competitors or those companies renowned as industry leaders. If other organizations are found to have more effective operations, then the company can try to understand how they work and why they are better. The company can then start to improve its own operations and will be able to set itself realistic performance targets.

Business process reengineering involves the significant reorganization of a company's business processes with the objective of making very large improvements in customer-service metrics. It involves redesign of the workflow and the application of information technology to the new workflow with the aim of obtaining competitive advantage.

Concurrent engineering is a systematic approach to the integrated, concurrent design of products and their related processes, including

FIGURE 5.8. Product Life Cycle

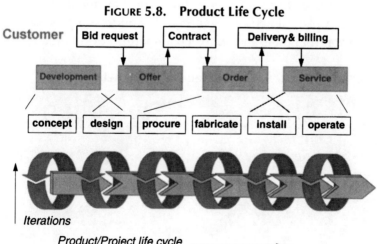

Iterations

Product/Project life cycle ⎯⎯⎯⎯⎯⎯➤

manufacture and support. Concurrent engineering brings together multidisciplinary teams that work together from the start of a project with the intention of getting things right as quickly as possible and as early as possible. Input is obtained from as many functional areas as possible before the specifications are finalized. This approach leads to consideration, from the outset, of all the elements (including quality, cost, schedule, and user requirements) affecting the product life cycle from conception through disposal.

GM's Cadillac Motor Car Division used concurrent engineering to reduce the time taken to develop a new car by a year. Using concurrent engineering, Hewlett-Packard reduced development time of its 54600 oscilloscope by over 50 percent. Using concurrent engineering, Boeing's Ballistic Systems Division reduced design time for a mobile missile launcher missile by 40 percent and cost by 10 percent. Du Pont brought radiologists into the development process of a new chest X-ray system, UltraVision. The product was developed in sixteen months—half the usual time.

Early manufacturing involvement (EMI) includes manufacturing engineers in design activities that take place early in the workflow, rather than waiting until the designers have finalized a product that will be difficult or impossible to manufacture.

The Plan-Do-Check-Act (PDCA as shown in Figure 5.9) cycle represents a generic approach to continuous improvement of any activity or process. A plan of action is generated to address a problem, corresponding control points and control parameters are generated, and the

FIGURE 5.9. The Plan-Do-Check-Act Cycle

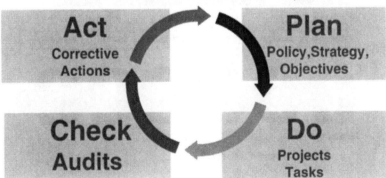

plan is reviewed and agreed. In the do step, the plan is implemented. In the check step, information is collected on the control parameters, and the actual results are compared to the expected results. In the act step, the results are analyzed, causes of discrepancies are identified and discussed, and corrective action is identified.

Design for Manufacture (DFM) techniques will be used for a variety of reasons, such as providing early estimates of product life-cycle characteristics, minimizing sensitivity to process and environmental variations, and yielding better control of manufacturing processes.

Design for Assembly (DFA) techniques aim to reduce the cost and time of assembly by simplifying the product and process through such means as reducing the number of parts, combining two or more parts into one, reducing or eliminating adjustments, simplifying assembly operations, designing for parts handling and presentation, selecting fasteners for ease of assembly, minimizing parts tangling, and ensuring that products are easy to test.

Design for Manufacture techniques are closely linked to Design for Assembly techniques but are oriented primarily to individual parts and components rather than to DFA's subassemblies, assemblies, and products. DFM aims to eliminate the often expensive and unnecessary features of a part that make it difficult to manufacture. It helps prevent the unnecessarily smooth surface, small radius, and high tolerance.

Rapid prototyping—producing a physical prototype directly from a CAD model—gives everyone involved with a new product an early opportunity to see and touch a physical prototype. Automotive manufacturer Rover Group used rapid prototyping to develop a prototype of a thermostat housing. Traditional techniques would have cost over $6,000 and taken nine weeks. With rapid prototyping, less than three weeks was needed, and the cost was under $2,000.

COMPUTER SYSTEMS

Computer systems will play a key role in supporting new product development processes designed to achieve corporate targets and provide customer satisfaction. Use of computers will go far beyond the traditional engineering environment of a few FORTRAN programs, some high-cost workstations, many low-cost PCs, and some isolated CAD systems.

The trend to off-the-shelf open systems for the product development process will continue, and relatively cheap yet massively powerful computing platforms will be available. The availability of inexpensive computers will open up new applications. Advances in communications technologies will provide opportunities for new types of products and will allow services to be provided in new ways. In the world of global business, telecommunications will play a key role, with EDI being an essential communication tool.

Current-generation Computer Aided Design tools will continue to add new functionality such as the incorporation of Design for Manufacture. However, they will face competition from a new generation of CAD tools that will take advantage of extremely cheap computing power and new organizational structures and address issues such as holistic CAD (aimed not at details but at the overall product), shared CAD (CAD for the team) as opposed to individual CAD, CAMCAD (the upstream feedback of information from manufacturing to design), "wrapped" CAD systems that adjust to running on any system, and CAD systems integrated in frameworks.

Boeing is doing all the design and engineering work for its 777 aircraft with CAD and will be able to carry out extensive analysis on a CAD-based mock-up. Boeing hopes this paperless design will save 20 percent of the 777's estimated $4 billion to $5 billion development cost.

As companies get better at mastering the issues of world-class quality, cost, and delivery, they will increasingly find themselves coming up against "softer" issues of design appeal—the attractiveness, feel, and culture of a product. By the end of the 1990s, virtual reality systems will be in the product family team's toolkit to meet this need. The Electric Boat Division of General Dynamics has already developed a virtual reality submarine torpedo-loading scenario.

As product family teams try to decrease lead times, analysis and simulation tools will play an increasingly important role. As development times decrease, products will be fully engineered and tested long before they can be manufactured. It will be possible for several alternatives of the product to be engineered and simulated, with the final choice being made by the customer.

Engineering data management (EDM) systems will underlie the other computer-based systems in the product development process, managing information and processes all the way along the product life cycle. Understanding the flow of work throughout the business process and linking and controlling information will be important. Frameworks will be provided to knit systems and data together.

Knowledge-based systems will be embedded in CAD and EDM systems to improve performance when accessing information, identifying similar designs, and developing new designs.

ENGINEERING INFORMATION

Engineering information will become a strategic resource, and its management a key issue. A high priority of the product-line organization will be to improve the use, quality, and flow of engineering information. Effective use and reuse of engineering information will play a key role in differentiating world-class companies from others. As the real value of information becomes apparent, metrics will be introduced to help maximize its contribution to the product family team's activities. Reuse of information will be a key metric.

The structure of the product family team will be such that it requires very little information flow up the ladder and considerably reduces the barriers to horizontal information flow. Nevertheless, the product family team will be faced with many information issues and with issues concerning the communication of information.

The team will have to define what constitutes the engineering data relating to their product lines. It will address information issues such as the availability of information in electronic form, legacy information, access to life-cycle data, and management of the information relating to customized products. Communication issues to be addressed by the team include information interchange with suppliers, customers, research groups, team members, and off-site team members and the productivity of information use in the business processes.

Project databases will be set up by the product family teams for each project. They will record information about the product and also about the activities and decisions of the project team.

Product family teams will want to control their information and achieve the maximum benefit from it, but they will be able to do this only if it is all available electronically. As a result, all relevant information will be converted to a computer-controllable electronic form. Paper documents will be converted to electronic form. Discussions will be recorded on electronic media. Products and processes will be videotaped. All relevant product and process information will be made available on electronic media as an electronic corporate memory. Engineering data management (EDM) systems will manage this data. They will include cross-functional data dictionaries so that everyone understands what they contain. See Figure 5.10.

Knowledge-based systems will be used to try to increase the ability to find and reuse information. As product family teams look at the engineering process, they will realize how much opportunity there is to use information better. As a result, they will focus more on information. They will set up groups to understand what information is used and

FIGURE 5.10.   A Simple Engineering Data Management System

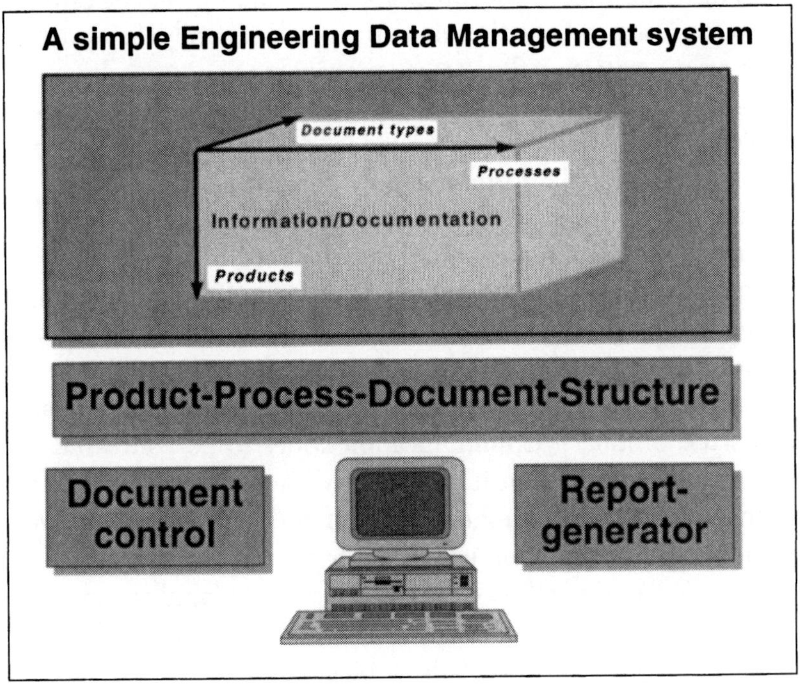

why it is needed. They will define and develop a common cross-functional vocabulary. They will look for collaborative tools that go beyond simple information storage and management. As business and product development processes are better understood and improved, the associated information needs will become clearer, and tools will be chosen to maximize the effectiveness of information use and flow.

The need for formal traditional meetings will decrease, and the format of meetings will change. Instead of sitting at the traditional table, people will congregate around models of the product and electronic surfaces displaying product information. Video conferencing will allow team members in other locations to participate.

The process of developing new products is already changing more rapidly than in the past, and within five years will be vastly different when compared to current practice in the average manufacturing company. Technology is advancing rapidly, customers are demanding more input into product features and functions, and competitors are learning that they can achieve superiority through product development. To respond to this situation, companies will have to organize differently, adopt new tools and techniques, maintain excellent quality, and get closer to their customers.

CHAPTER 6

The Evolution of Product Development

PROGRESS IN PRODUCT DEVELOPMENT

New product development is already moving from a sequential departmental process performed primarily by engineers to an integrated process accomplished by a cross-functional team. The steps of the process are essentially the same in either case, but they are accomplished simultaneously and with greater speed in the integrated environment.

There are four logical groups of activity in the creation of a new product:

- Identifying an opportunity or demand for a new product,

- Creating the technical specifications for the new-product idea,

- Developing the manufacturing process to produce the new product, and

- Fabricating the new product.

In the first group, customers and potential customers generate requirements for the desired features and functions they want in a product. This information is usually compiled by marketing specialists, who translate it into a set of product features that are intended to satisfy a target customer base. During this process, product offerings from competitors are evaluated to find weaknesses that can be overcome or improved in the new product. Pricing of similar products is also taken into consideration to estimate selling price ranges and cost targets. This data are analyzed and translated into cost and quality specifications.

Next, the product takes on concept and form. From the product feature set identified by marketing, a first vision of how the product will look and perform is created. The technical capabilities of the product are developed and refined. From this initial conceptual vision, work proceeds to design the product and test the technical concepts that form the basis of the features and functions. Once a preliminary design is completed, prototypes may be created and tested to ensure that the product performs as specified. "Bugs" and areas that need refinement may be identified as a result of prototype testing, and modifications based on these results are incorporated into the design. Once prototype testing is complete, and the new product is performing as it was intended to, the design is documented and finalized.

To prepare to produce the product, the manufacturing process must be created so that the product can be made in production facilities. If new technology is involved, this may require purchasing new equipment and training production workers. Based on the building of prototypes, one method of production will have been defined. But this method may not be suited to production equipment, especially if the prototype was created in an engineering development lab. Tools, fixtures, and the sequence of steps in the manufacturing process must all be developed to allow rapid, high-quality production. Layout of production facilities may need to be rearranged, and automated production equipment may need programming.

When the designs for the product and the manufacturing process have been completed, the business of producing and shipping the product proceeds. Raw material can be purchased, and the production facilities go into operation. During first production, technical problems may occur as a result of unfamiliarity on the part of manufacturing or insufficient involvement of manufacturing in the proto-type phase. Design changes or process changes may be necessary and serve to slow the introduction of the new product.

THE "OLD" PRODUCT DEVELOPMENT MODEL

In the traditional environment, each of these four logical activity groups happened in sequence, with few exceptions. The sequential nature of the steps was reinforced by the division of labor among distinct and separate departments. Research preceded development of the new product concept. Once a concept was formed, a formal evaluation process often caused a return to the concept-development phase for revisions. After revisions, another formal evaluation occurred, and the process continued through a number of iterations until all agreed on the product concept.

A similar sequence of design work, review, and rework of design followed as the concept was developed by engineering. When the design had been completed by engineering, it was "released" to manu-facturing, which began work to define the manufacturing process. A step that was often included in the definition of the manufacturing process was to determine which components would be made and which would be purchased. Until the make/buy decisions were made, those responsible for planning production and procuring material could not act.

Finally, material was ordered, necessary production equipment was installed, fixtures were completed, workers were trained, and the prod-uct was produced and shipped. Each department had performed its role in the long sequence of events leading to production of the new product. For the most part, each department had completed its work within its own functional area, consulting other departments only to obtain needed information or to review the results of a task in the sequence. The process took a relatively long period of time to com-plete, due to the sequential manner of operation. It was also prone to technical problems as a result of the lack of communication across functional borders.

The technical problems caused design changes if they were discovered before the product went into production and caused rework, scrap, and customer complaints in addition to design changes if discovered later. Both the design changes and the time required for the sequential method of new product development were undesirable and expensive. This very sequential step-by-step process fostered an environment where changes were virtually inevitable, and the changes made the process longer.

A Newer Model Emerges

Although there are still companies operating their design process in the traditional, sequential way of doing things, this method began to be displaced by the mid-1970s. The main disadvantages of the sequential method are the weak links between functions that should be cooperating to produce the new product, the sequential and iterative nature of the process, and the manual methods (draftsmen creating paper records of the design), which are slow and costly. Additionally, the number of designs tends to grow large when there is no method of rapidly identifying previous work that could be reused in the new product. The proverbial "reinvention of the wheel" continues daily in engineering departments worldwide.

In an effort to increase design productivity and reduce engineering time, manufacturers turned to a semi-automated process next. Through the application of computer systems, automation was applied to speed the completion of some of the manual tasks involved in product development, such as drafting. Stand-alone computer solutions were used to replace manual methods, but the sequence of tasks wasn't changed. Nothing was accomplished in terms of strengthening the links between functions involved in the design, and the iterative, sequential process continued. Now there were "islands of automation" that simply replaced human memory with computer memory. Although the ability to readily find and reuse previous designs was an advantage, it was often ignored and rarely implemented. The productivity gained from automation was usually lost in administering systems and entering data from one incompatible computer system into the next. In fact, the semi-automated environment only increased the complexity of managing the design process.

Current Practice

There are still a large number of companies operating their product design process in the semi-automated mode, though it is rapidly becoming out of date. A number of leading companies are using a more automated and interfaced process. This more modern method still includes an iterative design process, but many of the steps occur simultaneously. Design concepts are evaluated and tested as they are produced, without waiting for all of the concepts to be finished. As design work progresses, prototypes are built to test segments of the design. Manufacturing is involved in testing prototypes and shares information with engineering. The number of redesigns is reduced as a result of improved communication between functions and within engineering via computer systems. Interfaces between engineering systems and links to manufacturing systems now support the process. Additional automated engineering tools are available and are used to simulate, often eliminating the need to produce physical prototypes until the end of the design process. Designs are reused and can be optimized to minimize cost and ensure high quality. Development of the manufacturing process for the product no longer waits until an engineering "release" and is developed as the product is being designed. Attaining this level of development sophistication indicates real progress in improving speed to market but is no longer enough to outdistance world-class competitors that are doing the same things.

Future Directions

Keeping in mind that the objective is to innovate, build in the necessary cost and quality factors, and beat competitors to market, the steps to new product development need to be even more simultaneous and less sequential. *A change in thinking* is necessary to see the new product development process as a continuous process of interrelated activities and no longer a sequence of steps.

The change can be compared to batch processing versus real-time transaction processing in computer operations.

In batch processing, only one job in a sequence of related tasks can be run at a time. The first job processes all the data available for its assigned task and passes the outcome on to another process only when it is finished. Then the next job can begin.

In real-time processing, submission of a transaction can trigger immediate processing, and the result is immediately available to the next process. Once the first transaction has been input, additional ones can be submitted while previous transactions are being processed. The concurrency of this method makes the end-to-end process time much shorter in most cases. The same is true for development of new products.

In an integrated, simultaneous-development environment, a "transaction" triggers the process (identification of a product concept). Concept development proceeds simultaneously with research into possible technologies, while engineers design the parts of the product that can be completed as information and technology become available. Automated engineering tools help to optimize designs for cost and reliability. Previous designs that fit the new application are reused or modified, reducing engineering time. Simulation and prototyping occur simultaneously within engineering design activity and replace most physical prototyping.

As design work progresses, development begins on the manufacturing process. All major functional areas participate in the design efforts from the inception of the project, forming a team. The team may be physically located in one area, or it may convene electronically. In either case, integrated computer systems support the technical activities and sharing of information among the team, functioning to alert members when data are available for their role in the process. This facilitates simultaneous execution of many tasks that would otherwise wait for a "batch" of information from the previous function before being worked on. Engineering software and technical tools are integrated with business information systems, providing full information and status of the project to all team members. This high level of integration provides synergy and discipline, which combine to prevent the costly and time-consuming design iterations that are common in more traditional and sequential environments. See Figure 6.1.

APPLICATION OF THE INTEGRATED DESIGN MODEL

Although the following scenario is fictional, each part of the story is drawn from work taking place in companies that are leading the movement toward integrated design.

At a major U.S. automobile manufacturer, customer and dealer comments on vibration problems suggest the need for a new engine mount. The need for the new engine mount is discovered from analysis of data collected and stored in a quality database. Comments and complaints received from customers and dealers are categorized by type and correlated with possible causes that are maintained within the system. The system identifies problems for analysis when the frequency exceeds preset tolerances established by quality assurance.

A drive-train design team convenes to analyze the problem and determines that the engine mount design needs to be changed. A design concept is formulated by the team, which includes vibration dampening in addition to the strength characteristics considered in the current production design. As soon as the team meeting concludes, the project and design concept are established on the companywide information system. Engineers on the team search for previous designs, including those used on other models that may have the desired characteristics. An existing design is identified, and simulation programs are run to evaluate the vibration characteristics of the mount in the car that is experiencing problems. The simulation suggests a slight modification of the design that has been selected, and engineers make the change on the CAD system, run more simulations, and store the design when satisfied that the new mount is ready for physical testing.

Manufacturing personnel have been involved throughout the process and participate in the modification of the reused design to help ensure ease of manufacture and assembly. They have looked at the

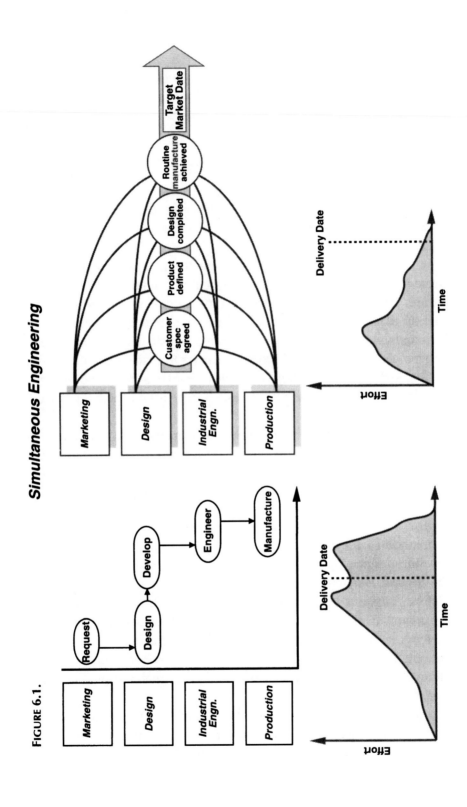

Simultaneous Engineering

FIGURE 6.1.

mating parts in particular, to make sure that assembly of the vehicle will not be made more difficult and that the procedure for securing the engine will not have to change significantly. Stereolithography (a method of making a solid model from CAD data, using plastic resins) is used to make a full-size model of the new part to check the fit with mating parts. A problem is discovered with the fit, and an error is discovered in the CAD design. The dimensional problem is quickly corrected on the CAD system, and a new model is produced the same day. This rapid prototyping capability and the team cooperation have combined to save several thousand dollars and many weeks of preproduction time. In a more traditional process, the company would have created tooling from the CAD design and made parts. Only then would the dimensional error have been discovered. The engineers have also used Design for Assembly (DFA) methods and tools to ensure that assembly of the new engine mount is as simple as possible.

As a result of the reuse of an existing design and manufacturing's involvement on the design team, the production process is ready to use by the time the design is finalized. The entire process of identifying the problem, analyzing it, formulating a design concept, and producing a new design has taken about forty hours of elapsed time.

In a typical semi-automated environment, the design process would probably ignore existing designs and create a new part from scratch. Most companies have not yet cataloged their CAD designs for ease of retrieval and reuse. Creating a part from scratch often takes three times as long as the total time used for the integrated process. Tooling adds another month or longer. Production of initial parts might take six to eight weeks more. Then when the dimensional error is discovered, additional time would be lost correcting the design and modifying the tooling. Add another six to eight weeks for production of new parts, for a total of five to six months' elapsed time.

These are conservative estimates, based on real-life experience. Comparison with the integrated design effort would have delivery of production parts in a significantly shorter time frame. Obvious time and cost advantages are possible after adoption of a truly integrated design process supported by modern systems and tools, and the technology exists to accomplish it now.

UNDERSTANDING THE DETAILS

One of the most common problems cited by experts in assessing the competitiveness of American industry is the lack of technical expertise within the ranks of top management. If U.S. companies are to adopt the new model of integrated product development, executives must understand a considerable amount of detail concerning the process and underlying technology. The major areas of concern are research, product design, process design, and transition to production.

New Product Research

Unless a company's product line is completely static and the marketplace doesn't require any innovation, a research function is essential to remain competitive. Research doesn't have to be an in-house capability, and many companies pay for the rights to technology developed by others. Depending on the circumstances, research may be limited to reviews of technical developments reported in journals. This information may suggest the need to incorporate the new technology into existing product lines as an enhancement or for cost-reduction purposes. Negotiations then begin with the developer of the technology for licensing purposes.

On the other end of the spectrum, large investments in new technology research may be required to meet challenges by competitors or to regain market share. Large-scale new technology research is generally used to make revolutionary product changes, as opposed to evolutionary ones. The effort is normally expensive and plays a major role in the market strategy of the firm.

The National Cash Register Company's transformation from a company that produced mechanical cash registers to one that primarily manufactures computer systems is a good example of a revolutionary change, supported by R&D in new technologies. In the early 1970s, the marketplace for point-of-sale equipment was shifting dramatically, and management recognized that the days of the mechanical cash register were numbered. Major investments were made in new technology research to produce products that would support a new strategic direction away from cash registers and toward transaction-oriented information technology. New technologies were developed that produced major new products. Computer systems, electronic point-of-sale data-collection systems, and cash machines were developed. Facilities were closed, workers were laid off or retrained, and new factories were built. Even the company name was changed from the National Cash Register Company to NCR Corporation. Today NCR is a major part of AT&T and is a strong player in computer systems ranging from notebook-sized machines to large processors. It is the leading manufacturer of cash machines and plays a large role in point-of-sale data-collection systems. If NCR had not made the revolutionary changes that it did, the company would have been unable to compete and would probably not exist today. New technology played a major role in this revolution, developed through a large investment in research. Controlling R&D was a major success factor for NCR and is evolving into a more critical success factor in the present world business climate.

Research is a necessary and important business function, but in far too many companies it is out of control. It is difficult to manage and requires close scrutiny to be sure that the money being spent results in the expected benefits. If management is unfamiliar with the technology and uninformed as to the types of research appropriate for their products and markets, the result will be disappointment and massive overspending. Not only is research difficult to control without knowledgeable management, but it is hard to evaluate in terms of its eventual contribution to new-product development. There may be a long and disjointed connection between the discovery of a new technology or process and its eventual application in a commercially viable product. It can be extremely hard to envision the eventual application of a new technology, and there is a strong temptation to discourage basic research for this reason. Unfortunately, without research the breakthrough products just don't get invented. What can be done to continue necessary research without incurring excess costs and suffering disappointing results?

One factor that seems to be escaping sufficient attention is the lack of technical orientation on the part of senior executives. Two-thirds of the CEOs in large Japanese manufacturing companies are engineers, or they have a technical or scientific background. In the United States, only one-third of the CEOs of large manufacturers have any technical background.

In the United States, most firms attempt to find legal or financial solutions to their competitive problems. In Japan, the more common solution to competitive pressures is based on new technology. Which is the best approach? So far, the results seem to indicate that the U.S. firms are not going to beat competitors through legal maneuvers, charges of dumping, or financial techniques. American companies that have succeeded in recapturing markets from the Japanese, such as Xerox, did it through product superiority.

Without technically savvy executives managing the strategic research efforts of their companies, the results are unlikely to support the ultimate objectives of the business. Either R&D spending will be too little, or it will be misdirected by a management that is unable to develop an appropriate strategy. Without knowledgeable management, spending is often excessive and time is wasted on projects that may be technically appealing to engineers but have little new product value.

Top management must take the time to understand the technology issues involved in the company's products to effectively control research. Management must make the difficult decisions concerning how heavily to staff research functions and which product lines the staff will support. Without adequate knowledge of the technology and techniques involved in research, the likelihood that either too few or too many resources will be applied grows ominously. The following guidelines suggest ways that management can keep research functions under control:

- Attempt to combine research groups to achieve critical mass. If there are sister companies or other groups within the firm with their own research function, combine them.

- Establish a formal process for justifying costs and allocating resources to research efforts.

- Initiate a regular review of objectives and strategy for research efforts. Document the objectives, and make certain that they are understood.

- Explore the possibility of establishing partnerships with academic institutions to conduct research. In the absence of academic possibilities, look for opportunities to subcontract research activities that are focused on achieving a specific result.

- Apply for government grants to supplement the costs of research.

- Establish a set of required skills that are needed to support research in the industry (what kinds of skills are employed at the most successful competitors), and recruit staff with these skills.

- Establish policies governing when changes to the level of research effort are indicated, and make an effort to understand when it is appropriate to raise or lower resource levels.

- Include all of the major functions of the company in setting and measuring objectives for research, not just marketing and engineering. Functions such as manufacturing and finance will bring valuable perspectives into the decision-making process.

- Review the history of previous research initiatives to measure the benefits that have been realized and the achievement of objectives. Determine what factors made particular efforts succeed or fail. Incorporate the lessons learned from the previous projects into the management and control of current and planned projects.

- Benchmark the level of research currently under way against research levels at other successful companies in the industry. Identify practices that support "best in class" performance and adopt them.

- Consider developing research centers that don't just research products, but also carry out research into processes, including the product development process.

The Product Design Process

The actual work of designing a product begins after the product concept is finalized and the technology to be used has been proven. In an integrated environment, design work may begin as soon as the product concept takes shape and potential technologies are identified. At this point in the development of a product, it is necessary to get very specific about the activities to be performed. Management must clearly communicate the objectives for the project and make team leaders accountable for results. A budget should be established and monitored at regular intervals, along with progress reviews for the project tasks.

The following checklist summarizes the points that should be considered to successfully manage the design phase of product development:

- Be certain that functional specifications and the methods of attaining these results are developed before allowing design work to begin.

- Identify one person to be responsible for control of a design project. If a team is performing the design work, identify a team leader to ensure that goals are met.

- Communicate the role this particular project plays in the company's long-term strategy to those working on the project. Knowledge of strategic objectives will help to produce a design focused on company and customer needs.

- Incorporate estimates of product cost in the regular progress reviews.

- Encourage make/buy decisions as soon as possible after individual parts are designed to allow material-planning activity to overlap the design process.

- Monitor resource levels and effort during progress reviews. Step in to resolve conflict over resource availability without delay.

- Use a formal method of establishing deadlines and reporting progress. Progress reporting can be electronic, making status information available instantly and avoiding the time wasted in meetings to discuss progress.

- Provide graphic media, not paper drawings, to communicate designs to all involved in the project.

- Reuse designs from previous efforts, stored and catalogued on CAD or other engineering data-management systems.

- Establish, maintain, and enforce design standards across all product development efforts.

- Encourage design teams to consider factors such as ease of service, cost of service to the consumer, tooling costs, manufacturing capabilities, ease of manufacture, and the product life cycle in addition to the essential product cost and quality considerations.

Process Design

Creating the manufacturing process for a product should be part of the design effort. There is no need to wait until the design activity is complete to determine how the product or part will be manufactured. In an integrated design environment, the manufacturing process will be developed concurrently with the product design. This implies a high level of involvement on the part of manufacturing, including immediate access to documentation or CAD data.

Members of the design team responsible for the manufacturing process should have significant input into design decisions that affect manufacture and need to be an integral part of the simulation and prototype-testing activities. Modifications to the design that arise out of simulation and prototyping need to be immediately evaluated and incorporated into the development of manufacturing procedures.

Management's role in supporting this phase of the design process should include the following:

- Review the availability of equipment and other resources necessary for development of the manufacturing process. Delays in introducing products into production are often the result of insufficient machinery, equipment, and software. Using an integrated product development process will not return the full potential to reduce time to market if work is delayed due to lack of equipment.

- Look for opportunities to automate manufacturing process development. Often the CAM component of CAD/CAM is overlooked. Catalog and store manufacturing processes, much the same as product designs are classified and saved for possible reuse. If product designers are going to standardize component designs and reuse them, the manufacturing processes that go along with the designs should also be reusable.

- Subcontract manufacturing process development when capabilities in-house are already utilized or there is an external resource that can do the job faster with high quality. There are commercial design firms that can take design data from an in-house CAD system, produce a rapid prototype directly from the CAD design, and build the tooling in far less time than traditional manual methods.

- Include manufacturing process development in the design project plan. It should include activities to identify any long lead time process equipment to be acquired, and to allow sufficient time to order it, install it, and train operators. Automated test equipment should be considered and included in the plan.

- Insist on having the final product prototypes built on production equipment, with production workers using the manufacturing process instructions. Building final prototypes in an engineering lab or at an outside supplier almost guarantees that there will be trouble with the first production run, probably including last-minute design modifications that are costly and very avoidable.

Information Requirements for the Design Process

One of the primary objectives of the integrated design process is to achieve commonality. This means that similar items should be coded and classified by material, manufacturing process, shape, and other characteristics.

Data such as the following should be stored and available for easy access:

- Item data, such as description, unit of measure, material type.

- Manufacturing process data, including detailed descriptions of the process and dimensions/specifications.

- Cost data, including process costs and purchased item costs.

- Statistical quality data collected from production runs of similar processes.

Storing this data on-line is essential to the integrated design process. Paper records are inefficient and cannot be easily reclassified or re-sorted to analyze commonality and other design aspects. Retrieval of paper records is slow and cumbersome.

In an engineering database, technical specifications and design stan-dards should be available on-line at all times for use by the design teams to ensure conformance to preestablished needs. Information on the "best" known design characteristics and manufacturing processes should be included. By storing the experience of the firm from existing product designs and manufacturing methods on-line, designers (even those physically located in other facilities, states, or countries) can access this information during the creation stages of a new product and incorporate it into their work. Not only does this information tend to produce a consistent level of product quality, it serves to speed up the design process.

This certainly does not mean that reuse of previous designs replaces the research effort and technological progress, but in many cases the purpose of a design effort is simply to apply an existing technology to solve a problem. If an existing technology solves the problem it should be used to save time, as in the example of the engine mount discussed previously. A completely new design might provide an increment of improved functionality, but in most cases it is just overkill. The time required to "reinvent the wheel" makes the organization less respon-sive to customers, who will not recognize the technical merits of the overdesigned solution anyway. In cases where an existing design does not appear to be applicable to the problem at hand, engineers should review the design concept to make certain that unnecessary require-ments are not driving the effort to create a new design.

The Design Process Varies by Industry

Although the examples given here have been oriented toward mechanical products, there is no reason why the new model of integrated design cannot be applied to other industry types. If the company is producing electronic products, the mechanical design effort will be involved primarily in packaging the product. There will be more simulation and prototyping of circuit designs, and less need for physical prototypes until the design is complete.

The integrated design process also applies to development of software products. Here, there is no mechanical design. CASE (computer-aided-software-engineering) tools, fourth-generation (English language-like) programming languages, and screen generation tools help to automate the process. Prototype applications can be quickly produced and evaluated with these tools. CASE tools often provide the capability to validate database designs, and fourth-generation languages usually check syntax and some program logic on-line. In software design, teams are less cross-functional since there is no real manufacturing involved. But segments of the design are normally divided between teams who work concurrently.

In the food, chemical, and pharmaceutical industries, there is less opportunity to reuse designs, particularly in pharmaceutical development where major research efforts are employed over long periods of time to produce a new "breakthrough" drug. There are also many more requirements to physically produce and test prototypes, due to the need to actually use the product to receive government agency approval. Still, there are significant opportunities to use integrated design concepts in these process-oriented industries particularly in the area of *process* design. Historically, inclusion of manufacturing people in the design process in these companies has been poor, information sharing across the design-related functions has been less than adequate, data management systems are generally fragmented, and design automation has been lagging behind other industries.

CHAPTER 7

New Techniques and Technologies

Although the executive management of a company must understand technology and its application to product development, it does not have unlimited time to become involved in the details of technology. However, management does need to be familiar enough with techniques and technologies to be able to execute a leadership strategy.

Toward this end, we offer an overview of techniques and technologies that can be applied to product development in an integrated environment. Reading this section will help you to become conversant with definitions and general applications of these essential tools and techniques. The final section of the chapter will help nontechnical managers assess the current state of affairs in their companies. More detailed coverage has been included in later chapters of the book for those who want in-depth coverage.

DESIGN FOR REUSABILITY OR GROUP TECHNOLOGY (GT)

Design for reusability—also known as group technology (GT)—is essentially a coding and classification technique that is used to classify designs by material, shape, and manufacturing process characteristics. New items that fit into an existing classification can take advantage of the similarities of the class to reduce design and manufacturing time by reusing existing designs to produce new parts. Current studies of new product development have shown that 80 percent of parts required for a new product can be created from existing designs; only a small percentage of parts needed for a new product must truly be designed as completely new.

The major objective of design for reusability is to reduce the time required to create a new product. It allows the designer to search for preexisting designs using the proposed material and shape attributes of the new item. It also supports quality goals through the reuse of designs that have been proven in use. Shorter design times result in reduced costs, increased reliability, and higher quality.

SIMULATION

Simulation allows engineers to test designs and processes without physically creating them. The savings in time and expense are considerable. Simulation can be used to synthesize and evaluate process problems and to predict design performance. Many what-if types of analyses can be performed in a short time, with reliable results.

In simulation, a model of the characteristics of the design is built on the simulator. The simulator includes logic to perform exactly as the physical product would perform in given situations, much as a popular computer game might realistically simulate flying an airplane. The same concept is used to test aircraft designs before building physical prototypes. Known characteristics of a technology or a production system are built into the simulator, allowing experiments to be conducted. Information resulting from the experiments is evaluated by the designer, and modifications may be made to the design. Further testing is conducted on the modified design, and the model is further refined until the designer is satisfied that the model meets the requirements of the design concept. As computer-aided engineering technology advances, simulation capability will become less expensive and more popular. Currently, simulation gives some leading companies a distinct advantage in time to market and cost of development and is indispensable in designing aircraft or other complex products.

COMPUTER-AIDED DESIGN (CAD)

Computer-aided design (CAD) is the generic name for all the computer-based systems that use interactive graphics techniques in translating a requirement or concept into an engineering design, the geometry of which is stored in a computerized database. The acronym CAD does not embrace computer-based systems for activities in manufacturing engineering. Activities that occur early in the design engineering cycle and in engineering analysis often are grouped under the CAE acronym.

In the 1980s, many companies primarily used CAD systems for drafting rather than design and engineering. During the 1990s, the use of CAD will change. Many new CAD applications aimed at specific activities—conceptual design, desktop manufacturing, detailed analysis, front-end analysis, machine control, modeling, simulation, and visualization—were introduced during the late 1980s. They have the potential to reduce product development cycle time as well as make the final product inherently more manufacturable. The key to this advance will be the integration of all of these systems.

Differences in data types, user interfaces, and hardware, however, make the integration of these packages difficult. Differing and incompatible data structures make complete integration of the newer technologies with the older, existing systems difficult. Today, many of the newer systems work in conjunction with the old through a series of cumbersome and inaccurate interfaces. For these systems to reach their full potential, vendors must work toward an applications framework. Such frameworks have been proposed and implemented for electronics applications and to a lesser extent for mechanical engineering applications.

A core requirement of integration of the many systems is a data model that is easily and accurately transferable between applications. Because of the differing demands that will arise, a comprehensive data model that represents information about use for all activities is required. Although all of the data may not reside in a single location, metadata models of a given part, supported by EDM systems, will enable users to find all the data they need to access. Without such a model even the most rudimentary data transfers between applications are fraught with errors and misrepresentations. Some current efforts (such as computer-aided acquisition and logistics support (CALS) and Standard for the Exchange of Product Modeling Data (STEP) will help. A short-term and more easily obtainable solution would be for all the major CAD vendors to standardize on a single solid-modeling kernel and provide defined parameters for the representation of key data. However, as for most standardization efforts, the gestation period is extremely long.

Although many companies focused on two-dimensional applications in the 1980s, by the end of the 1990s, 3-D will be the preferred method of mechanical design. Solid modelers using techniques such as parametric modeling and variational geometry, which control and constrain object relationships based on size or orientation, are getting more flexible, and solid modeling is at the core of many of the new systems.

Because in the 1980s so many CAD systems concentrated only on two-dimensional design applications, many users will upgrade to systems that will better allow them to attack the upstream activities of product design and development where the costs are built into the product. For example, visualization systems can, by creating soft prototypes rather than hard ones, help engineers refine an optimal final design before any money is committed for tooling.

COMPUTER-AIDED ENGINEERING (CAE)

Computer-aided engineering (CAE) is the umbrella acronym for all computer-based systems used in the design engineering and manufacturing engineering functions. It sometimes is used to mean only all computer-based tools used in design engineering—proposal preparation, styling, conceptual design, structural analysis, aerodynamic analysis, kinematic analysis, simulation, geometric modeling, engineering design, engineering tests, detailed design, schematic and wiring layout design, drafting, parts list preparation, and preparation of technical documentation. It also may be used to mean all computer-based tools used at the front end of the design engineering process, prior to detailed design.

In the electronics design environment, CAE is the use of computer-based systems to assist in the processes from specification through layout to test.

COMPUTER-AIDED MANUFACTURING (CAM)

Computer-aided manufacturing (CAM) has become nearly as popular as CAD in recent years and is often mentioned in conjunction with CAD. CAD/CAM systems have been in existence for some time, although the CAM portion of CAD/CAM systems often is underused.

CAM entails the use of computers to monitor and control manufacturing operations and may include process-monitoring equipment, machine programming and control, or linking CAD directly to the shop floor. One of the reasons CAM is not more widely implemented is that it requires cooperation between engineering and manufacturing, and this is often lacking in firms that have not progressed toward an integrated design environment. Adversarial relationships between manufacturing and engineering are still common and contribute to the low CAM implementation rate.

CAM's main benefit is to link design and manufacturing, to the extent that an integrated design team can approve of a design that has been documented on a CAD system and electronically transmit instructions for producing the design directly to the shop floor. CAD data can be used to generate programs for machinery in the manufacturing facility, to allow programming of machine tools, and to manufacture physical prototypes (when required) quickly. Manufacturing set-up times can be significantly reduced and flexibility increased. Overall, the time from documentation of design through production of product is reduced.

COMPUTER-AIDED SOFTWARE ENGINEERING (CASE)

Computer-aided software engineering (CASE) makes its biggest contribution in firms that develop software as a major part of their business, but it also can contribute significantly where large amounts of custom-developed applications are needed. This definitely includes engineering organizations that are developing computer-aided engineering applications for their own use, and software that goes into their products.

CASE is the use of specialized computer software to create and maintain computer application systems. Design concepts can be entered graphically, and program logic can be validated by the CASE tool set. In addition, CASE may include the ability to create database specifications and data dictionaries and provide facilities to generate program code.

The main benefits of CASE are the speed with which applications can be generated and the greater reliability of the resulting systems due to its validation capabilities. CASE allows rapid prototyping of applications and can help generate screens and other user interfaces quickly for testing and user approval. Modifications and subsequent customization of systems created under CASE are simplified, requiring less effort and fewer people to maintain them. Although significant effort is required to implement CASE technology due to the training required to use it correctly, the investment usually pays off handsomely in terms of time savings and quality of end product.

Additional Techniques

Hoshin Kanri (Policy Deployment) is a step-by-step planning, implementation, and review approach to the management of change in critical business processes. Its aim is to translate top management vision into a set of coherent, consistent, understandable, and attainable policies and actions that can be applied at all levels of the company and in all functions of the company. Policy Deployment cascades, or deploys, top management policies and targets down the management hierarchy. At each level, the policy is translated into policies, targets, and actions for the next level down. At each level, managers and employees participate in the definition, from the overall vision and their annual targets, of the strategy and detailed action plan they will use to attain their targets. They also define the measures that will be used to demonstrate that they have successfully achieved their targets. They, in turn, pass on targets to the next level down. Each level under top management is involved with the level above it to make sure that its proposed strategy corresponds to requirements.

Performance metrics are needed to set targets, monitor progress, track results, and fix problems. They help identify, analyze, and report operating behavior. Without the ability to measure performance, it is not possible to ensure performance improvement. Metrics are needed to measure all aspects of a company's performance. Some will be related to financial performance, many to operating performance. Typical metrics address areas such as business performance, market satisfaction, quality, and development performance (metrics include lead time, number of engineering changes, change activity in a software module).

Benchmarking is a technique for comparing a company's performance with that of other organizations that are believed to have more effective operations. If other organizations are found to have more effective operations, then the company can try to understand how they work and why they are better. The company can then start to improve its own operations and will be able to set itself realistic performance targets. One purpose of benchmarking is to establish credible goals and pursue continuous improvement. This is primarily a direction-setting process; more important, however, it is a means by which the practices needed to reach new goals are discovered and understood. Benchmarking also legitimizes goals and direction by basing them on external realities. It is an alternative to the traditional method of establishing targets by extrapolation of past practices and trends. Conventional goal setting often fails because the external environment changes at a pace significantly faster than projected. The ultimate benefit of benchmarking is that end-user requirements are more adequately met because the process forces a continual focus on the external environment.

The cost of quality is the sum of all the costs incurred throughout the product life cycle due to poor quality—by the product not having perfect quality the first time and every subsequent time. The cost of quality is usually expressed as a percentage of sales and is made up of four types of quality costs—internal failure costs, external failure costs, appraisal costs, and prevention costs. Internal failure costs are due to failures such as rework, scrap, and poor design that the customer does not see. External failure costs are due to failures that occur after the product has been delivered to the customer and include warranty claims, product liability claims, and field returns. Appraisal costs are the costs of measuring quality and maintaining conformance by such activities as inspection, testing, process monitoring, and equipment calibration. Prevention costs are the costs of activities to reduce failure and appraisal costs, and to achieve first-time quality, such as education, training, and supplies certification. Before embarking on quality improvement activities, companies typically have failure costs of about 10 percent of sales, appraisal costs of about 8 percent of sales, and prevention costs of about 2 percent of sales—a cost of quality of about 20 percent of sales. Quality improvement activities aim to reduce this to about 2 or 3 percent of sales.

Traditional cost management is largely accomplished through variance reporting. The underlying principle is that if the cost center is under budget, then costs are under control. Traditionally, cost has been controlled at the point of occurrence rather than at the source. The cost centers that actually incur the expenditure may not be responsible for the factors that contribute to the actual costs. The result is that under some circumstances, traditional cost management results in inaccurate product costs and inappropriate performance measures. The reason for these errors is often that the attributes chosen to characterize the costs related to a product are attributes of unit products (such as direct labor hours per product), whereas in practice many of the costs (such as set-up time or engineering change time) are related to batches of products, families of products, or even all of a company's products. Additionally, traditional product-costing systems have spread overhead as a function of direct labor hours per unit product. But the cost of direct labor hours is becoming a smaller and smaller percentage of product cost, giving an inaccurate view of real product costs, masking the need to clearly account for and reduce overhead costs, and focusing attention on dollar costs rather than on time cycles.

Accurate product costs are at the heart of pricing decisions for new product introductions, obsolete product withdrawal, and responses to competitive products. Activity-based costing starts by matching the resources of the business with the activities that are performed, by determining what tasks are performed on a routine basis and then identifying the personnel and other resources that are required to perform each activity. Product costs are then calculated by driving the activity costs down to products based on how each product "consumes" the activities.

Product life-cycle accounting distributes costs and potential profitability of a product among categories over the life of the product. The product life cycle is made up of the stages a product moves through as it evolves from a concept through development and production to operational use. The actual product life cycle of a particular product depends on the nature of the product and the environment in which it is developed and used. The most critical time for controlling a product's cost is in the development stage even though most of the product's costs are not incurred until much later. The discrepancy between when costs are committed to (in the development stage) and when they are actually incurred (during the manufacturing and distribution phases of the product's life cycle) must be clear.

Design for Assembly (DFA) techniques reduce the cost and time of assembly by simplifying the product and process—by reducing the number of parts, combining two or more parts into one, reducing or eliminating adjustments, simplifying assembly operations, designing for parts handling and presentation, selecting fasteners for ease of assembly, minimizing parts tangling, and ensuring that products are easy to test. For example, tabs and notches in mating parts make assembly easier and also reduce the need for assembly and testing documentation. Simple z-axis assembly can minimize handling and insertion time.

Design for Manufacture (DFM) techniques are closely linked to Design for Assembly techniques but are oriented primarily to individual parts and components rather than to DFA's subassemblies, assemblies, and products. DFM aims to eliminate the often expensive and unnecessary features of a part that make it difficult to manufacture. It helps prevent the unnecessarily smooth surface, the unnecessarily small radius, and the unnecessarily high tolerances.

Waste Removal. Waste is anything that exceeds the minimum amount of time, money, effort, materials, equipment, and space required to produce the product. In the plant, waste includes unnecessarily long manufacturing cycles, damaged goods, unnecessary transportation of goods, unnecessary storage areas, and many non–value-adding activities such as unpacking, inspecting, returning, storing, material handling, and rework. There are similar non–value-adding vices in the product development process, such as reentry of data, transportation of paper drawings, failure to use existing information, poor office layout, working on different projects at the same time, and engineering change handling.

Concurrent engineering brings together multidisciplinary teams that work together from the start of a project with the intention of getting things right as quickly as possible and as early as possible. Getting the design correct at the start will reduce downstream difficulties in the workflow. The need for expensive engineering changes later in the cycle will be reduced. Sometimes only design engineers and manufacturing engineers are involved together in concurrent product and process development. In other cases, the cross-functional teams also include representatives from other functional groups. Sometimes customers and suppliers are also included in the team. Multidisciplinary groups acting together early in the workflow can take informed and agreed decisions relating to product, process, cost, and quality issues. They can make tradeoffs between design features, part manufacturability, assembly requirements, material needs, reliability issues, serviceability requirements, and cost and time constraints.

Life-Cycle Design. Concerns about environmental protection and safe working conditions have affected the demand for industrial products. Companies now have to cope with these issues as well as those of cost, quality, and time that have already been established by global competition. Life-Cycle Design ensures that not only the issues related to a product's useful life are considered at the outset but also those issues (such as recycling and disposal) involving the product once its useful life is over. Life-cycle design includes evaluation of environmental protection, working conditions, resource optimization, life-cycle costs, and ease of manufacture. Life-Cycle Design goals in a specific case could include ease of disassembly, ease of assembly, fast and safe decomposition, lowest cost to find/recover, and lowest cost to recycle.

ASSESSING USE OF THESE TECHNIQUES AND TECHNOLOGIES

The following checklist provides a method of assessing potential opportunities to improve your company's product development process. Based on the results of rating your company's performance against the checklist, areas of opportunity for improvement (and advantage) can be prioritized for implementation.

Manufacturing Process Development

1. What percentage of current processes are documented and stored electronically?

- Electronic storage is a first step toward reusability and helps avoid the reinvention of the wheel syndrome. Most modern manufacturing systems provide this capability. If this hasn't been implemented yet, it should be an immediate priority.

2. Is software implemented to support development of manufacturing processes?

- CAM and CAE are the primary technologies available to help automate the development of the manufacturing process. If CAD and electronic storage or classification of manufacturing processes have been implemented, progression to automated support for process development should be a high priority.

3. Are manufacturing processes categorized and stored according to item type to support reusability?

- Electronic storage and categorization lay the groundwork for process reusability and automated support for process development, greatly shortening the time required to produce a manufacturing process for a part or product.

4. Are there formal procedures for creation and maintenance of all process-related data?

- Formal procedures simply ensure that the most efficient method for producing a process has been defined and can be used to enforce standards.

5. Do procedures include standards to be adhered to in the development of a new process?

- Inclusion of design standards in process-creation procedures is an essential element in establishing basic disciplines to support an integrated development process.

6. What is the level of compliance with the procedures?

- All too often, companies develop procedures and design standards and then fail to enforce their use. Less than 100 percent compliance with procedures may indicate a number of conditions, including invalid procedures, unrealistic design standards, poor morale, and incompetent technical management.

7. At what stage of the product development process are manufacturing process methods determined?

- Development of the manufacturing process should begin during the design phase of the part, as soon as the performance characteristics and geometry of the part have been determined.

8. When are make-versus-buy decisions made during product development?

- Make/buy decisions should be made as early in the design process as practical, to allow concurrent manufacturing and vendor process development.

9. How are programs generated for computer-controlled machinery?

- If programs are not being generated with the aid of CAE applications or automated tools and are still created and maintained with traditional programming languages, there is significant opportunity to compress development time and expenses.

10. How many different languages are used to generate part programs for computer-controlled machinery?

- Proliferation of programming languages complicates the development and maintenance process and causes inefficiency in the use of programming resources due to specialization.

11. Are part program revision levels controlled and referenced or linked back to the process?

- Failure to use the most recent version of a program can cause scrap and rework or may cause production to use a less efficient, lower-quality process in production.

12. How much time is spent testing part programs, and is this testing done on production machinery?

- Programs created with CAE support and incorporating reusability will require little testing. Where the ability to simulate operation of the machinery has been developed, it is possible that no on-machine testing may be conducted at all.

13. Are any test specifications developed via automation?

- Test specifications developed via automation will reduce the time required for development and help ensure reliability of the process.

14. Who is responsible for developing jigs, tools, and fixtures?

- If your company still develops production tooling within an island known as "manufacturing engineering," there is potential time and quality improvement available through the use of a multifunctional design team or outsourcing.

15. Are jigs, tools, and fixtures standardized, modular, or "soft"?

- Using "soft" tooling allows maximum flexibility and can often help to reduce set-up or changeover times, providing the ability to respond quickly to changes in schedule, and ultimately reducing manufacturing costs.

16. Are there standard methods for documenting process data?

- Documentation should follow standards for ease of maintenance and clarity in use. Standardization of format helps to reduce maintenance effort and mistakes in manufacturing.

17. Is process data integrated into the materials management or scheduling systems?

- Accurate process steps and operation times need to be available to production scheduling personnel to support achievable schedules.

18. Are method sheets produced for use in manufacturing, or is process data communicated to the shop floor electronically?

• Using electronic work instructions on the shop floor helps to ensure that the most current version of the process is used and helps to eliminate delays in starting production.

19. How are programs input to the automated production machinery?

• Technology can transmit programs directly to production machinery. This can significantly reduce set-up or changeover times, increasing flexibility and reducing costs.

20. Is there a significant backlog of programs waiting to be written or modified?

• Programming backlogs may result from excessive programmer specialization, "old" programming languages, or insufficient resources. They delay introduction of products and will not support the objectives of simultaneously completing product and process design.

21. How many people are employed in the creation and maintenance of programs?

• The number of people involved in programming tends to be larger in shops utilizing "old" design methods.

22. Are programming and the CAD systems integrated?

• The ability of the programming staff to display the geometry of a part, and to simulate characteristics during development of the manufacturing process can eliminate process design iterations, speeding the completion of the manufacturing process.

23. Are jigs, tools, and fixtures designed on the CAD systems?

• Using CAD to design manufacturing tooling reduces development time through categorization and reuse of similar designs.

Product Development

1. To what extent are the following types of data stored electronically within engineering data management systems?

- Drawings
- Specifications
- Parts lists
- Procurement specifications
- Part standards
- Design standards

- Electronic storage is a necessary step toward reusing designs and should be implemented as a high priority.

2. What proportion of current designs is documented and stored electronically?

- This measurement indicates the current state of automation of design information. A low percentage suggests insufficient focus on basic enabling technology and too much manual documentation effort.

3. Is software implemented to support product design functions?

- If systems have not been implemented to support the design function, a high priority should be assigned to achieving the basic functionality (such as CAD) immediately. If more advanced systems have been implemented, it is worthwhile to question whether the intended benefits have been achieved. If not, corrective action should be initiated.

4. Does software used to support design include functions that extend beyond the scope of a CAD system (DFA, etc.)?

- Assess the level of progress toward automation and integration of part and product designs. At a basic level, CAD has been implemented, while an advanced level is represented by CAE and integration of engineering systems with company business systems.

Operation at a basic level suggests that it may be time to plan implementation of more advanced capability.

5. Are designs stored and categorized to support reusability?

- Electronic storage and categorization lay the groundwork for design reusability and automated support for product development, greatly shortening the time required to produce a new part or product.

6. Are there formal procedures for creation and maintenance of all design data?

- Formal procedures simply ensure that the most efficient method for producing a design has been defined and can be used to enforce standards.

7. Do procedures include standards to be adhered to in the development of designs?

- Inclusion of design standards in product development procedures is an essential element in establishing basic disciplines to support an integrated development process.

8. To what extent are standards incorporated into software used to support design?

- If CAE applications are implemented, established design standards should be incorporated to analyze designs for conformance.

9. What is the level of adherence to standards?

- Failure to conform to design standards may indicate a number of things, including invalid procedures, unrealistic design standards, insufficient training, or incompetent management.

10. How much time is spent building and testing product or part prototypes?

- Time (and expenses) devoted to building and testing product or part prototypes is an indicator of the potential savings available from technologies such as simulation and rapid prototyping.

11. Is prototyping supported by software or automation such as rapid prototyping equipment?

- If rapid prototyping or simulation capabilities are available, new product development time should be reduced compared to historical averages. If not, money has been spent to acquire technology that is not returning the intended benefits. The technology may not be implemented or used correctly.

12. Who is responsible for developing and testing prototypes?

- In traditional environments, prototyping is largely restricted to the engineering department. In an integrated design environment, the entire design team has the opportunity to develop and evaluate prototypes.

13. Is product design documentation integrated into the materials management or manufacturing scheduling systems?

- An important component of achieving an advanced state of integration in product development is the availability of product documentation and technical data on demand throughout the company. Integration of engineering and business systems indicates achievement of this important capability.

14. How many people are employed in the creation and maintenance of product design data?

- The number of people engaged in creating and maintaining product design data is usually proportional to the level of automated support used to maintain product documentation. In environments where documentation is still created and stored primarily on paper, a significant portion of engineering and drafting workhours is spent on clerical tasks. In an environment supported by design automation tools, a comparatively minor amount of human resources is engaged in documenting and maintaining design data.

15. What method of part classification (if any) is used?
  - Drawing
  - Geometry
  - Description

- Classification is an important basic requirement for supporting reusability. The primary classification scheme for supporting reusability is geometry.

16. What controls are in place to ensure that only the latest versions of product designs are used?

- Integration of engineering and manufacturing systems is vital to ensure that the latest production version of a design is produced. Revision levels are normally part of the documentation carried on the system. If this level of integration has not yet been achieved, manual systems are usually employed to ensure that current revisions are used by manufacturing. These tend to consume more engineering and clerical resources.

17. What is the speed of access to product data throughout the company?

- Speed of access to product data and documentation is an important support requirement. Immediate access is usually achieved by implementation of integrated engineering and business information systems. Immediate, on-line access eliminates delays in purchasing or making parts.

18. What is the average amount of elapsed time for the development of new products (from concept to shipment) versus the amount of value-added time spent actually working on the design?

- Although this measurement may be difficult to obtain, reasonable estimates are possible by observing current development efforts for a short period. It is not uncommon in traditional sequential environments to find only 20 percent of total development time was spent actually adding value to the process, with the remainder being spent waiting for another function to perform its role or reworking a design due to the functional separation inherent in the traditional, sequential process.

19. How many new products are developed each year compared to the competition?

- If competitors are introducing significantly more new products, they are probably ahead of you in implementing advanced organizational techniques and design technologies. A major effort will be required to catch up to or surpass these competitors, who will not be standing still while you are improving your own capability.

20. What percentage of drawings is created on paper each year?

- The amount of paper documentation produced by the product development process is another indication of progress. While it is not possible to completely eliminate paper in all stages of the process, graphically oriented electronic systems allow for major reductions in the need for hard-copy documentation.

21. What does design and development activity cost the company each year versus major competitors?

- If product development spending is significantly equal to or greater than the competition in real terms but the number of new products is the same or less than the competition, improvements in the product development process will be necessary to avoid losing competitive ground.

22. To what extent are functions other than engineering involved in the design and development activity?

- Progress toward reducing time to market is indicated by the establishment of functionally integrated design teams, including marketing, manufacturing, and finance.

23. What has been the annual level of capital investment in systems and equipment to support product development?

- Little or no investment in CAE technologies may indicate that the product development function in your company has not recognized the importance of these capabilities or has been unable to justify the expense. Competitive factors must be given weight in the process of gaining approval to invest in CAE.

24. What is the annual level of investment in engineering technology education and training?

- Leading companies realize that they must continually train employees to maintain a dominant position. Without a significant investment in technology training and education, engineers will be unable to keep up with advances, handicapping R&D capability.

25. How often do designs have to be revised before release to production?

- Designs that must frequently be reworked before release to production are likely in a traditional, sequential development process.

26. How often do designs have to be revised after release to production?

- If a significant number of designs needs to be revised after release to production, it is likely that manufacturing is not playing any major role in new product development and needs to be integrated into the process.

27. How many new products are released on time (according to the originally set project release date)?

- If new product development projects are continually late, the process is probably still too sequential or the project planning mechanism is flawed. Barring a poor project planning and estimating method, rework and numerous design iterations are major contributors to delay and should point to areas of the development process that can be improved.

CHAPTER 8

Defining the Improvement Strategy for Product Development: From Vision to Plan

WHY ONE AUTOMAKER IS PLAYING CATCH-UP

The strategic importance of the design function and its role in the success of the enterprise are expanding. Recognizing this fact will propel some companies to make changes in the way they develop products. In fact, some companies have already begun to adopt new methods in product development and engineering that are having significant marketplace impact.

In the automobile industry, luxury models and sports cars capture the attention of the press and car enthusiasts, but the venerable and often unexciting family sedan earns the most revenue. About one-quarter of the entire U.S. auto market is family sedans, a competitive market traditionally dominated by General Motors.

Recently, however, GM has been losing share in this major market segment to rivals Ford, Toyota, Honda, and now Chrysler. GM's inability to update its flagship Lumina sedan has been a significant contributor to the car maker's financial troubles as sales have weakened. All of

GM's rivals have been able to reduce product development time and time-to-market to levels that GM has been unable to match. The current projection for delivery of the redesigned Lumina will be the culmination of a six-year effort. Most other major players in this market have shaved time to market to half that amount of time and are still improving. Consequently, when the redesigned Lumina finally hits the showroom floors in the 1995 model year, it will compete against features and styling that are no longer present in models of rival manufacturers. Toyota, Honda, and Chrysler will have redesigned their offerings again by the 1995 model year and will be offering features that the Lumina does not address and will not be able to respond to. Why is the once-dominant General Motors steadily losing ground in a market it owned?

It is not surprising that GM has made no significant progress in improving its product development process since the 1980s. While first the Japanese and then Ford and Chrysler adopted team approaches to product development, GM scoffed at the idea and continued with a more traditional approach. On the Lumina project, work is distributed across a few thousand engineers who also work on other models. The process is very sequential, communication is poor, and the number of component redesign iterations is very large. Fortunately, this is the last major GM project to be organized in such a fashion. After a recent reorganization of the engineering function at GM (and recognition that they are being left behind), all new development projects are to be performed by cross-functional, product-dedicated teams. Results of this realignment will begin to bear fruit by 1996, assuming that GM successfully implements the team organization and culture. In the meantime, the competition is not standing still.

Over in Dearborn, at Ford Motor Company, the design process was revised to incorporate multidisciplined design teams during development of the Taurus during the 1980s. Recently, Ford has linked its worldwide design operations in North America, Europe, Japan, and Australia electronically on a single international network. The team working on a particular design for a new car may be physically located around the globe but can communicate electronically to facilitate working together. A design created in one location can be transmitted to all other locations, and designers in a number of locations can view the same design at the same time, while discussing and actually making changes to the design in real time on graphical workstations. This capability allows Ford to take advantage of expertise no matter where in the company the capability resides. Once a design is finalized, the data files can be transmitted by satellite on the same day, to the design studio in Italy where computer-controlled machinery creates a clay or plastic model and work begins on the body of the car. Today Ford is able to produce a new model in about three years; it intends to reduce new product development time to two years.

PRODUCT DESIGN AFFECTS OPERATING RESULTS

Not surprisingly, the product development process has a major effect on the bottom line and not just because a popular new product earns more than a failure. As demonstrated by the contrast between Ford and General Motors, time to market can be a major factor in the cost of developing products. Ford has made a substantial investment over a number of years in the underlying culture, processes, and technologies that makes it possible for design teams to be scattered around the world. But it has gained market share and reduced development costs as a result of the capability it has developed in time to market. In contrast, GM will take six years to deliver a redesigned car that is the flagship in their most important market. The costs resulting from three extra years of development time and the loss of market share to rivals are likely to substantially exceed the costs rival Ford has invested, when viewed with an eye to long-term results. While GM has been spending merely on product development, its competitors have been investing in new techniques and the necessary enabling technologies.

This is but one example of the strategic importance of the design function. It contrasts a traditional approach against some of the newer techniques being applied to product development and also vividly demonstrates the potential benefits available to those who implement some of the new ideas. Those who are late in recognizing and acting on this information may be permanently hurt by their delayed reaction, as is possible with General Motors. Only time will tell whether GM can regain the ground it has lost by waiting so long to acknowledge the viability of a team-centered approach. The bigger message in this story is that delay can be very costly and that many companies are already competing on the basis of product development capabilities. Any firm that expects to play a major competitive role in its industry in the future should be acting *now* to take control of the product development process at the highest level in the organization and dramatically improve it.

HOW TO IMPROVE THE PROCESS

Most companies have a number of improvement initiatives in place that address areas that top management believes to be important to success. These might include total quality programs, reduction of manufacturing cycle time and inventories, implementation of integrated business information systems, and a host of other "flavors of the month." There is nothing inherently wrong with initiatives such as these, which are often focused on continuous improvement and are probably being undertaken because everyone else in the industry is doing similar things. They must be addressed just to maintain competitive parity.

In fact, none of these flavors of the month will substantially differentiate one company from the next. If all the competitors in a market are embarking on similar internal capability-improvement programs, parity will be maintained. Those who want to surpass their competition must do something more. If everyone is focused on continuous-improvement programs, then only those who find a "step change" improvement will jump ahead of the rest and enjoy a real breakthrough competitive advantage until others can duplicate what they have done.

Achieving the breakthrough type of improvement requires that top management be *committed to and involved in radical change*. Core business processes will have to be redesigned, supported by changes in organization structure, performance measures, and management style. Outside observers have termed the changes made by Chrysler and Ford as "brave and bold" moves, but in reality these changes were absolutely necessary to meet the challenge posed by Japanese rivals that had succeeded in achieving breakthrough improvements in time to market. The changes may be bold or radical, but they are certainly not reckless. In fact, it is reckless not to react to major capability improvements at rival companies. Responding to this challenge requires a carefully controlled cross-functional approach and unwavering commitment on the part of management. It also requires highly visible leadership.

To take advantage of the breakthrough improvement potential in product development, a strategy must be developed and implemented. Some of the important considerations to be included in developing a strategy and policies for product development are

- Understanding of the financial and operational requirements of the development process,

- Knowledge of the potential of the company to produce, compete, and grow, and

- Consideration of costs, quality, capacity, and time-to-market factors.

The Effect of Design Technology

Considering the influence on costs, market share, and profits from the product development function, it is important to understand the effect that technology can have on the design function and its pass-through effect on operating results. If you are selling hundreds of thousands of automobiles, you can justify an investment in technology that helps to automate and speed the production of new or enhanced designs. Rapid prototyping, solid modeling, simulation, worldwide concurrent design, and virtual reality are all possibilities. In fact, these tools and techniques may be essential to effective competition with others who also have the motivation and funding to invest in new techniques and technology.

If you are building one-of-a-kind, custom-built products, you may also be able to afford the investment in the latest technology by passing the cost along to customers who are willing to pay for the luxury of custom design and production. But if you are producing a standard product in a very competitive and price-conscious market, your ability to afford advanced technology may be severely limited. Using older technology may keep the bottom line in the black for the present, but failure to invest in new technology and implement advances could eventually result in loss of market and unprofitable results as others use these advances to lower their manufacturing costs or discover other ways to differentiate their product from yours. Strategies must be developed to incorporate technology that addresses long-term competitive needs, through outsourcing, consortia, or cost sharing with a noncompetitor that has similar needs.

In a highly competitive market situation, the rate of product change will provide advantages to those who have invested in techniques and technologies that allow rapid development of new or enhanced products. Those who have been unable to reduce their time to market will face a constant stream of new features coming from a rival who is closely monitoring customer needs and rapidly satisfying them. Even if an effort is made to respond, it will take longer and therefore cost more, watering down any financial benefits to be gained from matching a competitor's new offerings. Delay in developing the appropriate capabilities could be disastrous.

Situations such as the one just described point to the need for management to consider technological strengths and product development capabilities in determining how to compete and how to respond to competitors' moves. As illustrated by the automobile industry example, a company like Ford can be confident that it will be able to produce a new model in about the same time as the Asian competition and in less time than General Motors. It also knows that Chrysler, Honda, and Toyota are continuing to shave months off the development time for new models, as they are. Knowledge of its own capability versus their competitors' allows Ford to make strategic decisions that have a high probability of success. It is also clear that others will have new models every two to three years and Ford must do the same. It knows it must continue to invest in techniques and technology at a fairly high rate if it is to retain the ability to compete effectively.

But technology by itself will not make the critical difference in the marketplace. Technology is an enabler that is used to respond to the features demanded by the customer. Focusing on customer requirements is the key determinant of strategy.

Customers Increasingly Affect Product Development

With the increasing importance of quality in all that we do, it is no surprise that quality has become a given—the price of entry into the competitive arena. Everyone seems to have a TQM effort under way, although some are just paying lip service without putting real substance into the effort. One of the basic concepts of TQM is the idea of incorporating the "voice of the customer." What this means in product development and market success is that no design will be successful unless the end user's requirements are satisfied. Of course, customer desires and requirements tend to change over time, indicating a continuing need for communication with customers to assess the degree of product conformance to requirements and to recognize enhancements.

Incorporating the voice of the customer (or Quality Function Deployment) is an *essential* product development and competitive factor that must be a part of policy and strategy. Customer needs must be correlated with design objectives and implemented. In practice, customers might be surveyed via questionnaire, or market studies might be purchased. Out of the data coming from the customers, specific customer requirements are categorized and then prioritized to identify the most important ones. Out of the list of high-priority requirements, characteristics are identified that are used to measure the current design against the voice of the customer. Those characteristics that correlate closely with the prioritized customer demands become the goals to be met in the product design, and these goals are translated into technical requirements for the product. These technical requirements will be deployed all the way down to the components and raw materials used in manufacturing the product, making the role of suppliers more important.

The Role of the Supplier

Suppliers are playing a much larger role in product development with the advent of partnering. Through the establishment of partnerships with major vendors, additional product development capabilities and resources are being added by outsourcing some of the component development for new products to major suppliers.

At a manufacturer of heavy industrial equipment, major components of their products are castings. In the past, this company's engineers designed the castings themselves, despite their lack of expertise in foundry technology. After establishing a partnership with their major casting supplier, the foundry engineers now participate in the earliest stages of new product design, essentially doing the casting design for this company. Both companies benefit, as the foundry can often design the part with its own unique capabilities in mind, resulting in lower cost and improved reliability. The manufacturing company applies the design effort normally expended on the castings to other areas of product development where it has expertise, while enjoying higher-quality castings at lower cost.

Competitive Threats

When Ronald Reagan took office back in 1981, he was determined to do something about ending the cold war. He began a military build-up unprecedented in peace time and initiated the Strategic Defense Initiative. Although many experts were doubtful of the viability of the Star Wars defense, merely announcing the program and funding the necessary research caused a reaction in the USSR. Just as in business competition, the Soviets knew they had to maintain parity in defense capability and were forced to dramatically increase their own defense budget to counter the growth of the U.S. military and the Star Wars threat. Already in shaky condition, the USSR eventually spent itself into oblivion.

The parallel with industry is not hard to draw. A company that has built superior capabilities in the development of new products can use this advantage to gain market share, while luring competitors into an expensive struggle to develop the same capabilities. While the competition is occupied with developing the new abilities, the leading company continues to introduce new products and features faster and continues to develop its capabilities. When a competitor reaches the targeted level of capability, the leader is ready with a newly developed advantage and the competitor finds itself in the same position it started in—spending considerable sums of money to build capabilities that do not provide the needed return when they are implemented because the battleground has moved. There are two ways out of this game:

- Spend yourself into oblivion (or a weakened financial state), or

- Develop a "step" improvement that leapfrogs the leader (or provides a different type of advantage that it will have to try to match) and that will provide enough return on investment to strengthen the company's position.

The choice is obvious and will increasingly need to be made. Leading companies have already developed the type of capabilities necessary to give themselves a distinct advantage, and the number of companies building advanced capabilities in new product development is increasing.

This points to some new realities for competition and product development in the near future:

- The business strategy needs to include a synergistic product development strategy, one that acknowledges existing capabilities, uses them to the fullest extent possible, and seeks to develop new ones.

- The product development process must support the business strategy. If the strategy targets introduction of a product in a specific timeframe, the development process must be able to respond or risk financial and market-share losses. Product development capabilities must be known at the inception of the strategy to ensure that realistic goals are established.

INTEGRATING MANAGEMENT PROCESS AND TECHNOLOGY

If the business strategy has to incorporate the product development process and its capabilities, what key areas should be considered in this integration of management process and technology? Cost, quality, and lead time (including capacity considerations) will all be significant and are discussed in the sections that follow.

Product Development Effect on Product Cost

Product cost is sensitive to the type of technology used in the design concept and is another area that must be considered in developing a strategy. Design for Manufacturability and Assembly (DFMA) is one of the tools used to make designs more efficient in their use of material and labor, which tends to reduce costs. In general, the technique reduces the number of parts and simplifies handling in the manufacture or assembly of the item. Companies that have developed expertise in the use of DFMA techniques recognize that they have a powerful capability. This contributes to their sense of what can be accomplished in the marketplace against competitors who can't match the cost or quality they are able to achieve.

At one electronic instrument manufacturer, a DFMA analysis yielded significant improvements. On one circuit board assembly, the number of parts was reduced from 100 to 30. The number of process steps was reduced from 140 to 40, and assembly time was reduced by 60 percent. This was only one subassembly of a major product, and similar or better results were obtained on other assemblies. Overall, approximately 70 percent of the assembly time was eliminated across this product's subassemblies, and corresponding savings were realized in the redesign by eliminating the number of components.

This is not an isolated case. IBM used DFMA in competing with Epson on its personal computer printer product lines. Although most of these dot matrix printers look pretty much the same, incorporate the same basic technology, and function almost identically, after DFMA analysis the IBM unit had achieved major advantages over the Epson. The IBM model has 80 percent fewer assembly operations, requires 90 percent less assembly time, and has 80 percent fewer parts. IBM is able to offer this unit for a competitive price and get excellent performance out of the unit, superior reliability due to the decreased number of parts, at a cost to produce that is lower than Epson's.

One of the other large components of product cost is overhead. DFMA tools can incorporate cost estimation capability, which helps designers determine when they are approaching target costs for an item. But when there is an incomplete understanding of the product cost structure and how cost is affected by various factors, it is impossible to make good design decisions. One problem with designing to cost or "value engineering" techniques is that they depend on the accuracy and validity of the costing system, which in many cases does a poor job in allocating overhead costs.

Traditional cost accounting does a fair job of explaining costs for public financial reporting needs but is limited in its ability to collect and report cost components that indicate actual consumption of resources used in the overhead categories. Using the direct labor content as a means to estimate the percentage of overhead to be allocated to a product tends to distort actual cost and conceal the real sources of resource consumption.

A simple example of how traditional cost accounting methods distort costs can be seen in a real-world example. A manufacturer of complex assembled and machined industrial equipment was unhappy with profitability and set out to analyze costs in great detail. True to Pareto's law, 20 percent of the product line brought in 80 percent of the sales. The accounting system reported that the remaining low-volume products were profitable, despite their minor contribution to overall sales and disproportionate consumption of support resources.

The accounting system allocated overhead expenses based on the direct labor content of the products, which was nearly the same percentage for all products, due to their similarity. As a result, all products had essentially the same overhead. Management knew from observation that the low-volume products (comprising 80 percent of the product numbers, but only 20 percent of the sales) consumed a greater portion of the resources included in overhead and embarked on an activity-based cost analysis that allocated overhead according to actual usage of resources to support each product. The outcome of the study resulted in far more accurate allocation of overhead expenses to products and revealed that more than half of the products were actually losing money at their current pricing levels.

A word of caution in situations like this. The result of the activity-based analysis should be used to set pricing and other strategies for the unprofitable products so that they may become profitable again but is not necessarily a criterion for eliminating them. Eliminating unprofitable products reduces the population of items to which overhead can be allocated, and when taken to extremes can have a negative effect on the remaining products by forcing overhead costs to be spread across a much smaller population. Removing products from the product line should be coupled with corresponding reductions in supporting overhead or replacement with new products.

A number of companies have implemented the capability to perform activity-based costing, initially driven by the need to identify profitable versus unprofitable products. What they realized as they continued to use the technique is that the more accurate cost information helps to enhance any process-improvement effort, including product development. The ability to know the true costs of each segment of the product development process can help the company optimize the whole. Leading companies such as Hewlett-Packard have recognized that DFMA and the enhanced knowledge of cost from activity-based analysis can contribute substantially to the development of a business strategy that is based on confidence that they can produce high-quality and low-cost products that are brought to market quickly.

Manufacturing and Engineering Capacity Constraints

A strategy and policies to harness the competitive potential contained in product development must address product design and production, whether done in-house or outside. The capacity of an engineering department, design team, or manufacturing facility will depend partially on the magnitude of facilities and the relationship between investment in human resources and equipment. It is a costly and wasteful situation to have more resources than necessary, but poorly staffed and equipped facilities will incur costs as well. Insufficient capacity will result in delayed projects, equipment breakdowns, and declining quality. Frequently, capacity will meet needs in some areas and fall short of needs in other areas along the product development chain. Bottleneck points and overcapacity situations within the process flow must be recognized and carefully considered in determining the product development strategy. Even so, unanticipated situations will arise due to changing conditions, and provisions should be included in the strategy for reacting to these cases.

Quality Requirements

In the world of competition, quality is required in everything that is done in the name of bringing products to market and meeting customer specifications. Much of the cost of quality can be traced back to the design phase of the product. Excess scrap, rework, warranty, and customer complaint costs result from decisions made in the product development process, compromising profitability through customer dissatisfaction and constant reprocessing of material in manufacturing. There is a point somewhere between overengineering products and designing with standards lax enough to allow a significant amount of product failure that must be identified and attained. The object is to achieve balance between the inevitable customer alienation resulting from one extreme, and the excessive cost and waste that occur at the other end of the spectrum. Continuous assessment of quality attainment is a prerequisite to determining the desired balance point.

Understanding current performance against standards established by the marketplace and internal policy helps to determine what needs to be improved. Policy needs to incorporate internally developed standards but also must be consistent with marketing objectives. This means actively seeking customer input to determine that market requirements are valid and are being attained. Validity in this case means not only communicating with customers to see that established performance standards are being met, but determining whether current standards drive product performance to the level expected by customers.

To achieve the correct balance of performance against standards, the product development strategy and quality policies have to provide a framework that will reliably produce the desired outcome. Performance measures should be established and continually monitored for compliance. Customers should be surveyed regularly, not just when there has been a problem or complaint. Constraints on achievement of quality levels must be identified and addressed. Unrealistic product cost targets, capacity limitations, lack of marketplace or customer input, and inappropriate or untested technologies can all have a major impact on attainment.

Time-to-Market Requirements

The culmination of the product development strategy is achievement of a position where products conform closely to validated customer requirements and exceed competitors' products in features, cost, quality, and lead time. There is significant competitive value in shortening design and development lead time, as has been demonstrated by companies like Hewlett-Packard, Toshiba, Chrysler, and others. Short time to market for a new product permits a quick response to emerging customer requirements and provides an opportunity to gather a bigger share of the market by being first.

Choices made in the product development cycle often affect the speed of design and production. Choice of technology is just one of many factors that can affect the speed of new-product development, but it has significant influence. The response of a new technology to specific conditions is often not known and may require experiments, simulation, or prototype testing. More mature technology is predictable due to a larger experience base and can be immediately incorporated in a design with little or no experimentation to determine its characteristics. Using untested technology without a strong case for its superiority and competitive potential is generally unwise when weighed against the longer development time and unforeseen technical problems that are almost always present.

Management should develop time-to-market goals that will make a difference in capturing market share and seek to quantify the benefits that will result from achieving the goals. Once goals have been established, a plan for achieving them can be established and implemented. Reengineering the product development processes to eliminate sequential processing and non–value-adding steps will help to achieve the desired goal. Reengineering the process will reveal needs to restructure the organization, redeploy resources, and incorporate new technologies.

THE BIGGER PICTURE: VISION

Overshadowing all of the individual components of the product development strategy is its link to the business strategy. If the business strategy recognizes product development as a strategic competitive weapon, then those who develop the strategy must have a vision of how the product development process should operate and what capabilities are necessary to support the vision. The future vision of product development will be very important to the success of the business strategy, and is the first step in planning for implementing the strategy.

The evidence is clear that product development and design can have a major effect on company operating results. Leading companies are now implementing strategic changes in their product development processes that will provide them with competitive advantages, profits, and dominant market positions. The roles of tools, techniques, redesigned business processes, and organization structures have been recognized. After recognizing the needs of your own company, you are ready to plan the necessary changes to improve your situation.

To develop an effective product development process requires a clear vision of the future product development process. Once quantified targets have been associated with the vision, the best strategy for achieving the vision can be selected. Only then can the corresponding plan be developed and implemented. If the strategy and plan are suitable and the plan implemented correctly, the envisioned product development process will occur.

A vision of the product development process is a conceptual description of a company's product development activities in five to ten years. The vision describes what the company wants to be doing in product development by providing a framework, setting the scope, and defining the focus. It says where the company wants to be, where it doesn't want to be, and where it wants its emphasis to be.

The vision is company-specific: no single vision will be correct for all companies. The only real test of whether a vision is correct for a particular company is the extent to which it allows a company to successfully carry out the product development process. See Figure 8.1.

FIGURE 8.1.   Consequences of Lack of Vision

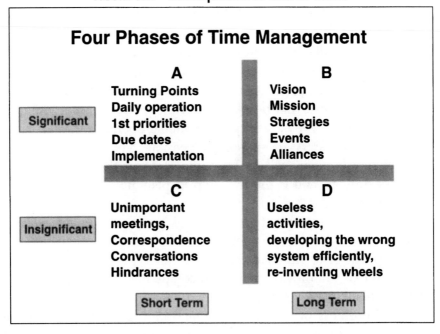

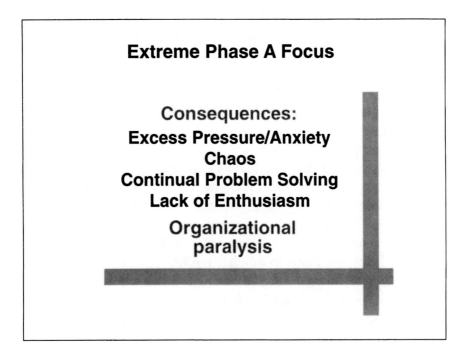

Few companies regularly develop or maintain a vision of their future development environment. Instead, they focus exclusively on fire-fighting today's operational problems. When a company does develop a vision, it usually is in response to an event that has created the need for change—the loss of a key order or customer, very poor financial results, marked change in a competitor's behavior, or change in the market environment. As a result the company begins to consider

- The need to control its destiny (without a vision, it is at the mercy of the market),

- The need to control its strategy (there are all sorts of ways to develop, but which is best?),

- The realization that today's operations will not be successful in the future (what will we do?),

- The need to overcome particular problems (what should we do?),

- The need for common approach (a shared vision helps everybody move forward along the same road),

- A desire to get more attention or resources (how can we justify it?), and

- A will to exploit a new opportunity (how should we do it?).

To actualize the vision is a three-stage process:

- In the first step, the vision must be clearly defined and communicated. After describing the overall desired state in mainly qualitative terms, the vision must define some clearly expressed quantitative targets. Because the vision describes a hazy view of the company in the future, top management needs to translate the vision into clear, reasonable and achievable targets that can be expressed in business terms.

- In the second step, (shown in Figure 8.2) a strategy must be chosen to take the organization from its current situation to the envisioned situation. The strategy describes how resources will be organized and the policies that will be used to manage them.

- Finally, detailed action plans have to be developed and implemented in line with the strategy.

The process of moving from a vision to targets to strategy to planning to implementation is easy to describe. It is much more difficult to implement. In practice, the process requires time and a lot of work, with initially very little to show for the effort.

Development of the vision requires active top-management involvement. In many companies only top managers have a sufficiently broad view of the current and future situations to be able to develop the vision. Often a task force is set up to develop the vision and then take responsibility for it. Development of the vision requires consideration of two major sets of factors:

- Forces external to the company—such as customers, competitors, other market players, technological and other developments, and key market requirements, and

- Forces internal to the company—such as expected corporate and business development, key success factors, sources of competitive advantage, and projected internal resources and capabilities.

Once a vision has been identified, top management must ensure that it is communicated and that a corresponding strategy is developed and implemented. A major step along the path to the strategy is the identification of performance targets.

FIGURE 8.2. Developing a Strategy to Reach the Vision

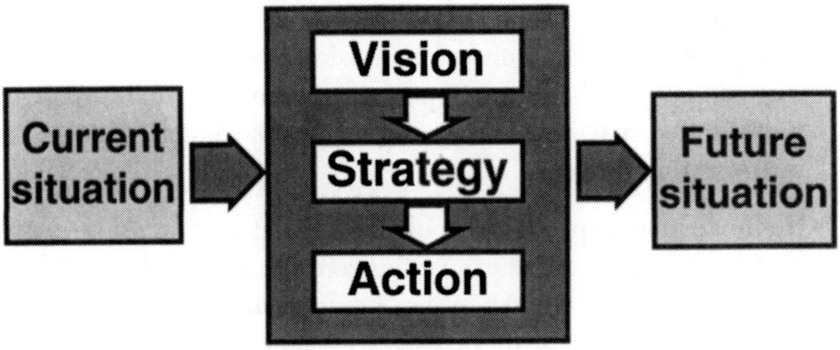

DEVELOPING TARGETS

Without clear, quantified targets, a vision is too abstract to be implemented. The targets that quantify the vision may be related to particular customer requirements or to general issues such as quality improvement or reduction in lead times. Vague targets are not useful: targets have to be defined and described in detail. For example, a target to reduce product development cycles by 50 percent over five years may not be clear enough. Does this target refer to completely new products or to modifications of existing products? Would it be suitable if a 5 percent reduction over the first four years was followed by 45 percent in the fifth year? Unless all the details are specified, there will be so much room for maneuvering during strategy setting and planning that there will be a high possibility of going off course.

Individual targets may appear to be separate and belong to different functions, levels, and time periods, but they are almost always intricately linked and can easily lead to conflict if they are accepted without close analysis and harmonization. It often takes longer to ensure that all targets are compatible than to identify and describe the individual targets.

Any strategy will produce some results, but they are unlikely to correspond to the vision. On the other hand, well-defined targets make the strategy definition process easier. Later in the implementation process they also provide a useful fixed reference against which progress can be measured and action plans detailed.

STRATEGY

To achieve the vision and the targets, the next step is to select a suitable strategy to position the organization for the future. The strategy defines the policies for how resources and capabilities will be organized to meet the vision.

Strategy setting is a three-stage process:

- Collect the information needed to develop the strategy. This information includes the vision and associated targets, details of the resources and capabilities, strengths and weaknesses, opportunities and threats.

- Identify and describe several potential strategies.

- Select and communicate the most appropriate strategy so that it becomes a key input for the planning process.

Generally, the strategy is developed by a task force made up of top and middle managers who determine the key requirements, resources, and capabilities required. It will determine organization structure and policies addressing people, processes, systems, and the use of information and practices.

KEY CAPABILITIES AND RESOURCES

The vision, the strategy, and the plan address a set of key requirements, resources, and capabilities. These include

- Customers

- Products

- Organization

- Processes

- The approach to new product development

- The approach to project management

- People

- Information

- Information systems

- Practices

- Facilities

- Metrics

- Finance

These key issues can be addressed, organized, and managed in different ways in response to the questions "What do we want to be?," "How do we want to do product development?," and "How do we implement the corresponding change?" For each issue there are several alternative directions that can be taken. Selecting particular alternatives leads to the vision, then to the strategy and implementation plan, and finally to a particular organizational and work approach and culture:

- People may be organized in hierarchical or flat organizations. They may be organized and work in teams, as individuals, or as departments. They may be geographically distributed near clients or work at a centralized location. All may be employed by the company, or some may be contractors.

- Information systems may be in-house or outsourced. They may be distributed or centralized, discrete or integrated.

- Processes may be sequential or concurrent. Some of them may be outsourced. They may be well organized and taut or poorly organized and tangled. There may be clearly defined project phases with strict milestones, gates, and phase reviews, or there may be an amorphous mess.

- Product development may be restricted to assemblies, with detail components being outsourced. Some assemblies may be outsourced.

- The approach to product development may be the (unlikely-to-succeed but glamorous) megaproject or the less exciting but more reliable process of continuous incremental improvement. Development may be primarily by individual functions, or it may be multifunctional.

- The techniques to be used may be the traditional ones of literature survey and physical prototype, or they may embrace all the latest discoveries.

- The allowable spending on product development is clearly going to influence many of the above choices.

It is clear that the answers to the questions that can be asked about each of the above key issues are going to be very company-specific. They will depend on factors such as

- The industry the company is in,

- The company's organizational structure,

- The company's culture,

- The company's resources,

- The development approach so far,

- The degree of risk accepted,

- The performance level expected,

- The geographical location of the company's units, and

- Company size.

Industry sector is an important characteristic. For example, vision, strategy, and plans will differ between an automotive company making a high-volume, standard product and an aerospace company making a make-to-order product that differs from one order to the next.

The organizational structure of the company is a determining characteristic. There will be many differences between companies that are organized by project and companies that have a strong departmental focus to their organizational structure.

The culture of the company is another important factor in determining strategy. In some companies, top management takes all decisions, and bottom-up initiatives are discouraged. In others, management actively tries to empower people lower down the hierarchy with decision-making authority.

The development approach taken by a company to date will have major implications for its approach in the future. Leopards don't change their spots overnight, and product development project managers don't change their behavior overnight. Without some strong motivation, major changes to behavior are difficult to bring about.

PLAN AND SCHEDULE

Once the strategy has been defined, it is possible to start planning the detailed activities and resources needed to meet the vision and targets. Individual projects have to be identified, and their financial and time requirements calculated. Their priorities have to be understood. The projects have to be organized in such a way that they result in the changes required by the vision within the allowed overall budget and time scale.

To achieve the type of improvement in product development that will be necessary to succeed, top management must lead the way. Only the leaders can implement the type of change that is necessary. The executives of the company must understand that competition is shifting to a new arena. They must be committed to making the necessary changes in management style, organization structure, and business processes. Management must have a vision of what the company will look like after the changes have been implemented, and a plan for making that vision a reality. In Chapter 7 we discussed some of the techniques and technologies that can be applied. In Chapter 9 and Chapter 10, we will provide specific ideas and essential concepts that should be included in an action plan.

CHAPTER 9

Improvement Requirements

VISIBILITY AND CONSENSUS
FOR REQUIREMENTS

Many companies run their improvement projects backward. Instead of defining their requirements and then looking for a solution, they choose a solution and then look for requirements to justify it. Before requirements can be defined, however, the objective of the improvement project has to be clear. The objective should be written down and communicated to everyone involved. The requirements also need to be discussed, written down, and—before they are acted on—agreed to.

For all improvement projects there is a hierarchy of requirements. At the top level are the requirements to directly improve business results and satisfy a particular customer. At the next level down are requirements to improve the key areas of the product development process, the flow, use, and communication of information in the process, human resources, and the computer systems. Each area has characteristic attributes, and metrics can be applied to these attributes. The principal requirement for any improvement project is to improve performance in one of the above areas—that is, to achieve improvement in one of the metrics used to measure an attribute. This should also result in an improvement in customer satisfaction or one of its key attributes—cost, time, and quality.

TWO WAYS TO LOOK AT REQUIREMENTS

The reasons for making improvements can be looked at in two different ways—by considering the position of the main customer for the improvement or by differentiating between improvements to overcome problems and improvements and then to increase performance levels. The requirement to improve may be made with the primary intention of improving internal performance (satisfying an internal customer) or of improving external performance (satisfying an external customer).

For example, the tool or technique may alleviate some problems that occur in the engineering environment, or it may positively affect engineering operations. Although these two classes can be treated separately, in practice, they are closely related.

The first class of improvements—those that overcome currently existing problems—often is related to the increasingly competitive business environment, the rapidly increasing amount of data in the engineering environment, and the general trend toward computerization.

The second class of improvements—those positively affecting product development performance—includes better use of resources, better access to information, better reuse of design information, better control of engineering changes, a reduction in design cost, a reduction in lead times, and improved security of engineering information. All these improvements increase the productivity of the engineering process, allowing companies to respond more flexibly to customers, to improve the quality of their products, and to be more adaptable to market requirements.

The two classes of improvements are closely linked: the first class addresses the resolution of existing problems; the second class goes one step further and addresses the potential for further improvement. Each class can be divided into several groups, and within each group improvement areas can be related both to resolution of current problems in the product development process and to overall improvement of the product development process. These groups are

- Overall business performance improvement,
- Functional performance improvement,
- Process management,
- Change management,
- Management of product development activities,
- Information management,
- Reuse of information,
- Better use of skilled human resources,
- Automation of product development activities,
- Information systems effectiveness improvement, and
- Provision of an infrastructure for effective product development.

Examples of improvement areas within each group include

- Overall business performance improvement:
  Improve product quality.
  Reduce overhead costs.

- Functional performance improvement:
  Increase engineering productivity.
  Reduce inventory.
  Develop better cost estimates.
  Reduce scrap.
  Reduce product-liability costs.

- Process management:
  Ensure the most appropriate process is followed.
  Improve distribution of work to developers.
  Ensure release procedures are followed.

- Change management:
  Speed up the distribution, review, and approval of changes.
  Provide status information on changes.

- Management of product development activities:
  Improve project coordination.
  Increase the reliability of schedules.
  Provide high-quality management information.

- Information management:
  Provide a single, controlled repository for information.
  Maintain different views of information.
  Provide faster access to data.
  Manage configurations.

- Reuse of information:
  Make available existing designs for use in new products.
  Reduce duplicate data entry.

- Better use of skilled human resources:
  Provide training for teamwork.
  Update skills.

- Automation of product development activities:
  Automate the sign-off process.
  Automate the transfer of data between applications.

- Information systems effectiveness improvement:
  Integrate islands of automation.
  Link databases.
  Remove unnecessary systems.

- Provision of an infrastructure for effective product development:
  Support agreed practices and computer systems.
  Distribute data, documents, and messages electronically.

Process

Attributes of the process include cost, time, and quality. Metrics to describe these attributes include

- Cost:
  Total development cost
  Labor cost
  Ratio of direct to indirect costs

- Time:
  Break-even time
  Elapsed time
  Time used

- Quality:
  Rejects
  Errors
  Manageability
  Degree of concurrency

Traditionally, the phases of the product development process are run in lengthy serial project cycles. Rules and procedures are difficult to enforce. Project planning exercises cannot draw on real data from the past but are based on overly optimistic estimates. Project managers find it difficult to monitor the progress of work and are unable to address slippage and other problems as soon as these occur.

In many companies, few people can really describe the flow of work, and even fewer know why it takes a particular shape. In most cases, the flow results not from a reasoned design but from a long series of minor reorganizations in departmental structures, product characteristics, and human resources.

Because engineering changes are poorly coordinated, unnecessary changes can be introduced. Design cycles are longer than necessary, and unreleased versions of data are acquired by manufacturing, causing confusion and waste. The time taken for raising, approving, and implementing changes is much longer than necessary. The change process takes days, weeks, or even months, whereas the actual processing time might be only minutes or hours. In large companies, it costs thousands of dollars to process an engineering change.

Engineering-change control systems are bureaucratic, paper intensive, complex, and slow. One company, for example, found that up to sixteen departments were involved for some changes. It can take several months and fifty or more different documents for a proposed change to be approved and incorporated into the product design. During this time, the product is produced with an unwanted design. Even when changes are agreed on and announced, months go by before the corresponding documentation reaches the field.

Because the management and change process appears inefficient and time consuming, some people avoid it. Minor modifications are not signaled; some might even have no formal change-control process. When something goes wrong or another change has to be made, unnecessary effort is needed to find out where the problem came from, and additional support staff members are employed to try to prevent further problems.

All these problems lead to improvement projects and to a requirement that people take control of the product development process. A review of the current workflow from initial product specification down to customer support will provide a solid base from which improvements can be made. Activities that do not add value should be removed, and activities that were previously carried out serially should, wherever possible, be run in parallel.

Information

Attributes of information in the process include cost, time, and quality. Metrics to describe these attributes include

- Cost:
  Information development cost
  Storage cost
  Information administration cost

- Time:
  Development time
  Access time

- Quality:
  Errors

Examples of problems that arise in the traditional product development process include reentry of data, manual transportation of paper drawings, failure to use existing information, working on different projects at the same time, and project and resource management tools not linked to product information.

In the typical company with large numbers of people involved in the engineering and associated functions, many problems arise from the lack of control over engineering data. People sometimes are unable to find the information they need or that corresponds to the actual state of the product. For example, a facility drawing might not correspond to the physical facility layout.

Developers are unable to rapidly access a particular design among the mass of existing designs. To find specific information, they search through tens of pages of listings, losing valuable time. Studies show that design engineers spend up to 80 percent of their time on administrative and information-retrieval activities—developing new designs that were almost identical to existing designs and generating unnecessary additional costs in the various activities necessary for manufacture and then for support during use.

As more and more data are generated on computer and other electronic systems, it becomes more difficult to use manual control and management procedures introduced when data volumes were twenty or even fifty times lower to track the location of data, prevent unauthorized access, and maintain up-to-date product configurations.

The increased computerization of engineering activities has led to an increase in the volume and availability of engineering data. Some of this information is on electronic media (disks, tapes, and cassettes), but much is on paper and other traditional media. Even in the 1990s, few companies have even 10 percent of their engineering information stored on electronic media. To further complicate information management, there are different types of data—numeric data (such as part geometry in a CAD system), text information (such as specifications and technical publications), graphic information (such as engineering drawings, photographs, and videos) and, increasingly, voice data.

In the traditional product development process, data entry is poorly controlled. Data are lost and might not be retrievable. They are recreated, and errors are introduced. The wrong product is sent to a customer. Product configuration data are not kept up to date. When a defective part is found in the field, many more products than necessary have to be recalled. Design history is not maintained, so it is next to impossible to draw on previous experience.

Several copies of the information describing the same part are maintained, and nobody knows which is the master copy. When a change is needed, not all copies are changed, and not all downstream functions alerted. Old, unwanted revisions of parts are machined, while the new, required versions are ignored. When there is no agreed master version of a particular item of information, and no agreed owner, all users of the information will behave as if they are the owners. Each user will define the item to suit his or her particular requirements, and all definitions may be different, leading to confusion when information is transferred between users.

Informal communications are developed between departments to cope with the lack of suitable formal communications, but few records are kept of this type of transfer and it often is impossible to find any trace of important information.

People wait hours, even days, for a given piece of information. When the person who should sign off on a design is called away for a few hours, work is held up because nobody knows who else has the authority to sign off. When people do receive information, they are not sure whether they have received the correct version. Sometimes they just want to make a simple request for information from a system that "belongs" to someone else and find they have to wait several days to get it.

Configuration documentation no longer corresponds to the actual product. Unexplained differences appear between as-designed, as-planned, and as-built bills of materials, resulting in increased scrap, rework, and stock. Incomplete products are assembled and delivered. Field problems are difficult to resolve, and inefficiencies occur in spare-parts management. New versions of computer programs are introduced without sufficient care being taken to ensure that, for example, data created with earlier versions are still usable. Programs are insufficiently documented.

Technical manuals become outdated and yet are not updated. Logistics support data are out of control. Inadequately documented configurations become difficult to maintain. Spares replenishment becomes inaccurate, and customers immobilize products while efforts are made to identify correct replacement parts. Sometimes, even when the right part arrives, the right handling equipment and maintenance tools are not in place.

Engineering data lie at the heart of the engineering function in today's computerized, information-based environment, yet few companies have it controlled. Often several groups of users have different versions of what should be one set of data. Each claims to be the legitimate owner of the data and hence the owner of the correct version. As companies invest in more and more engineering workstations, thus creating a truly distributed computing environment, it will become even more difficult to maintain control of the company's engineering computers—and to maintain control of engineering information, a valuable company resource.

The engineering data in use must be of a high quality. Without reliable, timely, and accurate information, managers and users cannot work efficiently. Quality has to be built in through the right procedures and a company culture that penalizes poor quality work.

It is essential to ensure that engineering data are reused and allowed to evolve to meet market requirements. Reuse of information was expected to be one of the major advantages of CAD/CAM, but in practice there has been less reuse than expected because even if users are aware of suitable existing information, it is difficult to find. Few users are prepared to spend hours, or even days, hunting for existing data. It is easier to take a clean sheet and design a new part.

Data must be available to users when they need them, or valuable time will be lost. Even though engineering data must flow smoothly through the organization, confidential and proprietary information must be protected from unauthorized access. An individual user might worry that a colleague might overwrite a file, or a company might worry that access rights granted to trusted suppliers might somehow be discovered by unscrupulous competitors.

People

Attributes of people in the product development process include cost, time, and quality. Metrics to describe these attributes include

- Cost:
  Labor cost
  Training cost

- Time:
  Time to carry out activities

- Quality:
  Ability to work with others
  Errors made
  Skills

In the traditional serial product development process, people in different departments work one after the other on successive phases of the development. Problems occur because some functions and people are not good at working with others.

There often is conflict between different functions such as design engineering and manufacturing engineering. There also is conflict between the central electronic data processing (EDP) staff and the computer system support staff in the product development process. The EDP staff are deeply involved in Finance and Accounting work and do not invest enough time in supporting the development process. They often are more interested in the theoretical aspects of EDP and new EDP technologies than in its practical use for development activities.

As the organization tries to increase the value-adding component of the work it does, it may find that it does not have people with appropriate skills or that some people are not motivated. Two of the best ways to improve performance are to train them and to have them work in teams. Other reasons for the increasing emphasis on teamwork in product development are to reduce costs, improve the speed of development, and improve quality.

Today, many companies use a concurrent (or simultaneous) engineering approach in which product developers from different functions work in parallel, sharing information and knowledge and producing better results faster than they would have done if operating in serial mode.

By using multifunctional development teams, a wide range of design and process knowledge from throughout the organization can be focused on the product development objectives. Team members come from functions such as marketing, design, service, manufacturing engineering, test, and purchasing. Key suppliers may also be part of the team.

The team involved in the early development of a product has a great influence on the product's costs and quality. When multifunctional teams are used in the early stage of a product's development, their composite knowledge of design, materials, manufacturing, quality, and customer requirements helps to develop the best definition of the product and its manufacturing, support, and disposal processes.

Teamwork is a new concept for many companies. It is a step in the unknown, requiring people to think, behave, make decisions, and be measured differently. Although such change can be difficult to implement, its potential benefits are great. If teamwork can be made to work, it can lead to much better and faster product development.

The improved communication resulting from team membership helps reduce the number of changes to specifications. Cross-training has the same effect. As people understand better how other functions work, they are less likely to create problems for downstream functions. Fewer changes means less rework and a shorter product development cycle. A reduction in the number of development hours has a direct effect on reducing development costs. The team approach also tends to prevent development-cost overrun as it focuses attention on the early identification and resolution of problems. The team approach can also improve product quality. The early involvement of downstream functions reduces the risk of potential problems.

As with all attempts to change the existing environment, teamwork can be difficult to implement. Representatives of some departments will not want to see themselves at the same hierarchical level in the team as representatives of other departments. Some managers will not want to lose their titles. Some people work best as individuals and not as members of a team. Some people cannot adapt to playing different roles as the development process progresses. Some people may not appreciate being expected to play a visible role within a team. Some people within the team may see no benefit for themselves from team participation and may try to destroy the team. Many people in the team will fear the unknown. People will fear that they could be punished or that their remuneration could be reduced because of poor performance by other team members.

A lot of effort has to be put into making teamwork succeed. Through suitable training, team members learn the techniques that teams use for team building, problem solving, decision making, resolving conflicts, meeting productively, and encouraging and helping each other. People who have always worked as individuals or with other specialists from their own department may find it very difficult to learn how to behave as a team member, but the team needs to share a vision of what it is trying, as a group, to achieve. Within this vision, the aspirations of individuals must be respected.

Computer Systems

Attributes of computer systems in the product development process include cost, time, and quality. Metrics to describe these attributes include

- Cost:
  Total development cost
  Operating cost
  Maintenance cost

- Time:
  Development time
  Development waiting time
  Response time

- Quality:
  Errors
  User-friendliness
  Degree of automation
  Degree of integration

Many companies have found that although hardware costs halve every two years, their computer system budgets spiral upward. Often maintenance costs represent 80 percent of the budget, and users have to wait two years for the IS team to make new developments. Many companies find 40 percent of projects come in late and another 40 percent come in over budget.

When product development systems and applications are discrete and poorly integrated, they create as many problems as they solve. Gaps between incompatible application programs mean that data must be transferred manually, and correcting the errors made during this process wastes time and money. For example, part descriptions and bills of materials developed on CAD systems might have to be manually transferred to an MRP II system in a computer that is not linked to the CAD system.

In many companies there is a low level of integration between the different systems supporting the engineering process, and time and effort are wasted in managing information in such an environment. It is difficult to control the exchange of data and the synchronization of activities between different systems in the absence of well-defined, enforced procedures.

In today's high-tech companies, the product development function cannot function without computer systems and a wide range of application programs and communications. Information system performance must be improved.

The Way We Work

Attributes of organizational behavior and culture in the product development process include cost, time, and quality.

Metrics to describe these attributes include

- Cost:
  Product development cost
  Cost of replacing unwanted departures

- Time:
  Product development cycle time
  Internal response time

- Quality:
  Customer satisfaction
  User satisfaction
  Product quality

In the traditional product development process, new product introductions in a whole range of manufacturing industries are delayed for a myriad of apparently random and minor but cumulatively significant reasons. Product quality is erratic despite vast investments in engineering and manufacturing technology and in quality programs. Lead times remain the same in spite of all the new investment. Overall, the costs associated with development rise instead of fall.

How can this situation be corrected? What has to be done to realize the potential of all the techniques that are available? The main improvement project to increase performance is management's belief in and introduction of TQM.

MANAGEMENT'S RESPONSIBILITY

Corporate management has the responsibility for developing a vision of the future competitive environment, developing a corresponding strategy for the corporation, and putting the appropriate corporate structure, people, and reward systems in place. Corporate management cannot be expected to clean up the product development process, but it can set the scene, put the right actors in place, and then watch the play.

The top management team is the only group in a company that can ensure that the product-development process is used to provide competitive advantage. They alone can link the product development process to the business mission and business strategy and ensure that the necessary changes occur throughout the company. Someone else in the company or an individual department may develop a product development process activity that offers competitive advantage, but for real benefits to occur, top management must support the development, ensure that it is focused properly, and apply it to developments in other areas of the company.

On organization charts, top management appears as a small rectangle above many other rectangles. Clearly top management runs the company and has to take responsibility for performance. People at the bottom of the pyramid do their best within the framework set by top management. If the company doesn't perform, the fault lies with top management—as many CEOs have found to their cost.

Corporate management's role in creating a vision and setting strategy may sometimes appear theoretical and trivial, but it is crucial to success. The wrong vision will lead to the wrong strategy, the wrong organization, and poor performance. In the 1990s, many CEOs have failed to adjust to the new competitive environment, and they and their corporations have paid the price. Other corporations in the same industry sector have succeeded, however. It appears that those who have failed have not been able to adapt, or to learn how to adapt, to change.

The one key differentiating factor between those who have failed and those who have succeeded is probably belief in and implementation of Total Quality Management (TQM). TQM underlies every decision made by corporate and business management—helping them develop an appropriate vision, developing the right organizational structure, and motivating and rewarding the right people. Some readers may throw down the book in disgust at reading this, but from our experience it is true. Companies that incorporate the principles of TQM are far more likely to succeed (other things being equal) than those that reject its principles or give them only a lukewarm reception.

TQM: KEY TO SUCCESS

TQM is the culture, attitude, and organization of a company that aims to provide its customers with products and services that satisfy their needs. The culture requires quality in all aspects of the company's operations, with things being done right first time and defects and waste eradicated from operations.

It's difficult to describe TQM in a few pages, but the following overview suggests how TQM and similar techniques must be incorporated in the corporate vision.

All company personnel must participate in Total Quality and take responsibility for their activities. Each part of the company operates as a customer to some functions and as a supplier to others. The company aims for continuous improvement by measuring and analyzing its own performance and that of other companies.

The primary characteristic of TQM is a customer-first orientation. Customer satisfaction is the company's highest priority and is obtained by providing a high-quality product and continuously improving the quality of the product to maintain a high level of customer satisfaction. Since product quality is the result of process quality, there is a focus on continuous improvement of the company's processes. To check progress, performance measures consistent with the objectives of the company are used.

TQM emphasizes elimination of waste and prevention over detection and hence emphasizes quality at the design stage. Statistical methods are used to reduce product and process variation.

Top management leads the quality-improvement process. Top management is responsible for Total Quality and must be totally committed to it. Maximum involvement in the quality-improvement process of all the company's employees is essential. Ongoing education and training involve all employees.

Continuous improvement lies at the heart of Total Quality. Continuous improvement implies continuously improving customer service, product performance, and process performance. It occurs only if management develops and puts in place corresponding processes, techniques, organizations, and systems. Management has to consistently reinforce continuous improvement attitudes and behavior, recognizing and rewarding the right performance, and recognizing and resolving problems. Without continuous improvement, attempts at improvement tend to be uncoordinated, unmeasured, inconsistently rewarded, and insignificant for the bottom line.

Product and process variation can be reduced by the use of statistical methods. Most companies already use statistical process control (SPC) during the production phase of the product life cycle to reduce variation and help correct whatever is wrong. The statistical problem-solving techniques usually grouped under the SPC acronym are the control chart, the cause-and-effect diagram (also called the fishbone chart or the Ishikawa diagram), the scatter diagram, Pareto analysis, the histogram, the process flow chart, and the check sheet. Just as SPC has been used to improve manufacturing processes, it can be applied to any other part of the product development process, such as reducing errors and cycle time in the engineering change process, the development of technical manuals, data entry, and processing a specification. For instance, by using control charts to measure process performance and Pareto analysis to identify the most frequently made errors, one company was able to achieve a BOM accuracy that now approaches 100 percent and reduce the 300 percent inspection previously performed to random-sample audits.

CORPORATE STRUCTURE

To meet customers' requirements, product development costs and overall product costs and product development cycle time need to be reduced and quality improved. To meet these targets, corporations will implement organizational structures based on small, independent product-line-oriented business units (BU).

Corporations will be made up of a lean corporate staff unit and multiple, small, independent, product-family-oriented business units, each of which will be focused on a particular product family. Within the overall corporate structure, there will also be some service units (treasury, finance, human resources) that sell their services to the BUs on a competitive basis.

The main role of the corporate staff unit will be to develop the corporate vision and strategic plans corresponding to corporate targets and to support BU management in its efforts to develop its own plans and objectives. The corporate staff unit members will also play an important role in initiating, monitoring, and supporting important cross-BU initiatives in areas such as product quality improvement, product introduction frequency, process improvement, and resource development and utilization.

The corporate staff unit, working with senior corporate management, defines the business philosophy and practices to be adopted throughout the corporation. It also defines the reward and recognition systems to be set up to encourage people to work in the direction of corporate success.

Each BU will be made up of a lean BU staff unit and one or more product family teams, each of which will be focused on a particular product family. This organization provides the appropriate focus on the customer. Although the organization appears to be primarily characterized by its product-line orientation, this exists only to focus on the satisfaction of customer requirements.

Each product family team is relatively independent, focused on its customers and its product family, and has responsibility for the complete life cycle of its products from concept to obsolescence. All the resources (personnel, technologies, techniques) required throughout the life cycle are dedicated to achieving the cost, quality, and time-to-market objectives of the product family. The product family team leader is responsible for everything to do with the product family— including profit and loss responsibility.

Product family teams are self-sufficient and contain all necessary expertise. These requirements help determine their size, but corporate, geographical, and business unit considerations also are a major influence. Due to the need to be near to customers and the need to make use of the skills of engineers resident throughout the world, many product family teams will be distributed across several geographical locations. In most industries, BUs will not exceed 2,000 people, with product family team sizes of 50 to 500 people.

Each product family team is charged with getting the next few generations of its products to market in the next few years. It is responsible for deciding when it should introduce new and upgraded products and when it should withdraw products.

Each product family team is responsible for its business processes and for meeting continuous improvement targets. At one end of the overall business process is the customer (and advanced technology and innovation); at the other end is use of the product and eventual obsolescence and recycling.

To better understand customer requirements, companies need to be closer to the customer—the prime source of product and service requirements. Some product family team members may work temporarily or even permanently on customer sites to find out what customers really want in terms of product, service, quality, price, and timeliness.

Companies also need to improve their relationships with suppliers by working closely with a small number of suppliers. As relationships become longer-term, closer, and quality-oriented, they will tend more toward partnership and away from the short-term, dollar-oriented, conflictual relationships common in the 1970s. Companies will see their chosen suppliers as assets and will help them to improve performance, providing training and process improvement assistance as applicable. Companies will look to suppliers to offer major components rather than minor parts.

TQM is the philosophy that has been proven to guide companies toward achieving their vision and strategy. It keeps companies from falling into the flavor-of-the-month pitfall and introduces an unparalleled level of consistency to the implementation of the changes necessary to remain competitive. When a good understanding of tools, techniques, technology, and management processes is coupled with TQM as the guiding principle, your company will be ready to begin the process of implementation.

CHAPTER 10

The Process of Implementing Tools and Techniques

THE PROCESS OF IMPLEMENTATION AND IMPROVEMENT

The implementation of all tools and techniques follows more or less the same process. Its major activities are

- Initial recognition of the need for change and initiation of a corresponding project,

- A clear description of the current ("as-is") situation,

- A clear description of the future ("hoped-for", "to-be") situation,

- Identification of a strategy to go from the current ("as-is") situation to the future ("to-be") situation,

- Justification of the strategy,

- Development of a justifiable implementation plan,

- Implementation,

- Use, and

- Review of the success of the implementation.

There are many differences between the various tools and techniques—some are more complex than others, some are cross-functional but some are not, some are heavily computer-related whereas others are not—but the overall process is much the same, whether the tool or technique is CAD, EDM, DFM, CIM, or QFD. The overall implementation process will be much the same: the steps are similar, the rules are similar, and the potential problems are similar.

Within any organization, management is a key client of an improvement project. Management wants to see improved performance, but management cannot be involved in all the details of selecting and implementing a solution. These have to be delegated to an implementation team.

The successful introduction of an improvement project is almost always hampered by a general lack of understanding and knowledge of the subject, resistance to change, departmental interests, different functional priorities, difficulties with cost justification, and various ongoing projects. In any large organization, there is high resistance to change. Most people are more than willing to do tomorrow what they did yesterday. The successful introduction of an improvement project requires changes in organizational behavior, and these are not achieved through half-hearted efforts by uncommitted individuals. The project's champions and catalysts must be identified, supported, and encouraged. The opponents of change—whether they prefer a quiet life or specifically fear that the project will reduce their power and privileges—must be identified and understood. Only then can they be influenced to modify their behavior. Only management can resolve many of the interdepartmental and interpersonal issues associated with a long-term, costly, and strategic project.

The Implementation Team

Management, the client of the need for the improvement project, must define the objectives and authority of the implementation team. The objective of the team probably will be to ensure that the project's activities are carried out efficiently and effectively to improve the company's overall business results.

The implementation team should be made up of people from all the functions that will be affected by the introduction of the improvement project. Depending on the project's scope, these functions may include R&D, design engineering, manufacturing engineering, marketing, sales, F&A, manufacturing planning, manufacturing, logistics, maintenance, and IT. It may also be useful to include in the team an individual who will represent the interests of suppliers, customers, and others outside the company.

For wide ranging, long-term, and costly projects, the team will be led by a top manager who has full responsibility for the project's success or failure. Major enterprisewide projects cannot be run successfully by individuals who lack the necessary organizational power to implement significant change to business practices.

Implementation of a strategic, costly, and time-consuming tool or technique should take place only once—right the first time. It should be sufficiently supported. A team secretary, reporting to the team leader, should run its day-to-day activities. The team secretary may work full-time on the project, whereas the team leader might have only part-time involvement. A project plan should be drawn up showing the major milestones, resources, activities, and costs and be kept up-to-date and visible. Management needs to be kept aware of any progress being made and problems that may arise.

As some people have difficulty in working in a team, it is important that only individuals who can both add value to the team's activities and work well together are selected for team membership.

Project Start-Up

Introduction and implementation of the improvement project will probably be a three-phase process. The first stage, in which the team plays a major role, leads to the development of a strategy that addresses technological, organizational, and financial issues and provides a long-term implementation plan. The major activities will be

- A clear description of the current ("as-is") situation,

- A clear description of the future ("hoped-for", "to-be") situation,

- Identification of a strategy to go from the current ("as-is") situation to the future ("to-be") situation,

- Justification of the strategy, and

- Development of a justifiable implementation plan. See Figure 10.1.

The second phase of introduction and implementation starts from the high-level results of the first phase. A rebuilt team, probably containing some members of the original team and some other managers and users, translates the high-level plans into detailed actions.

The third phase sees the improvement solution in everyday use, leading to requests for modifications and further improvements. Its implementation will have to be reviewed and compared against the original targets.

Before the project can start, the terms of reference of the implementation team have to be defined by management. What is the objective? What is the budget? When do team members have to report? To whom do they report?

Effort may have to be put into making team members work well

FIGURE 10.1.   Deployment of the Vision

together. In addition to learning techniques for team building, problem solving, decision making, resolving conflicts, meeting productively, and encouraging and helping each other, team members need to share a vision of what the group is trying to achieve. People who have always worked as individuals or with other specialists from their own department may find it difficult to learn how to behave as a team member. An early task of the team will probably be to carry out a feasibility study to demonstrate potential scope, areas of application, costs, and benefits. This is a good opportunity to see how team members work together.

Awareness and Understanding

Probably some team members will not know much about the improvement project. Although they will learn much from their participation in various project activities, it is helpful to receive basic information at the beginning of the project to avoid circular reasoning and attachment to the idea that the project is being implemented mainly to solve their everyday problems. The assistance of a neutral, experienced expert at an early stage can prevent a lot of time being wasted.

It may be possible for team members to attend an introductory course on the basic points and vocabulary of the improvement project. Useful information also can be gathered from books and journals, conferences and seminars, demonstrations by vendors, and visits to other companies using the technique or system. Engineering journals generally provide some information about the selection and use of various tools and techniques as well as typical costs and benefits.

Initially, many people in the company will find it hard to understand the aims of the improvement project. It is important for the team to develop a clearly understandable and easy-to-communicate vision that it can use to enlist support from potential users and managers. The team leader must understand what is being done and be able to communicate concepts and progress to the rest of the team, to management, and to potential users.

The team's initial understanding of the improvement project should be shared with management and potential users: the more that management knows, the more supportive it will be; the more that users know, the more supportive they will be and the less likely they will start competing activities and overlapping projects. If users are aware of potential changes before they take place and are asked for their help, they usually contribute and by doing so become involved and identified with the eventual solution.

Different Points of View

The many people involved with the introduction of the improvement process will have different objectives and points of view. An engineering manager may expect to reduce lead time, a manufacturing manager may expect to improve quality, and an individual engineer may only see a way to ease the pain of everyday work. Many individual engineers expect to have better tools and techniques available immediately and without any effort on their part. They are not interested in the overall product development process or in the procedure that is taken to implement a new tool or technique. Other people involved in defining the new system will have a different, if not opposite, approach: they may be more interested in the design of the overall system but have no interest at all in the technique or tool itself or in its use.

Parallel to the different viewpoints described above may well be differences over the best implementation approach. Individual engineers, looking for a quick solution to their own problems, may prefer a prototyping approach—an iterative approach that accepts that user requirements cannot be clearly defined initially and in any case will change as the users get to know the new system. A prototype is built to meet the user's apparent requirements and then used. Experience of its use provides input for the development of a more advanced prototype. On the other hand, other people involved with the introduction of the new project may prefer the life-cycle approach of feasibility study, requirements analysis, system design, detailed design, programming, testing, and use.

Some people prefer the use of a more business-oriented approach to the improvement project to ensure that its introduction meets major business requirements so they give these priority. Typical approaches of this type look at critical success factors and the value chain. Critical success factor analysis identifies the factors that are essential to meeting business goals. If management focuses on a limited number of critical issues that are essential to business success, then its chances of success are higher than if less well-focused goals are addressed. Focusing only on lead-time reduction and product-cost reduction means there is more chance of attaining these goals than if a larger and less well-defined set of goals is chosen. Value-chain theory recognizes that a company's product development process is made up of a set of activities such as sales, development, logistics, production, and service, each of which adds value to the company's product. By understanding where the company is most effective at adding value and focusing resources on such areas, the company can improve its market position. These business-oriented approaches help to ensure that the improvement project will be used to meet business objectives and not only to solve technical problems.

MODELING

A prerequisite for effective use of most tools and techniques is a clear and complete description of the engineering processes and engineering information that are associated with the improvement project. This description is usually in the form of a simple model—probably in the form of graphics and text.

A model helps clarify engineering processes and the flow and use of engineering information. As the relationships between activities, systems, and people become clearer, the events that link activities, and the major management milestones used to control them, also become clearer.

The development of a model is generally an iterative approach. The first attempt at a model will probably lack detail and be incorrect, but it provides a starting point from which further refinement can take place. The modeling activity should be approached in several ways, some of which are complementary. It is useful to build models of both the current ("as-is") situation and the future ("to-be") situation. These will eventually be related by the implementation strategy. Another useful pair of models is the "top-down" model and the "bottom-up" model. The top-down model is derived from a business-oriented description of the engineering process, working down toward individual operations and detailed descriptions of data and activities. The complementary bottom-up approach starts from individual operations and detailed descriptions of data and activities, then links data and operations, and builds successively higher levels of information and processes. The top-down and bottom-up models should agree in the middle.

Development of models should involve all the people affected by the new tool or technique. Their involvement at this stage will increase their commitment to eventual use. The model acts as a common basis for communication and provides a way to reach agreement for people who might previously have had different views and definitions of the environment. Involvement in the modeling activity will help them better understand the work they do and the way it fits into the overall workings of the company.

Four types of model are often used to describe process and data flow, control flow, data structure, and control structure. Control-structure models focus on top-down decomposition of the control organization. The typical organization chart is an example of a control-structure model. It shows the various departments of a company, the groups within the departments, the teams within the groups, and the individuals within teams. Another example of a control-structure model is the hierarchical structure involved in release of design work.

Control-flow models describe the allowed values and combinations for the inputs and outputs of functions and show how these are related to detailed product development activities. An example of a control-flow model is a programming flow chart showing the sequence of instructions to be executed and the points where flow is dependent on the value of particular variables.

Process- and data-flow models show the activities that make up a process, and the way data flows, is used, and is stored. For each activity, the model shows the input, output, reference, and control information. Usually, process- and data-flow modeling is carried out as a top-down exercise with as many decompositions or hierarchical levels being introduced as necessary. The system is first described as a set of elements at the top level, often called Level 0. Then each element of the top level is separately described in more detail. The process of decomposition can be repeated as many times as necessary to provide the required level of detail.

Data-structure modeling focuses on the structure of data elements and the static relationships between data. Data-structure models are often based on the entity-relationship model. An entity is a class of similar items each of which can be characterized in the same way and will be used in the same way in the engineering process. Customers, products, suppliers, processes, locations, documents, and employees are all examples of entities. The common properties and characteristics of an entity are referred to as its attributes. Examples of an aircraft's attributes could include weight, fuselage length, and wing span. Relationships are associations that describe the link between entities.

Computer-aided software engineering (CASE) tools are methodologies and software used to automate the software development life cycle. Their software for producing data-flow diagrams, data-structure and entity-relationship diagrams, and data dictionaries is of great benefit in modeling, since the amount of data generated by the modeling activity is all but impossible to handle by purely manual means.

DESCRIPTION OF THE CURRENT SITUATION

The description of the current situation, prior to the implementation of the improvement project, will probably have to address part or all of the following subjects:

- Products and their life cycles,

- Processes used to support the product life cycle,

- The people who work in the process,

- The use and flow of information,

- Computer systems,

- The organization of engineering, and

- Performance metrics.

The implementation team can take two complementary approaches to understanding the part of the new product development process that is relevant: the first of these is a top-down functional decomposition approach; the other is a "sideways," or horizontal, product path approach that follows product information through successive activities. A particular product may start in marketing and then go through conceptual design, engineering design, analysis, testing, detailed design, manufacturing engineering, process planning, tooling, NC programming, production planning, purchasing, sales order processing, machining, assembly, testing, packaging, distribution, use, and maintenance. Other new products will follow a different route as will minor changes to existing products. In some cases, the path leads out of the company to suppliers and partners. In most cases, it eventually leads back to customers. Detailed process flow, or workflow, models will be needed to help understand the flow of work and information and to communicate this understanding.

The team should identify the structure of product paths, typical milestones, events, and management activities along these paths. Different structures are needed for different product lines, and some individual projects will follow specific rules. This information will help team members gain understanding of the generic product life cycles, which is necessary for an effective new product development process. The project management techniques in use should be identified.

In addition to understanding the overall flow of the product development process, the team also should address the individual activities in the process that are related to, or will be affected by, the introduction and use of the new process. These "application" areas—such as engineering design, process planning, and NC programming—will probably be partly automated but still have a significant manual content. The team needs to understand the tools and techniques in use and the tasks and information needs (input, processing, output, and storage) of each application area.

As the individual activities are examined, the team will begin to understand the characteristic parameters and volumes involved. These include the life cycles of products, the number of existing products, parts, and tools, the annual number of new products, parts, and tools, the number of software versions, the number of modifications, the number of new and modified drawings and other documents, the number of drawings released daily, typical design times, the number of engineering changes, the timing of engineering changes, the time taken to process engineering changes, and the number of levels and constituents of bills of materials.

The current organization of the company needs to be described from the points of view of processes, people, systems, and information. This will show the number of users, their location, both geographically and functionally, and the way they work.

Even during the earliest stages of the development of the as-is model, it is helpful to use computer-based tools to manage the process and information models. A top-down hierarchical breakdown of requirements may be a suitable modeling approach. The amount of detail in the model can be progressively increased until a user feels that all information use and flow is shown on the diagram. Other users can be asked to comment on the model, and models produced by users in neighboring activities can be put together to see how information is transferred.

It is important to understand how users store, share, and communicate information. Sources and users of engineering information should be identified. An attempt should be made to understand how users create, access, modify, store, and communicate information. Some surveys indicate that designers spend more than one-third of their time looking for information and that drafters spend more time looking for information than drafting. Many users spend most of their time moving, preparing, and controlling information and little time adding value to it. The access needs and rights of users and groups of users need to be understood by the team. Shared and redundant data need to be identified. Data standards and data ownership have to be understood.

The different structures of engineering information such as bills of materials, assemblies, and parts lists should be identified, and other associations such as product/drawing relationships clarified. The way that packets of information are created and moved between activities will become clear. The management of engineering information, in particular at departmental boundaries, needs to be understood. Data-security and data-integrity issues need to be addressed.

Review, release, and engineering change processes need to be understood. The team should discover how many engineering changes are made and the way they are made and recorded. The time and effort required to carry through changes should be brought to light. The roles and rights of users and managers at change and release time must be understood.

An inventory of existing IT systems related to the new product development process should be drawn up. The list should include obvious candidates, such as CAD and CAM systems, as well as systems used in analysis, CASE, project management, technical publications, documentation management, configuration management, and release control. The corresponding computers and networks should be identified. The programs in use should be listed and analyzed. Their use of engineering information needs to be understood. Any database management systems in use should be closely examined. Information transfer between systems should be described. Transfer of information to and from supplier and customer systems should be included in the survey.

The performance measures associated with the improvement project should be understood. These should be related to business characteristics such as lead times, cycle times, engineering changes, number of parts, number of defects, and cost of designs and cost of production, not to tool or technique characteristics, such as number of users, the frequency of use, or the volume of data generated.

THE TO-BE SITUATION

The description of the to-be situation should complement the description of the as-is situation, so it should also address

- Products and their life cycles,

- Processes used to support the product life cycle,

- The people who work in the process,

- The use and flow of information,

- Computer systems,

- The organization of engineering, and

- Performance metrics.

The to-be situation is developed from an understanding of user requirements, business objectives, and competitive analysis.

The implementation team evaluates the way that competitors are organized and the steps that they have taken toward implementing similar solutions. The team also should look at the way that competitors' suppliers and customers are using the new technique or system. This may help the team to understand competitors' behavior. In some cases, competitors will be willing to invite the team for an open exchange of information. If this is not possible, something may be learned from presentations made at conferences and seminars or from articles in journals and magazines.

Another major source of information for the team is the current and potential users of the new technique or system within the company. Many of these users probably never have thought about the overall requirements of the company, but users often are the best source of information about everyday activities, the information that is used in such activities, and short-term improvements. They find it more difficult to address long-term and cross-functional issues. The team should encourage users to discuss their problems and bring issues into the open.

The business objectives are an important component of the description of the future situation. The team should identify the four or five factors that seem to be most important for management. There could be a need to reduce lead times significantly or to improve product quality and reliability. There could be specific problems that have to be avoided or relationships with powerful customers that need to be improved. There may be the intention to delete some product lines, or to develop new or improved products. There could be plans to change the way clients and markets are addressed. Product development costs and product costs may be too high. Support staff costs may need to be reduced.

These high-level issues are just as important as the low-level user requirements. If, for example, a particular product or process is to be abandoned, then it may be excluded from the analysis. A company intent on market dominance through lowest unit cost may have very different requirements from one that provides highest-performance products to specification in a specialty niche market.

The information obtained about business objectives should be quantified because quantified information has more meaning and can be used both as a target and as a measure of progress. Without business objectives, the team can easily produce a solution that is of no benefit to the business. With business objectives, the team has clear targets in sight and can focus its activities and prioritize its recommendations.

The team needs to develop a list of features believed necessary for a solution. Preparation of such a list helps provoke discussion and get agreement on the scope of the solution to be proposed. It will show the various issues that have been raised, even if they may not be answered in the eventual solution. The team should indicate if each individual feature is an essential part of the solution and, if not, assign it a relative importance factor.

A CHOICE OF STRATEGIES

The implementation team must develop a strategy that meets management objectives and define a corresponding implementation plan. The first step is to develop and describe the strategy and get management agreement. In some companies, management examines several possible alternatives for the strategy in detail and then makes the decision. In other cases, the team defines a strategy that management then reviews. Definition of the strategy is all-important because the rest of the implementation is guided by the strategy. If the strategy is wrong, implementation probably will fail to meet the objectives.

Before the strategy can be finalized and before the detailed implementation plan can be developed, the team needs to clarify three major areas of concern—business benefits, organizational issues, and architectures.

The primary aim of the improvement project is to improve the company's business position, so the team needs to show how the solution it proposes meets requirements and how it will be possible to measure progress toward achieving specified targets. The identified needs will have to be quantified. The related benefits to the company, such as decreased product costs and increased sales, should be evaluated. How much would be gained from the proposed implementation? To what extent will customer responsiveness be improved?

How much time will be saved? What is the cost of not having it? What will be the effect on engineering changes? Will there be a reduction in the number of developers? What would be the effect on configuration control and traceability? What would be the effect on the overall product development process? What are the risks associated with implementing it? What is the risk associated with not implementing it?

The other side of the cost-benefit equation is the investment required to implement the new strategy. The cost of the tools and techniques, their operation and maintenance, and other technical and organizational costs should be identified. It is important to understand the total cost of a tool or technique over its expected lifetime, taking account of the cost of introduction, customization, upgrades or extensions, and maintenance costs. Among the organizational aspects that need to be examined and costed are implementation planning, system installation, training, development of procedures and documentation, use of standards, standardization, system management and support, security, work methods, work flow, management roles and responsibilities, and potential reorganization and reassignment of roles and responsibilities.

Usually organizational costs are the largest component of the total cost of an improvement project. They often are of the same magnitude as the combined cost of computer hardware, software, and telecommunications.

The full-scale introduction of many techniques and tools is a lengthy process. For medium and large companies it may take anything from two to seven years. The combination of cross-functional and long-term project characteristics implies that the process will be difficult to cost justify. Cost-justification techniques that take account of only short-term, task-oriented benefits will fail. Management must ensure that cross-functional and long-term benefits related to time-to-market and product quality are included in such cost justification.

Cost-justification calculations address expected benefits. Sometimes it is difficult to know what type of benefits should be considered and how they should be measured. The approach taken for cost-justifying local, short-term, operational improvements is not the same as for cross-functional and long-term improvements. Many of the benefits that are easiest to measure in a short-term project are the least important in a long-term project. A balance must be found between short-term costs, short-term benefits, and long-term benefits. A short-term reduction in personnel may be easy to measure but may not be the major benefit. The ability to reduce lead times by 50 percent would be a major benefit, but it is difficult to measure exactly how much of this might be due to the new improvement as there are so many other variables in the long term.

The right measures of performance must be used in the cost-justification calculation. Measures should be related to business characteristics and products, and could include lead times, cycle times, number of engineering changes, number of parts, number of defects, cost of design, and cost of production.

Most improvement activities affect several functions and many people. If such an activity succeeds, its effect on the organization will be widely felt. Minimizing negative effects and maximizing potential benefits require a clear understanding of the organizational issues. These range from basic issues such as training, through the development of system and working procedures, to standards and policies defining the use of the improvement, and major functional reorganization. The former issues, closer to the tool or technique, are usually easier to address. The less technological and the more purely organizational the issues, the more difficult they are to resolve. However, unless they are resolved, benefits promised by the team will not be achieved.

The many very good reasons for the improvement should not be allowed to mask the difficulty of achieving real benefits from its use. Although, at first glance, the implementation team may believe that the improvement looks very much like a win-win opportunity, successful implementation and use of new tools and techniques are difficult to achieve. As many companies have now realized from their attempts to introduce new tools and techniques, a purely technological solution is rarely successful without a corresponding organizational solution.

Benefits will not occur just because a tool or technique has been chosen. Many other actions will be needed, such as setting targets for use of the improvement, deciding how to manage related systems, training people to take advantage of the improvement, training the support team, defining use procedures, clarifying information structures, defining the best overall product development process, modifying workflows, and defining and using a suitable design methodology.

When introducing new tools, the key architectural components to be defined include the data architecture (flow and structure by function and by system), organizational structure, the structure of control procedures, the information flow network, the life cycle of projects and products, the computer systems, and the structure of the support organization.

Once the implementation team has completed the above steps, it is in a position to identify potential solutions, or scenarios. These should take into account not only the new process itself but also the general environment surrounding the new process. It is useful to investigate three or four alternative solutions, describing each in detail with its strengths and weaknesses. This exercise is extremely useful in gaining an in-depth understanding of a proposed solution. Often it is by trying to understand the strengths of an alternative that the weaknesses of the others become more apparent.

Proposing a Way Forward

Having evaluated the scenarios and selected the most appropriate solution, the implementation team needs to obtain management approval to move forward to the next step. The team will have collected a mass of data about the company, but little of this will be of interest to management. The team has to stand back for a moment and recall its objective—to propose a solution to management, not to waste management's time with unnecessary information. The team must distill the information into a form in which management can easily understand it. It must recognize the way in which it relates to the company and to the objectives set for the project.

The team should produce a one-page overview that shows how the business objectives are to be met by the proposed solution. Starting from this one-page, top-level picture, the team can then develop one-page pictures of each of the major issues related to the improvement project.

The strategy document defines the overall objectives, vision, scope, function, and policies of the improvement project and the relationship between it and other activities. The accompanying overall implementation plan produced at this stage by the team should address both the long term and the short term. For the long term, it provides management with the information necessary to understand the resources that the project will require. It shows the activities that will be required in related areas. It shows how the initial installation fits into a long-term development plan. The more specific the plan is, the better. It should define an overall implementation timetable showing how the implementation will be split into manageable projects. For each project in the plan, the timing, objectives, resources, investments, relationships, priorities, and expected benefits should be detailed. The plan should show which people will be required to work on the projects, for how long, and when. It should show the project organizational structure. As the project will be interdepartmental, responsibilities and authority need to be clearly defined and confirmed by management.

The short-term plan should show management which actions need to be taken in the short term. Many of these will inevitably be linked to investment in technology and organization. The plan is more likely to be accepted if it also includes some actions that will lead to short-term savings and other short-term benefits.

Implementation, Use, and Review

Wherever possible, implementation should be incremental and based on successful pilot studies. During pilot activities, full support should be given to users. Users and their managers should be involved in the pilots as much as possible. It is much better to be able to show small but early success from real implementation than to show theoretical results and thick reports full of detailed plans unrelated to business objectives.

The overall implementation plan produced by the team for management approval addressed both the long term and the short term. A detailed implementation plan should now be produced addressing the short term. The more specific it is, the better. This plan should identify all necessary short-term activities. It should show which people will be required to work on the projects, for how long, and when. It should show the organizational structure of projects and the structure of the new support organization.

Before the new technique or system can be used, the overall solution has to be built, integrated, and installed. A detailed requirements document may be needed as a basis for the development or acquisition of individual subsystems. Architectures will have to be detailed. One important sub-project will address the engineering workflow and engineering activities. Project life cycles and associated technical activities, systems, users, information, events, and management activities need to be detailed. Users have to be trained. Test procedures have to be developed and put in place. Standards have to be chosen, defined, and communicated. Detailed questions have to be answered. How will the whole solution run on an everyday basis? What interfaces to other techniques and systems will be required?

Modifications to individual activities, the workflow, the organizational structure, and other control structures may also be necessary. Policies and working procedures need to be defined. Users and managers from many parts of the company have to be trained, and a support team needs to be formed and trained to develop procedures and documentation for system use, management, and control.

In addition to the purchase and installation of new systems, it may also be necessary to carry out some in-house tailoring and development. New systems may have to be tailored so that they meet the specific requirements of the company. Interfaces may have to be developed between existing and new systems. Associated system administration and system management procedures will have to be defined. Unless the company has been very successful in the past at developing new applications, the team should try to keep system development work to a minimum and ensure that whatever development work does take place is kept under strict management control.

One of the major responsibilities of the team at this stage is to ensure that the implementation takes place within the agreed-on budget and time limits. The team also is responsible for ensuring close integration between organizational and technological activities.

The third phase in the process of implementation is actual use. In a way, this is only the beginning of the process of using the new technique or system to produce business benefits. Before it can be used, the solution needs to be up and running, with new procedures in place and users trained to use them. Soon after the new technique or system is in place, users will find that it can be improved, and adaptation will take place.

Use will be monitored to see that it meets expectations. Occasionally, formal reviews should take place to see what progress is being made toward meeting the targets agreed on with management. Reports will be issued to management and appropriate actions taken.

A successful implementation involves some simple but very essential activities:

- A clear need for the changes to be implemented,
- Description of the current situation,
- Description of the future situation,
- A strategy for achieving the future vison,
- Formation of an implementation team,
- Indoctrination and education of the team,
- Identification and neutralization of those who oppose change,
- Development of a detailed implementation plan,
- Modeling and testing of new techniques and technologies, and
- Project monitoring and performance measurement.

When these factors are present, achievement of the vison and goals will occur.

Key Issues for Implementing Improvements

R&D AND MANUFACTURING NEED TO COOPERATE!

In recent years, more and more emphasis has been placed on using teamwork to meet the challenges posed by competition that is increasingly global. Teamwork is an important ingredient in implementing Total Quality and Just-in-Time disciplines, and those of us in North America and Europe are constantly barraged with examples of how our competitors in Japan and the Pacific Rim use teamwork and intercompany cooperation to take an increasing share of world markets. The following example illustrates what is so important about teamwork.

During the mid-1970s, I worked for a Fortune 50 corporation in a division making precision medical instruments. The products allow medical researchers to make extremely thin sections of tissue for analysis under the microscope and to separate blood into fractions.

I was in the manufacturing and materials management side of the business and was a member of a product committee that controlled the destiny of a product called an ultracentrifuge. This machine spins a titanium rotor loaded with test tubes at speeds up to 65,000 RPM in an evacuated, refrigerated chamber. The product committee included a marketing manager, a design engineer, a manufacturing engineer, a field service manager, a materials planner, a director of manufacturing, and the assembly department supervisor. The charter of this group was to work together as a team to control the design enhancements for the product, ensure that customers received quality product, provide excellent service to the installed base, and ensure that production quotas were met.

This was a relatively new product at the time, and after being introduced to the market, a number of design refinements and cost reductions were suggested by various quarters. One refinement that design engineering decided to implement was the redesign of the hydraulic control mechanism, which was machined from various castings. The design change included a nearly complete redesign of the components of this assembly, which were now to be made out of machined steel. As was typical at that time (and is still today in many companies), design engineering produced a complete new set of blueprints without involving manufacturing or the product team in the actual design process and without a preproduction test of prototypes made in production departments.

The introduction of the new design was carefully planned and introduced into production with very little trouble until the assembly department attempted to put the new design into production. Once in operation under hydraulic pressure, the control valve mechanism didn't work properly, and the moving parts of the assembly interfered with each other so badly that the units had to be disassembled to free them. This stopped all production at a critical time when we were attempting to prove the superiority of our hydraulic engine over the competition's electric motor and gear transmission assembly. Panic ensued.

All parts made to the new design were pulled out of inventory, and all were reinspected by quality control to be certain that they were made "to print." After spending much time and effort inspecting the parts, we could not find any out of tolerance. It seems that design engineering had produced an enhancement that rendered the machine useless when all the components were made exactly to the specifications. Instead of waiting for the engineers to redesign the unit and functionally test it as they should have done (with manufacturing participating), one of our assembly technicians devised a method of assembly that used a lapping technique to overcome the tolerance build-up between parts. Production resumed, the units operated flawlessly, and the design engineer was furious that manufacturing technicians had "overstepped their authority" by correcting the problem themselves without the advice or consent of engineering.

Unfortunately, this was not an isolated case. Management created a climate where design engineering and manufacturing were encouraged to be adversaries. Rather than working with a real spirit of cooperation and teamwork, which would enhance the success of our products in the marketplace, engineering and manufacturing were constantly at odds.

A short time later, the product committee determined that it would be a major performance advantage if the ultracentrifuge could be air cooled rather than water cooled. This would dispense with the need for a plumbing hook-up and make it more convenient to move machines around the laboratory. The design engineering contingent determined that there were too many technical barriers to achieving a reliable air cooling system for the unit and predicted that it would likely take years to come up with a design that would be acceptable.

Meanwhile, those of us in manufacturing determined that the product really needed an air cooling capability to succeed in the marketplace, since the competition was using their product's ability to run without a water hook-up as a selling point. Realizing that by the time engineering came up with a design that worked we could be out of business on this product line, we undertook the development on our own. We designed a completely self-contained cooling unit, built a prototype, incorporated it into a production unit, and tested it severely for weeks with no major problems. In the space of about three months we had designed, built, and completely tested the new design.

Once again, engineering was outraged that we had "invaded their territory" without even consulting them. Marketing was overjoyed and proceeded to clear the way for us to market the new model, which was quite successful. Engineering was reduced to sending a draftsman to the assembly department to make blueprints of our design. Although we were the winners in this skirmish, it was a risky thing to do and did nothing to foster cooperation between engineering and manufacturing. If engineering and manufacturing were really working as a team, perhaps the design could have been even more successful and cost less to produce. We were actually lucky to have succeeded in this case, and without a clever manufacturing engineer on our team, we might never have produced a workable design. The loser in this case was not really engineering, but the company itself and the employees. This type of adversarial relationship fostered by management (either actively or by default) is costly in terms of time wasted on politics and jockeying for position, and even more costly in lost synergy, which impedes the ability to compete.

A Quality Design Process

What was needed in that situation was the application of Total Quality concepts to the design process. Those familiar with TQM know that each of us has customers within the organization and to service these customers properly we must communicate with them to understand their requirements. For our organization to produce a quality product, we must understand our customer's needs and meet or exceed them. Quality is not what *we* think it is; quality is what the *customer* says it is.

In a quality product-design process, each participant in the process must know who his or her customer is and what that customer needs and expects. Internal customers are as important in the product-development process as the external customer is in defining the market requirements for the product itself. Manufacturing personnel must be involved from the earliest stages of product development to help determine the best way to manufacture components and assemble the product, all of which have a real effect on the technical aspects of the design. Purchasing, material control, field service, marketing, customer service, QA, and accounting personnel all have important contributions to make to the design process as well. Just think for a moment of all the times you have heard field service lamenting about the difficulty of repairing a product, or customer service complaining about the difficulty of configuring a product for a customer order, material control wrestling with the implementation of a design change "thrown over the wall" by engineering, and on and on.

Quality is one of the missing ingredients in the product development process, despite the great progress that has been made in technology. As in so many other areas of business, technology is a tool that can help companies advance but it is *how we manage* that will make the difference. People use the technology, and those people must work in an environment that makes the best use of the available tools. A customer-oriented R&D process or organization will outperform the more common adversarial one, regardless of technological advantages.

Production/Operations Takes On a Design Role

Another aspect of the teamwork required to make the new paradigm work is the education of production and operations people in current technology. These same people need to educate the design engineers in all the techniques of production:

- Core technologies needed to produce product now and in the future must be understood, from engineering through manufacturing.

- Manufacturing people must be educated and trained in existing and upcoming production techniques.

- Programs must be started to keep everyone aware of new technology, illustrate the cost drivers in the company, and teach process reengineering skills that will be indispensable in a fluid and flexible organization.

- Most important, there must be a clear awareness of the customer's requirements (both internal and external customers).

Football Versus Rugby

The sport of rugby is an excellent example of the type of teamwork that is desirable, and comparing it to football illustrates what is not as effective. In rugby, players pass the ball back and forth among themselves, improvise as the game progresses, and substitute for each other when another player is out of reach. The game never stops, and no timeouts are allowed. In rugby, all the players may carry the ball. There is lots of passing, improvising, overlapped roles, and players who back up each other. With no timeouts, the players must decide for themselves what to do when situations change.

Football, in contrast, is focused on the specialist who plays on an offensive, defensive, or special team. It *requires* specialization, significant amounts of careful planning, and near perfect execution to win. Only certain players can carry the ball, and when something goes wrong, a timeout is called, and the players wait for instructions from the coaches.

In too many companies, as in football, we are looking for individual heroes. The goal is to be inducted into the hall of fame. Statistics are collected on individual performance, and players are rewarded on their individual performance. Team objectives never seem to be as important.

What is becoming clearer is that individuals cannot save us from competitors that are increasingly more nimble due to their ability to work as a team. If your company's product design process (and your company as a whole for that matter) is to work at its peak capability, you must work together like a rugby team.

There is a new emphasis on speed and agility that is required to stay in the game—to meet and beat the competition. Speed and agility will require cross-training, improvisation, and mutual back-up, just as in rugby. Specialized job titles will need to be abolished. Engineers cannot be a design engineer, a manufacturing engineer, or a service engineer. They must be assigned to product line teams. Employees from all the operating departments of the enterprise will have to share equally in the work of designing the product. Design will now include consideration of material availability, cost, use of appropriate technology, and manufacturing methods. No longer will that familiar refrain "It's not my job" be heard. The functional walls that separated the specialists of the past will, like the Berlin Wall, be taken down and disappear. The rules of the game have been changed by those who have already learned to work as a team, and those who do not adapt will not only be losers, they will eventually be out of the game. It is time to dispose of the football model.

ENGINEERING CHANGE CONTROL

The following is a true story. Only the name of the company has been omitted to protect a firm that has a number of problems with its reputation in the marketplace and is in serious financial trouble. Management of its R&D function is a major contributor to manufacturing problems that underlie the reputation and financial problems.

At a meeting of the engineering change committee at this electro-mechanical manufacturing company, there is a disagreement on how to respond to yet another engineering change "thrown over the wall" from R&D. Contained in the engineering release is a requirement to immediately phase in a modification to a circuit board, due to failures in the field. As is customary in this company, the change has been released by engineering and sent to the manufacturing engineering department for implementation.

The manager of the department has assigned one of the least qualified people in the department to handle the releases from engineering because the more talented ones are busy trying to put out the numerous "fires" in production. Problems due to design and quality flaws are making it extremely difficult to build a product that meets advertised specifications. One major new product (which is in its first production run) cannot be manufactured to meet the specifications that product management is advertising to the marketplace. A large percentage of production fails functional tests repeatedly, and a critical subassembly cannot be manufactured at all due to technical difficulties resulting from a design that was not tested sufficiently in production facilities.

And so our friend in manufacturing engineering dutifully analyzes what must be done to implement this change and begins to make the necessary arrangements to put it into effect. Due to the nature of the function of this circuit board, the change will make it noninterchangeable with previous revisions in the field. But engineering has not changed the part number. A number of similar changes have been made in the past, creating interchangeability problems for field service and confusion in the repair depot.

Engineering in this particular company, as in so many others, has enough power to force implementation of most changes exactly the way it wants them done. Senior management in this company is not technically oriented, doesn't understand the problems associated with implementing engineering releases, and doesn't believe that it is of critical importance. Our manufacturing engineer knows that efforts to formally control engineering releases in the past have been failures, and so he begins implementation of the change at hand just as engineering has recommended. He knows that this change will cause difficulties later on in the repair depot and with field service, but he also knows he has little choice.

The form for approval of engineering releases requires the top manager of each operating function in the company to sign off. Each of these departments is represented at an engineering release meeting that is supposed to be a forum for discussion of releases, culminating in the approval and sign-off of the engineering change notice. This meeting is just a formality, and the outcome is usually to "rubber stamp" the course of action recommended by engineering.

Although this particular example is illustrative of a company that was not working as a team, the more common scenario is one of confrontation and adversarial relationships. There are many companies where engineering has released new products or changes to existing products with little or no warning to any other operating department. The other departments in turn analyze the engineering change notice to decipher what effect it may have on them. Often an engineering change meeting brings the various parties together to discuss the issues of implementation, and it is not uncommon for the operating departments to refuse to implement what engineering has recommended. Top management settles the dispute based on political clout, not merit.

What is missing in these companies is an enlightened management that understands the great competitive consequence of bringing product and product change out of R&D and into manufacturing and the marketplace smoothly and quickly. To do this requires a formal, controlled process that eliminates adversarial relationships and includes all the operating departments of the company from the earliest stage and throughout the product life cycle.

COMPONENTS OF A CONTROLLED, COOPERATIVE PROCESS

Engineering Change Request (ECR)

Companies that have their product development process under control seem to use the engineering change request (ECR) (or a similar document) as the vehicle for starting new development projects. The ECR is a form, much like a capital appropriation request, on which the project is described and justified. ECRs that involve significant dollar amounts or the release of new products should be reviewed by senior company management. This review must be conducted promptly after submission of the ECR and should include the following:

- Demonstration of a clear need for this particular project,

- Major customers, products, or other items that will be affected by the project,

- Cost of the project and expected benefits,

- Technology that will be required versus current manufacturing capability, and

- Safety and product liability issues.

Project Team

Once a major project has passed the ECR review, a project team is formed, with representation from each operating department in the company. If a project involves an existing product line, a product-line team will most likely already exist. As the development progresses, members work together to

- Design the product or components required,

- Ensure the manufacturability of the product and identify appropriate technology,

- Create preliminary product documentation that can be used for obtaining vendor quotations, cost estimating, and making prototypes,

- Determine an introduction date and forecast demand or usage for the item,

- Begin planning for production facilities, staffing, and training requirements, and

- Determine how to evaluate product quality.

This process varies very little from industry to industry in terms of these major steps and will differ only in terms of scale and the number of people involved in small companies.

Release to Manufacturing

Instead of the "throw it over the wall" sort of process described in the previous example of the troubled electromechanical company, release of a new design to production is almost a non-event when product development is under control and accomplished by a multidisciplined team. An engineering change notice (ECN) is not required. The project is approved at its inception by top management, and a team of people from all the functions in the company works to produce the design. All the necessary concerns are addressed as part of the design process. Required documentation, costs, and planning all take place as the development project is in process. When the product or modification goes into production, everyone knows what to do and is highly confident that there will be no glitches. All necessary preparations to produce the new design are made, so there is no need to have a separate process to implement changes released by engineering.

Contrast this with the company that still employs the traditional approach: engineering produces designs with little or no input from other functions and releases the result of their work to the rest of the company. At the point of release, most of the work involved in determining how to manufacture, how to cost, who to train, and how many to make is just beginning. Not only does this method take a lot longer, but it is full of opportunities to fail. Engineering may have made some technical decisions that are not easily produced in manufacturing, require technology that is not proven or well understood, put unreasonable resource demands on facilities, cost too much, or are based on insufficient or misinterpreted data from marketing.

CONSEQUENCES OF FAILURE TO CHANGE

What is happening to companies that today are still operating their product development process with obsolete process technology?

- Introduction of new models and marketplace-driven features are being delayed, which results in lost business to competitors and loss of reputation. Witness the disaster experienced by Ashton-Tate software a few years ago when it failed to bring its Dbase IV product to market on schedule. Competitive database products saw an opening to take market share away from the dominant player in the business and succeeded in doing so. Marketing had announced features in the new product that the development team was unable to easily produce. Until those features could be included in the product, it could not ship.

- Planned cost reductions are not being achieved, as extra effort and cost are expended to get product manufactured despite unproven designs and inappropriate use of technology. Poorly coordinated implementation of new designs also causes rework, overtime, and other premium costs. The result is often a loss of product profitability and even more often a shortened product life span.

- Substantial excess and obsolete inventory are almost always created by the uncoordinated implementation of design change. In one company we visited, a significant inventory problem had been created by ignoring the accumulation of obsolete inventory over a period of years. Even if the company had not ignored the accumulation, there would have been significant inventory write-off each year as a result of poorly implemented design change. Delay in addressing the problem only made the eventual adjustment more painful.

ORGANIZATIONAL REQUIREMENTS

The organization required to support the new model of product development and product introduction is more process-oriented than functional. People may still report to functional management for administrative ease but have to operate independently of a rigidly defined department to support the teams that they work with. Team goals and objectives must be the primary means of measurement to instill the value that individual heroes are not desirable and will not be rewarded.

In the past, many companies created an engineering change control committee composed of representatives from each function to meet periodically and determine how to handle the engineering releases. Under the new model, there is no need for this committee when there are teams working together throughout the product-development cycle. Functional roles to be included in the makeup of the team include technical design, manufacturing process design, cost estimating, market research and planning, manufacturability and serviceability assurance, inventory planning, purchasing, product testing, and manufacturing supervision. Functional roles do not necessarily indicate that one person is assigned to each function. If a team has a member who can fill two or more roles competently, there is no need for additional persons unless there is more work than one person can handle. Eventually, with the cross-training that occurs in a teamwork environment, work overloads on particular members will occur less frequently or not at all due to the blurring of functional distinctions within the team.

To evolve into the type of organization required by the new model of product development, we suggest the following:

- Identify the key customers of engineering in your company.

- Educate these persons to understand the new model.

- Provide teamwork training and facilitation for everyone.

- Reengineer the product development process to fit the new model.

- Form product line teams.

- Make organizational adjustments required by the new process.

SELF-ASSESSMENT

- How is the engineering change or new product introduction function organized in your company?

- Is the atmosphere conducive to the formation of teams that are empowered to make the necessary decisions, or will change require a major adjustment in attitudes and possibly require replacement of some players?

- If you are already moving toward concurrent development and process-oriented organizations, have you included the ECR concept or other mechanism to provide top management with a guidance mechanism?

- Are design changes and new products introduced on schedule and within budget?

- Is there conflict among management over who will control the new product development process, or does one function seem to dominate all the decision making?

- If there is an ECR or top management approval process for acceptance of major development projects, are there preestablished rules for acceptance of a project?

- Do product changes and new products move smoothly from development into production, without major technical problems or delays due to poor coordination?

HARD TIPS FOR SOFT ISSUES

Awareness

The product development process has changed so little over the last few decades that many people assume it is unlikely to change in the near future. However, the forces of change are building up and corporations will be forced to organize themselves differently so that high-quality products can be developed very quickly in response to customer requirements. Those organizations that recognize the opportunity first, and act fast, will benefit most from the change.

Benchmarking—the process of measuring the company's products, services, and practices against its toughest competitors or those companies renowned as industry leaders—is an ideal way of making people aware of the need for change.

The product development process is a companywide activity. Its improvement must be addressed as a cross-functional, high-level activity reporting directly to top management. It is not a departmental issue that can be solved by a few engineers, programmers, and data analysts. Improving the process will be lengthy, costly, and cross-functional. Don't look for a quick, cheap solution for one department before getting the overall picture.

To achieve the major performance improvements required if costs and time cycles are to be reduced sufficiently for it to be possible to meet customer requirements, top management has to take the lead and set the improvement targets. Top management support is crucial for a cross-functional, long-term project like the improvement of the product development process. Top management support must be gained and maintained, and it must be visible to all. In particular it must be visible to middle managers who may feel threatened by change and unwilling to support it. The improvement of the process needs the full support of top management throughout many years. Only top management will be able to resolve the interdepartmental issues that will arise from trying to change a cross-functional process. Top management involvement is necessary for long-term, costly, and strategic projects of this nature. However, top management cannot be expected to be involved in all the details of the solution. These tasks have to be delegated.

From Vision to Planning

Initially, people will find it hard to understand the new appearance of the product development activity, so it is important to develop a clear vision of its future shape. If the vision is not easy to understand and easy to communicate, it will be difficult to enlist support for change.

The only justification for introducing the product development process is to improve business results. The business objectives have to be understood and quantified before the implementation of change to the product development process can be planned. The criteria by which the success of the new product development process will be judged should be defined before implementation is started. Progress toward these targets has to be monitored regularly.

A strategic plan for process improvement must be developed to support the overall goals of the corporation. This will provide a basis from which product family team leaders can develop team objectives and initiate, monitor, and support change to the product development process.

Planning for change to the product development process should be top down, starting from customer needs and business benefits. Implementation should be bottom up, starting from individual activities in the process and working up toward the business benefits. During planning, it is useful to identify several possible solutions, including those chosen by other companies, and understand their strengths and weaknesses. During both planning and implementation, the organizational issues should not be ignored. Often, they are as, or more, important than the technological issues.

Moving Forward

People often find it hard to understand a changing environment, so it is important to communicate regularly to them the reasons for and status of change. It is best if all the people who are affected by change to the product development process are involved with it from the beginning. This increases their commitment to its success.

Changing People

It is important to take account of organizational and cultural issues. Deciding to make change is not the same thing as making change. The culture in the new organization will be different from that in traditional organizations, and many people will find it hard to adjust.

In most companies it is felt that there are only a few key people able to make things happen, and these people soon become overloaded with all sorts of tasks. When changing the product development process it is important to identify a few individuals who will act as change agents. Their only objective is to implement the changes required by management, and they should not be responsible for day-to-day firefighting.

In the traditional product development process, people in different departments work one after the other on successive phases of development. In the new process, a group of individuals, often from several functions, works together sharing information and knowledge and producing better and faster results than they would have done if operating in serial mode. Teamwork is a new concept for many companies. It requires people to behave differently, to take decisions differently, to be measured differently. Team objectives have to be set and controlled. New techniques will be needed for managing and training team members.

In any large organization, there is always resistance to change. The successful introduction of changes to the product development process requires product development process champions, catalysts, change agents, and change makers. They must be identified, supported and encouraged. The many opponents of change must be identified and understood and influenced to modify their behavior.

From Customer to Customer

When changing the product development process, don't focus exclusively on internal activities. The process starts and ends with the customer, so to better understand customer requirements, get closer to the customer—the prime source of product and service requirements. Ask customers what they want.

Aim to develop closer and better relationships with suppliers. Treat them as assets by taking advantage of a supplier's strong points. Help them to improve their performance by getting individuals from each company to work closely together.

The new corporate organization is built around the product development process, so this must be understood in detail. Key product development process steps include defining customer and performance requirements, planning the position and evolution of products within their families, planning for the entire life cycle of a product, and concurrently designing products and the processes to manufacture, support, and recycle them. The individual steps of the process need to be mapped, analyzed, and improved. Opportunities to make major improvements by restructuring the process can also be seen once the process has been mapped.

Engineering information will become a strategic resource and its management a key issue. A high priority of the product-line organization will be to improve the use, quality, and flow of engineering information. Effective use and reuse of engineering information will play a key role in differentiating the best companies from the rest.

In recent years, many new techniques have been introduced to support the product development process. Among the most important business philosophies and practices to be applied are TQM and top-down planning. Within the product development process techniques exist to support both the product life cycle and individual steps in the process. Both types of technique are needed, and they must be closely supported by computer systems. The best available techniques (such as QFD) and tools (such as CAE) should be used and systematically incorporated into the process. Engineering data management (EDM) systems will become the infrastructure for all the other computer-based systems in the product development process and will manage information and processes all the way along the product life cycle.

Wherever possible, standards should be used. This will increase the efficiency of the product development process activity. When developing the new product development process, international standards should be used wherever possible. This will reduce the workload both internally and when communicating with business partners. Unless it can be clearly proved that the company can not achieve the business benefits it is looking for through the use of standard systems and techniques, in-house development work for the product development process should be kept to the bare minimum.

Implementation

Wherever possible, implementation should be incremental and based on successful pilot activities. During pilot activities, full support should be given to users. Users and their managers should be involved in the pilots as much as possible. It is much better to be able to show small but early success from real implementation than to show theoretical results and three-inch-thick reports. The conclusions of a three-year project to define how to improve the product development process will probably be out of date before they are distributed.

When implementing change to the product development process it is always useful to bear in mind that the product development process in most companies has changed little in previous years and probably contains many wasteful activities. The implementation of a new process provides a good opportunity to identify and improve, or eliminate, inefficient activities.

Improvement of the product development process never ends. Continuous improvement implies continuously improving customer service, product performance, and process performance. Unless a continuous improvement approach is taken, attempts at improvement tend to be uncoordinated and insignificant for the bottom line.

Change cannot be bought off the shelf and does not occur overnight. Management cannot expect to set up a new process and then walk away. Change can occur only if management ensures that corresponding processes, techniques, organizations, and systems are put in place. Management has to consistently reinforce attitudes, behavior, and performance and recognize and resolve problems.

Technology watch activities should be set up to make sure that the organization stays abreast of advances in technology, systems, and practices. Benchmarking can play an important role in learning how other organizations modify their performance.

Getting the Numbers Right

Metrics are needed to set targets, monitor progress, track results, and fix problems. They help identify, analyze, and report behavior. Without the ability to measure performance, it is not possible to ensure performance improvement.

Product family teams target the five dimensions of product, process, regional, functional, and cultural performance. In each dimension, appropriate metrics, often related to cost, quality, and cycle time, are needed. The metrics by which performance are measured include a mixture of external metrics (such as sales volume, profit per engineer, product cost, and time to market) and internal metrics (such as development cost, number of iterations of the design cycle, and number of design changes). Reward and recognition systems will motivate people to perform as individuals and to contribute to team performance, along the five dimensions, with performance judged by superiors, peers, and subordinates.

Implementing change is not an easy task, and the "people" issues are invariably more difficult than the technological ones. Customers, vendors, employees, and their relationships are going to be more complex than technology. There are numerous multifaceted interactions between the people involved in changing the way products are developed. In addition, humans tend to adjust their attitudes and outlook on a daily basis. Technology is much more constant and predictable. While techniques and technology are essential tools that support the product development process, management of the people involved will determine success or failure.

CHAPTER 12

New Approaches to Engineering: The Techniques

DESIGN FOR ASSEMBLY (DFA)

One of the best ways to reduce time to market and to improve process and product quality is to *design in* the ability to easily manufacture or assemble the product. It has been estimated that between 50 and 90 percent of manufacturing costs (and process time) are committed during the design phase of product development. The manufacturing departments in many companies have already responded to competition and cost pressures and have reduced cycle times and non–value-adding steps. The "low hanging fruit" in manufacturing in many cases has already been picked. If we are to further reduce product cost, maintain high quality, and continue reducing the time it takes to manufacture or assemble the product, we must first reduce the number of parts to be assembled and then make sure that the rest of the components of the product are put together as simply and efficiently as possible.

Design for Assembly (DFA) has been developed as a technique to aid in accomplishing the goal of eliminating unnecessary parts and helping designers determine the best way to assemble the product. It incorporates a methodology and uses tools to analyze an assembly for DFA opportunities. In general, the DFA methodology incorporates techniques to

- Reduce the number of parts in an assembly by combining the function of several parts into one;

- Make the assembly simple by designing it to be assembled in only one fashion with a series of simple procedures;

- Make the product modular to facilitate alternative configurations and options;

- Keep manufacturing tolerances reasonable and achievable given the product's performance requirements;

- Facilitate quality assurance and ease of testing; and

- Ensure that parts from previous designs are reused where possible.

Software is available for DFA to perform such things as tolerance analysis, three-dimensional simulation, economic analysis, and expert analysis. DFA software was originally developed by Geoffrey Boothroyd and Peter Dewhurst at the University of Rhode Island, where the curriculum is focused on designing for manufacturability. Now a number of software packages support DFA concepts, and Boothroyd Dewhurst Inc. sells a "Design for Assembly Toolkit." This software performs cost estimating functions, helps to optimize designs for manual assembly techniques, and suggests preferred methods for assembling a product based on its characteristics.

When to Use DFA

DFA can be used in two different modes—when a new product is being designed and when an existing product is being redesigned. While DFA is valuable in all but the most simple assemblies, it applies extremely well in cases where

- A large number of component parts are used,

- There is a high labor content to the assembly,

- The assembly process is relatively complex, and

- There are lots of different fasteners.

Other situations that suggest good potential for DFA are where assembly times are extremely long, significantly affecting time to market; where cost reduction is a major competitive factor; where there have been real problems with field maintainability on a product; and where the ability to reclaim or recycle (disassemble and reuse) products is an important consideration.

DFA Examples

In practice, then, Design for Assembly concentrates on arriving at the best mix of materials and methods for the component parts used in an assembly. This is done by analyzing the structure of the product to be assembled, selecting the most appropriate materials, eliminating unnecessary parts, reusing existing parts that will function correctly in the new design, and selecting assembly and handling methods that are simple and easy to perform. If it is used on an existing assembly, the item is disassembled and evaluated. After evaluation an improved design is developed, guided by the DFA software. Fasteners and handling are minimized, and multifunctional components are used wherever possible.

At a major computer manufacturer's printer division, some excellent results were achieved with DFA. On one particular printer model (which was identified as an excellent candidate for DFA analysis because of the complexity of the assembly process and the number of component parts), dramatic reductions were made in time and cost. This unit had in excess of 200 components, took nearly three hours to assemble, and involved more than 200 operations to complete. After redesign with DFA, this same unit used approximately fifty components, required only twenty operations, and was completed in fifteen minutes.

During the design of a new consumer appliance at another manufacturer, DFA was utilized from the beginning of the design process. A completely new product was developed using a number of parts from existing product lines, a process that cleverly has all the internal parts fit together without fasteners and less than ten fasteners used to hold it together. Major savings in time to market and manufacturing cost were realized, product quality and reliability have been high, and the product has been quite successful in achieving a major share of its intended market.

Benefits

DFA has extremely high potential and costs relatively little to implement. Desktop-level systems are available to perform DFA analysis, making the technology available to almost anyone. Typical benefits return many times the investment to implement DFA. In nearly all cases, product reliability is improved, the number of parts is reduced, manufacturing labor is reduced, fewer drawings are required to document the design, simpler fastening methods are developed, maintainability and ease of disassembly are enhanced, fewer parts suppliers are needed, and manufacturing tooling costs are reduced.

DESIGNING FOR QUALITY RESULTS

Designing for quality is a concept that incorporates design experience, failure analysis, standards, and other information in a database used by engineers and designers. Although off-the-shelf software doesn't exist for this application, it is not complex and can be developed under the umbrella of CAE. It is intended to be a repository of engineering and design information that has been organized to support quality in product development through consistency and discipline in the application of design concepts to specific situations. It is intended to include a methodical, step-by-step approach that leads the designer through a series of activities that ensure that design standards and other references are incorporated into the product at the item level and that occurrence of defects is prevented.

In an actual application of the concept, engineers would be responsible for maintaining the database with data that can be useful in future design projects. Experience with existing products is used to draw conclusions about desirable and undesirable attributes of specific designs, to extract information from failure mode analysis, and to store these learnings so that new designs can avoid repetition of previous mistakes. Put simply, such a system would keep records of what works and what doesn't.

In addition to experiential data, engineers would maintain design standards and other references on the system and link these to instruction sets that designers could use when creating new items. Once the engineer has created the instruction sets, other designers would be able to access the information and create new designs that incorporate proven technology applications while conforming to company or industry standards.

As a result of using this system, preferred design methods can be available to anyone working on the design of a new part, design standards are enforced and correctly implemented, problems and open design issues are documented, and interaction between designers is enhanced. The overall quality and reliability of parts produced under this method are improved, and more important, the level of quality is consistent. The main benefits resulting from these efforts are that defects in products are *prevented*, and exposure to product liability actions is reduced. The costs associated with defects are also reduced, manifested in fewer manufacturing problems, less rework, and fewer field failures. Due to the reduction in manufacturing problems and rework, it also takes less time to produce the product.

DESIGN FOR REUSABILITY

Design for reusability is also called group technology (GT) to reflect the fact that parts are grouped together to take advantage of similarities. Parts are coded for reusability using the type of material they are made from, the shape or geometry of the part, and the manufacturing process used to create them.

Reusability can play a major part in reducing design time, as studies have shown that 80 percent of parts required for a new product design already exist or can be modified from existing part designs. In companies with no GT effort in place, proliferation of nearly identical parts tends to get out of control as time marches on and different designers come and go.

A few years ago, a situation that illustrates how parts proliferation occurs was observed at a division of a major corporation, which manufactured hydraulic and pneumatic equipment.

A new assembly department supervisor noticed that component parts of many product lines were very similar, often being different in only one dimension. For each of these families of parts the designs of individual items had been created by different designers at different times. No effort had been made to relate items into families, and each design had been created without knowledge of the similarities of existing parts because no coding scheme had been set up. In addition, there were multiple versions of purchased items such as fasteners to perform exactly the same function. No one could explain why there were six different kinds of 10–32 socket head cap screws that could all be used interchangeably but were each specified for different products. The same situation existed for nearly every other common fastener used in the plant. As you might guess, they proceeded to eliminate redundant purchased items and to classify and code the families of parts they had identified. The coding and classification process was then expanded to the rest of the products in the business, and the classifications were stored in the information systems.

This story illustrates a type of situation that has been observed in a large number of companies and contributes heavily to excess design and manufacturing costs and unnecessarily long product development times. Once a company moves beyond recognizing the problem (or opportunity), GT can be implemented in a straightforward way. A coding and classification scheme is worked out that matches the kind of product being produced. Then an effort gets under way to classify existing designs according to their shape or other important characteristics that will reveal similarities. Usually, the classifications are entered into a database of some type that makes retrieval and evaluation easier. As design concepts are developed for new products or parts, they are classified according to the coding scheme established for GT. Once classified, the designer can inquire into the database to retrieve similar items, then use them as-is, or modify them to fit the application. In cases where there are no preexisting parts that can be used, the design concept should be reevaluated before a decision is made to proceed with a completely new design.

Design for reusability is a valuable technique. It costs relatively little to implement in terms of computer support, and many existing systems have the capability to support it. It does require some effort to evaluate and classify existing items, but this can be done gradually, starting with product lines that are judged most likely to provide a basis for reusable designs. These could be products that are similar to new product concepts currently under consideration.

As design for reusability is implemented, benefits will be realized in the following areas:

- The time to design new products will be reduced as a result of the reuse of existing designs, either as-is or with modifications.

- As the time to design new products is decreased and the number of engineering resources required goes down due to reuse of existing designs, cost savings are realized.

- Proliferation and duplication of parts will be eliminated, leading to real reductions in the amount of drawings and other documentation that has to be maintained and stored. This can again lead to cost and headcount reductions.

- Manufacturing processes can also be reused, as similar items will be manufactured using similar processes and techniques. Once again, cost and headcount reductions are possible. The need for new or different manufacturing equipment may also be reduced, while existing equipment will be better utilized.

SIMULATION

Simulation is a method of describing complex systems or interactions and predicting the outcome of particular actions within those systems. This technique is heavily dependent on computer support and frequently requires custom programming. But it is unsurpassed as a tool to evaluate alternative methods of design or manufacture. Obviously though, there should be significant identifiable benefits to be realized from simulation, given the cost and level of effort normally required to set up and operate a valid simulation tool. An example will serve to show the level of effort required for a manufacturing process simulation.

Simulation can be used to evaluate the effect of designs on manufacturing costs by predicting such things as processing time, bottlenecks, and machine utilization. In this example, a model of the manufacturing facility would be described in the simulation, including all pertinent information regarding capabilities and predicted or known work loads. Information would also be required to describe the load imposed by specific designs and their respective manufacturing processes. Once the model is built, tests are conducted with historical information where the outcome is already known, to check the simulation against known values. Based on the results of the tests, the model may be refined and tested again and again until there is confidence that the simulator is a good representation of the system.

The effort required to set up the data required for the simulation and to go through numerous test and adjustment iterations can be substantial without even considering the effort to acquire or build the software itself. However, there are real benefits that can make simulation worthwhile. In situations where producing prototypes of a design can be very expensive, or where destructive testing may be required, simulation can reduce the number of prototypes or test products by helping to ensure success on the first physical trial. Put more simply, designs can be evaluated without physically producing them. Operations can be improved by simulating process time, bottlenecks, and machine or labor utilization before making changes to the manufacturing facility or part designs. Once the simulator has been created and tested, it becomes possible to evaluate a number of different alternatives in a short amount of time, reducing the time required to solve problems or decide between alternative strategies.

NEW PRODUCT INTRODUCTION PROCEDURES

In the traditional method of developing new products, engineering is responsible for a project once marketing defines the specifications and management approves. Engineering assigns a task force composed of designers and engineers to work on the project and appoints a project leader. The project leader typically coordinates the efforts of other engineering personnel assigned to the project, sets up and administers the project plan (if one was even created), monitors progress, and may also perform significant design work on the product. All the design and development effort is typically restricted to the engineering department. Once engineering produces a satisfactory design, the drawings are "thrown over the wall" to manufacturing and the real work of producing the product begins. Frequently, manufacturing discovers that the product designed by engineering cannot be made in the real world of production, and engineering receives numerous change requests from manufacturing after releasing a new product, to reflect the redesign the production engineers developed to reliably produce the product.

A typical traditional new product development situation was observed at an engineering and manufacturing division of the NCR Corporation, some time before the recent acquisition by AT&T. This particular division produced microcomputers used in retail point-of-sale and banking-transaction systems. These machines were essentially boxes stuffed with printed circuit boards and a power supply. As is typical in the electronics industry, marketing was constantly driving engineering to innovate and add features to remain competitive in this fast-paced industry. New product development often centered around the design of new printed circuit boards that incorporated desirable new features.

Predictably, the same scenario was played out nearly every time a new circuit board design was undertaken. Marketing would identify the functional characteristics needed to enhance the product, and meetings would be held with design engineering to determine feasibility and performance specifications. Once they had agreed on a course of action, the project was presented to the vice president and general manager of the division for approval.

After a design project was approved, engineering would assign a project manager and design engineers to develop the new functionality. No manufacturing involvement would be solicited at this stage, despite considerable expertise available in board layout, component reliability, and automated testing requirements. During the design phase, the project manager would schedule a number of design reviews to assess progress and tackle technical problems. In addition to the internal technical design reviews, the marketing people and the division VP would also schedule progress reviews. Within engineering, different sections of the design were parceled out to subfunction specialties. Initial circuit design was performed by one or two designers working together, who then passed the design to technicians to make a working prototype. The prototype would be delivered back to the circuit designers, who would test the prototype and make modifications to the design, which would now be introduced in a new version of the prototype. A number of iterations back and forth between the two groups was common.

Following production of a working prototype and a revised circuit design, a review meeting would be held within engineering to ensure that the design conformed to standards and met the required performance specifications. After the engineering design review, there would be a progress review with management. Initial cost estimates would be discussed, which might result in a directive to go back and take cost out of the design. This would produce another round of design/prototype/ design review iterations.

Once the circuit design was agreed on, the project went to the CAD department for development of the printed circuit board. Circuit diagrams, component layout, and artwork were finalized in this stage, including additional back and forth iterations to resolve component placement problems or other issues that arose in taking the design from a "breadboard" to a finished design. Once the CAD department was finished with this stage of the work, there would be final engineering department design reviews, and a management review prior to release.

Finally, engineering would release the new design to manufacturing. Only now would the work of designing the manufacturing, QA, and automated testing processes begin. Preproduction staff would take the engineering documentation and build preproduction units for evaluation. These units would be built in small quantities, using the engineering documentation. (In some cases, engineering might let preproduction have documentation before release of the unit so they could begin work as soon as possible.) The result of testing the preproduction units almost inevitably surfaced problems, which would result in design changes to accommodate manufacturing requirements. Once these changes made it through the engineering cycle, the revised design would be released to manufacturing. In the meantime, production may have started with units incorporating the change by way of "cuts and jumpers" on the board, or component substitutions. Of course, there are real costs resulting from this way of doing things, but they were never measured.

This was, and still is in many cases, a typical situation in that it describes a new product development and product-introduction process that is segmented, full of opportunities for rework, sequential for the most part, and primarily focused on the engineering department. Other company functions do not play a major role, though they do have much expertise to offer. Even within engineering, the work is departmentalized between functions that operate somewhat independently.

BREAKING THE MOLD

The time has come to change the traditional methods and organization structure for new product introduction. The process should be reengineered based on individual company needs but should follow the model of integrated development we have outlined. A model process is described here that can be adapted to each company.

New product introduction is a critical success factor that must be executed quickly and with quality in mind for success in the marketplace. Ineffective product introductions may result in loss of business to competitors, loss of reputation in the marketplace, failure to realize planned cost reductions, reduced (or negative) profits, shortened product life cycles, premium freight and overtime charges, and a substantial amount of excess or obsolete inventory.

Companies that have organized product development into multifunctional teams assign a new product project to an existing team or create a new one. A team leader is designated to coordinate and facilitate the activities of the group. But the team leader is not solely responsible for the successful completion of the assigned project; the entire team is. Together they will create a formal work plan for each design project and manage to follow it. The team will normally consist of design and process engineers, and representatives from material planning, purchasing, manufacturing management, quality assurance, product management, and sales/marketing.

Although there may be a period of time in the beginning of the project when only the engineers are involved in formulating technical details of the design, the entire team is involved as soon as initial design work begins to produce results that can be reviewed within the group. As soon as a preliminary design concept is completed, intended methods of manufacture and required technology can be discussed. Shortly thereafter, a bill of material structure can be created for the material planning and purchasing representatives to work with to use in procuring long lead time items and in planning the introduction of the product into production. Marketing's assessment of potential sales volumes is also valuable at this stage of the planning process. Manufacturing will assess the effect on production facilities and begin planning for resource requirements, training, and facilities. Likewise, QA will be working on the need for testing, test facilities, training, and staffing. As pieces of the design are created, purchasing can begin working to secure material suppliers, and financial analysts can develop cost estimates.

If prototypes are to be created, all members of the team will participate in building and evaluating the prototypes. After an intial prototype meets with the approval of the team and a complete set of documentation is produced, a small number of preproduction units will be built in manufacturing facilities. This provides manufacturing, materials, and process engineers with early experience on the product and proves the manufacturability of the design. Units such as these are often used as demos at trade shows, or delivered to selected customers who may have helped to identify the need for the product and specified its performance characteristics.

Notice that in a cross-functional team setting, some things are quite different. The project leader has been replaced with a team leader and the overall success of a particular project is now the responsibility of the team as a whole. The team's activities are managed using a formal work plan, which all members have a hand in developing. Notice also that the design review meetings and management review meetings are gone from the process. Designs are created in an atmosphere where all functions are represented and are aware of the status of the design because they are working on it together. Management reviews are unnecessary because management communication is continuous throughout the process. Review meetings are not value-adding in this environment and were mostly a waste of time in the old process. Everyone knew who the real decision makers were and essentially had decisions dictated to them in the meetings. Now management relies on people knowing their job and doing it right—an essential for empowered, cross-functional teams to succeed.

Activities such as creation of bills of material, assessment of impact on manufacturing, training and equipment needs, testing and QA facilities, and creation of prototypes are performed as part of the design process, not as activities that occur separately and in a sequential manner after engineering releases a product design. In fact, there is no need for a formal release process anymore. When the team determines that the product is ready to go into production, the product just starts to be made and shipped. All of the functions that would have had to sign off on an engineering release are part of the team, and when the team's work is done the approvals are, by definition, achieved.

ENGINEERING CHANGE NOTICES

Does lack of a formal engineering release or engineering change notice indicate that there is no longer any need to record revision levels and historical configurations of products and parts? Certainly not. While the use of teams obviates the need for formal release review meetings and such groups as an engineering change control board, the documentation requirements and implementation decisions must still be dealt with. The team working on any particular design project must consider the following:

- Is there a genuine need for this change or new product concept?

- What will be the cost versus projected benefits?

- If a product is being modified or changed, what stage of its life cycle is it in? Mature products should have essentially no change activity.

- What interchangeability problems must be considered? Changes to form, fit, or function will affect compatibility with previous designs.

- What are the purchased part considerations?
  Projected costs
  Quoted lead time
  Existing material and capacity commitments with the supplier that will be affected
  Revision or purchase of vendor tooling

- What will be the cost of obsolete or scrap inventory resulting from a design change?

- By what date could existing material be used up?

- Does manufacturing currently have the capability to produce the newly designed or changed items?

- What are the training needs or needs for additional people or equipment?

- How does the design affect QA facilities, equipment, and staffing?

- For new designs, is manufacturing technology reliable and readily available?

- What changes will be required to existing manufacturing process and equipment layout?

- What are the requirements for new or revised production tooling?

- Which newly designed items should be made and which ones should be purchased?

- What will the new design cost to produce?

- Are there any required field retrofit or upgrade requirements?

- What are the projected needs for spare parts for field service?

- What changes are required for product instruction manuals and price lists?

Additionally, the documentation and information needs of the company cannot be ignored. The team must ensure that the status of work in process on a design is available to everyone in the company, preferably on real-time information systems. Design projects and changes to existing designs must still be identified with a numbering system that allows them to be documented and tracked. It is often important to know the design level of product currently being manufactured and the planned incorporation point of a new design. For traceability, liability, and government reporting purposes, it may also be critical to know what a product's configuration was at a certain revision level in the past. Without documentation and numbering of design levels, this information can be exceedingly difficult to find.

In the past, cumbersome paper engineering change control systems were used. The engineering change notice or similar document recorded all the necessary information about the design at that point in time and referenced revision levels incorporated as a result of the design work. This paper system was slow, prone to errors, and produced lots of hard-copy documentation that had to be stored or microfilmed eventually. Systems are now available that can accommodate electronic engineering change notices and integrate these with all the related product data to identify and link product drawings, material lists, manufacturing processes, and production records. Not only is the hard-copy documentation eliminated or sharply reduced, but there is integration with and instant accessibility to all the related product data.

At this point, it should be evident that there are a number of new approaches to engineering that are already in use in some companies, and which offer significant advantages. Designing for manufacturability, ease of assembly, quality, and reusability significantly reduce time and costs involved in bringing products to market. Simulation technologies continue to advance and offer additional time and cost saving advantages by reducing the need to physically test designs and production techniques. Finally, reengineering the product development process itself eliminates the cumbersome, manually intensive, sequential methods of working that caused so much time and effort to be wasted.

CHAPTER 13

The Technologies

COMPUTER-AIDED DESIGN/COMPUTER-AIDED MANUFACTURE (CAD/CAM)

Computer-aided design/computer-aided manufacture (CAD/CAM) is a generic name for computer-based tools used to assist both design engineering and manufacturing engineering activities. Distinguishing features are the use of interactive graphics, geometry modeling, and reuse, in a manufacturing engineering activity, of computer-based information generated upstream.

CAD/CAM and CAE (computer-aided engineering) are two of the most important systems in the product development environment. Although CAD/CAM is most often associated with mechanical engineering and CAE with electronic engineering, conceptually they are similar, and these acronyms are often used interchangeably. They both refer to the application of computers to the design engineering and manufacturing engineering processes of a product and therefore refer to the total product development process. The objective of their use is to increase the quality, flow, and use of engineering information throughout the activities of defining what the product is to be, and the processes that will be used to produce, use, and dispose of it.

The use of CAD/CAM in mechanical engineering activities illustrates many important features of computer systems used in the product development process. First, modeling the part in the computer provides information that is reused at later stages of the process.

Geometry modeling is the process of building a model (in the computer) that contains all the necessary information about the part's geometry. The model should be unique (so that the part will not be mistaken for another) and complete (it should contain all the geometry information required in later activities). Product modeling covers the process of building up a computer-based model containing all the necessary information on the part or product. This information includes attributes such as color and type of material, in addition to the geometry. Among the most important features of CAD/CAM is the potential it offers to reuse product and part information, and the associated computer-based model of the part, in several application areas, thus saving time and money.

The CAD/CAM concept also includes the use of a set of application programs to carry out specialized tasks in particular application areas. These include finite-element analysis, NC programming, and drafting. Engineering drawings can be built on the graphics screen and, if necessary, modified. Once a drawing is satisfactory, it can be automatically drawn on paper by a plotter. Another application that benefits from the use of CAD/CAM is simulation. A designer may investigate on the screen, and from a variety of viewpoints, how a mechanism will move and whether it will interfere with another part. As well as aiding the programming of NC machine tools such as milling machines, CAD/CAM can be used to program robots and quality-control machines. Tool loads, feeds, and speeds can be optimized. CAD/CAM also can be used to aid design of tools and the preparation of process plans. Programs can be used, for example, to determine the best shape for dies of forged parts.

CAD/CAM can enable more designs and products to be produced within a given time frame to meet customer demand for shorter product development cycles. It can be used for a significant amount of design work in the product development process and, hence, shorten the development cycle. CAD/CAM also can lead to an increase in the reuse of existing designs, thus reducing the cost of the design process. Used in conjunction with group technology, it can lead to a reduction in the number of parts that are needed to produce a wide variety of customized products. This reduction will, in turn, reduce process planning costs and lead to a reduction in manufacturing engineering and inventory costs. All these gains can be directed toward reaching corporate targets aimed at providing customer satisfaction.

In the past, with manual techniques, information on part data was transmitted from person to person on drawings. Manually produced drawings of typical mechanical parts do not always exactly reflect what the part is: they tend to be incomplete, ambiguous, and incorrect. The use of three-dimensional design and display of a part on a graphics screen allows the product developer to identify errors in the early design stages rather than in manufacturing, when major costs have already been incurred. Many of the analysis programs involve carrying out a large number of calculations that just would not be feasible by hand. Reuse of the same model of the part by different application programs reduces the time previously wasted in reproducing and modifying drawings.

COMPUTER-AIDED INDUSTRIAL DESIGN

Computer-aided industrial design is one of the newest computer-based design systems. It allows designers to model and evaluate product designs in three dimensions and to generate and describe the surfaces of a product with a high degree of accuracy. Through the use of shading, color, movement, and rotation, it allows designers to create photorealistic images and animation from the basic geometric design. The model thus designed can be used to communicate designs to other individuals in the product development cycle and even to customers. In response to feedback from these people the designer can rework the design until it is satisfactory.

COMPUTER-AIDED MANUFACTURING

Computer-aided manufacturing is the generic name for all computer-based systems used in manufacturing engineering activities. These include CAPP (computer-aided process planning), computer-aided tool and fixture design, NC (numerical control) programming, and PLC (programmable logic controller) programming.

COMPUTER-AIDED PROCESS PLANNING (CAPP)

Computer-aided process planning (CAPP) systems are computer-based systems used in the generation of process plans. Process plans describe the operations that a part must undergo. They define the sequence of production operations, specify tooling, detail speeds, feeds, and coolants, and define setup and run times. CAPP systems work with either a variant or a generative approach. In the variant approach, a new plan is created by modification and adaptation of an existing plan to meet the specific requirements of a new part. In the generative approach, predefined algorithms are used to generate the plan on the basis of the characteristics of the part.

COMPUTER-AIDED SOFTWARE ENGINEERING (CASE)

Computer-aided software engineering (CASE) products are methodologies and software systems used to support some or all phases of the software life cycle. CASE products can help (or perhaps force) analysts and programmers to develop more thoroughly documented programs and more easily maintainable systems. Their function is to automate all stages of the systems development life cycle—from analysis and design through documentation, programming, testing, implementation, and maintenance. The ideal set of CASE tools generates updated documentation as well as updated source and object code.

There are three basic types of CASE tools—those that are used in planning, analysis and design, and code-related activities. Planning tools are used in the development of enterprise models and IT strategies and plans. The long-term objective of CASE at this level is to automatically translate the business requirements and environment, as specified by the user of a computer system, into a working piece of software. This would represent the complete automation of the software development process. So far, the complete process can only be automated for very simple applications. However, CASE has already proved invaluable for separate parts of the process.

It is not easy to agree on a proper specification for an information system, translate this into separate, independently testable modules, and generate the code. At the front end of a project, CASE helps in achieving agreement about the precise specification for software, building a conceptual model of the total system, and then breaking this down into small manageable independent parts. Apart from the very visible activities of analysis, coding, and testing there are other, more administrative activities, for which CASE is useful. These include project management and control, quality and configuration management, and the production of useful and accurate documentation.

Analysis and design tools, such as process modeling tools and data modeling tools, support the analysis and design phases of the software life cycle. At the design and analysis stages of software development, CASE tools help eliminate errors that would otherwise not be found until much later in the process, at which time their elimination would be expensive in both time and money. Common use of CASE among a group of software developers leads to improved communication, documentation, project management, and configuration management.

Most CASE tools provide support for other analysis and design activities as well as for modeling. Diagramming tools are used to capture and record the overall system specifications. Prototyping tools facilitate the creation of models of systems so that end users can evaluate the output. Often CASE tools for producing data flow diagrams, data structure and entity relationship diagrams, and data dictionaries can be used independently of other modules. This type of software is of great benefit in modeling, since the amount of data generated by the modeling activity is all but impossible to handle by purely manual means.

Code-level tools generate code or analyze existing code. Analyzer and checker tools are used to ensure that the information systems function is developing the applications appropriate to an organization's objectives and in line with its resources. Code generator tools are used to generate source program code and documentation from specifications. Importer and exporter tools can be applied to software maintenance. They are used as interfaces between CASE tools, facilitating either the transfer of information among the products from various vendors or providing these products access to the information in one another's files. Reengineering tools can be applied to software mainte-nance. They include restructuring tools, reverse-engineering tools, and migration tools.

RAPID PROTOTYPING

Rapid prototyping, or desktop manufacturing (DTM), is used to pro-duce a three-dimensional prototype from a CAD model. The prototype can be in a variety of materials including investment casting wax, some ceramics, photosensitive polymers, PVC, and polycarbonates. Rapid prototyping technologies include selective laser sintering, ballistic par-ticle manufacturing, stereolithography, instant slice curing, and direct shell production casting.

The stereolithography process uses liquid resins that solidify when exposed to ultraviolet energy. A fine beam of laser-produced ultraviolet energy is focused onto the surface of a liquid resin. Using CAD data that represents the object to be built, mirrors deflect the ultraviolet beam to draw a layer of the object on the surface of the liquid resin. After a complete layer has been drawn, the result is a thin, solid slice of the object. The slice is then submerged under the resin so that it is covered by a thin layer of liquid. In the same way as the first, a second layer of the object is drawn. This process continues, layer by layer, until the solid object is complete.

In the past, the creation of a physical prototype was often expensive and led to long lead times. A DTM system can produce a prototype in a few hours compared to the days or weeks of conventional prototyping, thus decreasing the cost and time required to create a physical model of a design.

ELECTRONIC DATA INTERCHANGE

Electronic data interchange (EDI) is the exchange of documents and other paper information such as engineering drawings, receipt advices, purchase orders, and advance shipping notices between the computer in one company and the computer in another company. The information is transmitted across a telecommunications network in a standard format in which the various contents of the documents are arranged in a predescribed way. EDI is already used in many industries for documents such as purchase orders, which do not contain a lot of information but are numerous. EDI is beginning to be used to transfer engineering documents. These may come from a CAD system and tend to contain a lot of information and be less numerous.

The potential gains from use of EDI are clear. When a paper drawing is sent by post, it may take several days to arrive at a supplier's site. When it is sent electronically, it may require only minutes. This opens up possibilities for much closer cooperation between companies and their suppliers at the product development stage. There can be a real interactive partnership between engineers in the two companies.

VIRTUAL REALITY (VR)

Virtual reality (VR) is a computer-based technology that provides its users with a synthetic environment in which they have the impression of being in a real-world environment. To achieve this, current VR peripherals include head-mounted displays and electronic gloves. Another approach relies on cameras that film a person's movements and blend the pictures with images on a big screen.

Potential applications of VR in the product development process include "walking through" products, visual simulation of manufacturing and assembly processes, and training. Virtual reality is thought to have the potential to change the way things are designed by enabling engineers to more clearly see their creations before completing them.

OBJECT-ORIENTED TECHNOLOGY

An object-oriented database contains objects defined by an object-oriented data model that covers objects, attributes, constraints, and relationships. Each object is an instance of a class of similar objects with common characteristics. Associated with each class is a description of common methods and procedures for building and handling objects within that class. The data and the methods are stored together. This technique of storing both information describing objects and the methods or processes that work on the objects is known as encapsulation. Users can work with an object only through its methods. A message is sent to the object capsule, requesting that a particular encapsulated procedure be applied to the object.

New objects can be created from existing objects, inheriting all the characteristics of the existing object. Compared to relational databases, object-oriented databases offer new features of encapsulation, inheritance, and polymorphism—the ability to uniformly apply processes to a variety of objects.

Object-oriented database management systems store items as objects rather than as hierarchically associated records or rows in tables. New data types (classes) can be added without affecting existing structure or methods.

As the description of an object also includes a description of the process and relations between objects, object-oriented technology offers possibilities for artificial intelligence applications. Specific know-how can be stored with the object.

The object-oriented approach is attractive in the engineering environment where objects—such as a product, a part, a drawing, or a manual—are natural units of work. However, object-oriented database technology is still in its infancy. In view of the amount of time that was needed before database systems based on traditional models were available for widespread, everyday use, it is likely that object-oriented databases will play a significant role in the engineering environment only by the end of the 1990s.

Object-oriented programming languages (OOPLs) provide a way of integrating data definitions and processing rules into objects. Each object in an object-oriented programming system (OOPS) is a free-standing entity that can be combined with other objects to form a complete application.

To be considered object-oriented, a programming environment must support four behaviors—inheritance, encapsulation, information hiding, and polymorphism. Information hiding refers to an encapsulation in which some details are not visible. In object-oriented programming systems, objects are encapsulated, or encased, from each other and have meaning without having relationships with other objects, so an object-oriented application is easy to maintain and modify. Its objects can be replaced without interruption to the systems they compose.

Objects can be grouped into classes. Classes are object categories that specify the data and process definitions for a particular object type. Each object within a class is called an instance. Instances share common definitions.

Inheritance facilitates the reuse of previously defined objects by allowing objects to pass their attributes (methods and data definitions) to other objects. Thus, inheritance creates new objects out of old ones. Classes are grouped into class hierarchies to facilitate inheritance. At the top of the hierarchy are the parent classes; at the lower levels are classes called children. A parent can pass its attributes to its children. Children can have their own attributes and can inherit from children above them in the hierarchy.

Methods are invoked when parameters, or messages, are passed between objects during program execution. After a method has been invoked, a corresponding message is produced that alters the content of one or more objects in the system.

Object-oriented programming's inheritance and encapsulation features help systems evolve gracefully, thus reducing the cost of application maintenance.

FRAMEWORKS

Frameworks are primarily aimed at design workgroups—small groups of product developers working together and carrying out similar and related design tasks. A framework provides an overall computer environment, including data management functionality.

In a typical engineering workgroup, users work with several computer systems from different vendors, repeatedly use each system to carry out a given type of task, create, use, store, and share a lot of short-lifetime data that are in various formats, and transfer data frequently from one system to another. These characteristics imply there will be several different user interfaces to be used, processes will be treated differently in different systems, file structures will be different, models will be different, versions can easily get out of control, errors will be introduced during data exchange, and time will be lost during data transfer.

To overcome these problems, frameworks provide support for a variety of applications on workstations in a networked heterogeneous computer environment, a standardized user interface through which users can access any application from a workstation on the network, and application integration. Since design tasks are generally carried out in a well-defined sequence, the environment can be set up to provide automated sequencing of design applications, automatic start-up of sequential applications, start-up of specific applications on request, and so forth. Frameworks also provide management of user rights, access control (including controlled simultaneous access by several work-group members), and data conversion and communication. Since only a limited number of known applications are used, data conversion requirements can be predetermined. Data from one application can be automatically converted to the format required for the following application. Data from a completed task can be communicated to predetermined applications and groups of people.

Many of these functions, such as the management of user rights, version management and control, audit trails, data conversion and communication, multiple-access control, and sequenced applications are similar to the functions found in engineering data management (EDM) systems. Frameworks are mainly oriented to the use of these functions by development engineers working in a highly interactive workgroup environment. Unlike engineering data management systems, typically they do not address functions such as release management and product structure control. However, a particular framework product may also offer some of these functions.

ENGINEERING DATA MANAGEMENT (EDM)

Engineering data management (EDM) systems manage, organize, access, and control engineering data. Engineering data is defined as all the data related to a product and to the processes used to design, manufacture, and support the product. EDM systems provide access and security controls, maintain relationships among product data items, define rules that describe data flows and processes, and provide notification and messaging facilities. Much of this data will be created with computer-based systems such as CAD, CAM, and CAE. EDM systems also manage the flow of work through activities that create or use engineering data. They support techniques, such as concurrent engineering, that aim to improve engineering workflow.

EDM systems, sometimes referred to as product data management systems, or engineering information management systems, or product information management systems, provide improved management of the engineering process through better control of engineering data, of engineering activities, of engineering changes and of product configurations. They provide support for the activities of product teams and for product development approaches such as concurrent engineering. They can help reduce engineering costs by at least 10 percent, reduce the product development cycle by at least 20 percent, reduce engineering change-handling time by at least 30 percent, and reduce the number of engineering changes by at least 40 percent.

EDM systems help reduce the time to introduce new products, reduce the cost of developing new products, reduce the cost of new products, improve the quality of products and services, and have a strong effect on competitivity, market share, and revenues.

EDM systems treat engineering information as an important resource that is used by many functions in a company. They allow companies to get control of engineering information and to manage activities in several departments. In the long term, EDM systems will allow companies to get control of all their engineering information and manage the overall engineering process. These characteristics set them apart from systems such as CAD that aim to improve the productivity of individual tasks in one functional area.

Viewed as data processing systems, EDM systems go beyond individual application programs such as CAD and NC. Viewed as organizational tools, they go beyond individual approaches such as DFA (Design for Assembly) and project-management systems. EDM systems provide a backbone for the controlled flow of engineering information throughout the product life cycle. Other systems using engineering data, such as CAD, NC, process planning, MRP, and field service applications, will be integrated to this backbone.

KNOWLEDGE-BASED SYSTEMS

Knowledge-based systems (KBS) are systems that aim to allow the experience and knowledge of humans to be represented and used on a computer so as to increase people's decision-making ability.

Knowledge-based systems are used in a wide range of applications involving research, engineering, planning, configuration, scheduling, analysis, monitoring, control, diagnostic, maintenance, and prediction. They use the same type of process as humans to get to an answer but draw on a much wider range of knowledge and experience and are not susceptible to emotional influences, fatigue, and other human weaknesses. They can provide support in situations where time or money constraints would make it impossible or impractical to rely on human support. For example the knowledge and experience of plant operators, design staff, and line managers can be encapsulated in a KBS to be available for plant operators around the world every minute of the year.

In the product development function, a KBS can make available to young engineers the knowledge and experience of their more experienced colleagues to help them to get products to market faster and with better quality. Knowledge-based engineering systems with embedded manufacturing knowledge will speed up design work. Knowledge-based systems will be used within engineering data management systems for a variety of tasks such as looking for similar parts and information.

COMPUTER-INTEGRATED MANUFACTURING

Computer-integrated manufacturing (CIM) is the use of computer techniques to integrate all the activities in the product development and product production cycle. These activities encompass all functions necessary to translate customer needs into a final product. CIM starts with the development of a product concept that may exist in the marketing organization. It takes in product design and specification and extends through production into delivery and after-sales activities. Integration of these activities requires that accurate information be available when needed and in the format required by the person or group requesting the data. Data may come directly from the originating source or through an intermediate database.

CIM is applicable to any manufacturing organization. The technologies used to automate the various manufacturing activities, however, depend on the industry and the specific manufacturing process. Similarly, the technologies used for integration and communications are determined by automation technologies and geographic considerations.

The benefits of CIM are realized through automation and integration. Repetitive activities are fully automated, and creative activities are computer-assisted. The computer does the routine portion, leaving people free to do the creative part. Benefits are also achieved just by integration. Time wasted in expediting information and errors due to obsolete, inaccurate data is eliminated with integration.

As more manufacturing activities use automated equipment, however, manual integration becomes cumbersome. Manual transfer of information from one automated piece of equipment to another is error-prone, inefficient, and unwarranted. More problematic, the same data reside in multiple places and can be changed in these different places by different people. Reconciliation becomes nearly impossible. In unintegrated environments, it has been estimated that 40 percent of the effort for data collection, verification, and entry is for creating and verifying redundant data. CIM not only eliminates these problems but results in additional benefits that help meet customer requirements.

Understanding the application of the various technologies is essential for management to be able to clearly define a vision of the future product development process. During the development of a vision, everyone involved needs to know which tools can be used to achieve the goals of the company, and they need to have a level of understanding that provides confidence that the technology applies to their circumstances. This helps avoid the situation some companies have found themselves in, where the technologies chosen were either poorly understood or new and untested. In particular, management needs to be conversant with current technology, to control the engineers' tendency to want to experiment with new technologies that may not be sufficiently stable or predictable.

CHAPTER 14

The Importance of Engineering Information

DATA REQUIRED TO SUPPORT DESIGN EFFORTS

Creating a product design is an information-intensive process. Product specifications have been developed by marketing in conjunction with major customers and state the intended performance characteristics of the product. Beyond these performance characteristics, there will be a significant amount of data related to the technical design in terms of drawings and other product characteristics such as manufacturing process specifications. Without the appropriate levels of documentation available to all who participate in the design effort, miscommunication is likely, and needless iterations will be introduced into the development process to correct the resulting errors. What should the requirements be for an information system to support product development? How do you incorporate all the diverse needs of the various people involved?

The term "engineering data management" (EDM) implies that product development is carried out solely by engineers, which is contrary to the most current thinking on how the design process should be managed. Engineers work only with a small subset of the total product documentation and in a team setting need to share design data across all the functions in the company. Therefore, the EDM system should be able to accommodate data ranging from product performance specifications to geometric data, manufacturing

259

process specifications, change orders, design standards, reusability data, and field failure rates.

People in different functional areas across the company will see the requirements for the EDM system differently. Those who deal with large volumes of data will be looking for a system that can efficiently store and retrieve data. Archiving capability and features that support configuration management and change control will be important. Others in the product development chain will be looking for a system that will store the classification and coding required to support reusability. Still other individuals will be looking for capabilities that support product costing, including cost estimation efforts during the design phase.

These requirements are not necessarily contradictory and can be provided by one system or integrated set of systems. This does not mean that such a system is easily developed and implemented. It can be difficult to accommodate the wide range of users and the variety of data types that need to be included. Data can be in the form of text, graphics, very large or very small numbers, or mathematical formulas. Logical groupings of data will be in different formats, requiring flexible database configuration capabilities.

The users of such systems, including design engineers and manufacturing shop floor supervisors, will be performing a wide variety of functions. The data in the system must be accessable by all, in a format that is understandable and usable. Data security also needs to reflect the types of access permitted to specific users: some users need to create and store data, some modify the data, and others only need to view it. Management must be able to establish and change access privileges as projects and needs change. Additionally, managers will want to review the status of projects and produce reports. All in all, this is a diverse but not unusual set of requirements.

Accordingly, the data in the system will have a range of structures, just as the system has a range of functions and users. At the lowest levels, the data are represented by specific items that are maintained by particular functions and users, such as a drawing of a machined part that is maintained by an engineer. At the highest level, the data may represent a complete product, such as a laser printer. The users who are working at this highest level of detail will not be interested in the dimensions of the front panel of the printer, but those involved in technical functions will. The system therefore has to support different views of the product at various levels of detail. These different views of the product require the system to organize data in different sets and allow users to define sets appropriate for their purposes. The system will need to be able to associate sets for the same product to link specifications, geometry, and physical characteristics. In addition, there will be relationships maintained by the system to support configuration and version control.

As if the complexity of types of data and the relationships between different sets is not enough, data in the EDM system may be physically distributed across a number of sites and local processors. This distributed data must be accessible to all users across the company, regardless of location. To further complicate matters, some of the data required to support the design function may not be stored on the computer systems at all. As a result, paper documentation will need to be catalogued so that rapid access to its physical location can be achieved. Long-term, hard-copy documentation should be captured on the EDM system.

In a distributed computing environment, the computer systems used in separate physical locations may be different. In all environments, the underlying file structures may differ between applications. Users will not want to be bothered with the details of translating data back and forth between applications that need to communicate, so the systems must have translation capability. In an ideal environment, all systems would use a common database management system. This would eliminate most of the need for data-translation capabilities and would make inquiries easier from any part of the system. Use of a common database has an additional benefit in that it supports the flexibility to modify and enhance the systems to meet changing needs. As technology changes, the requirements for an EDM system will change also. Overall, the systems must be designed to respond quickly to a wide range of requirements and an environment that can change very rapidly. Although standards are continually being developed for such things as exchange of graphical information, the speed of change quickly renders standards obsolete. Flexibility of the underlying infrastructure of EDM systems is therefore crucial.

INCLUDE THE MANUFACTURING DEPARTMENT

In a traditional design environment, engineering data are strictly the province of the engineering department. Manufacturing personnel and other company functions have to request paper drawings from engineering and wait for the request to be filled. In a more modern environment where product-development functions are being performed simultaneously, everyone needs immediate access to product documentation. While the design of the paper-handling subassembly for our fictional laser printer is being finalized by the engineers, finance is working on a preliminary cost and manufacturing is developing the process for producing it. All those involved are accessing the same product documentation. There is no reason for engineering to be the sole channel of access to product data. Only certain users need to modify data, but all should be able to inquire as necessary, with immediate access.

In our vision of an integrated, simultaneous development environment, product concept development proceeds in parallel with research into applicable technologies, and engineers design the segments of the product that can be completed as soon as information and technology become available. Automated engineering tools help to optimize designs for cost and reliability. Previous designs that fit the new application are reused or modified, reducing engineering time. Simulation and prototyping occur during engineering design activity and replace most physical prototyping.

As design work progresses, development begins on the manufacturing process. All major functional areas participate in the design efforts from the inception of the project, forming a team. The team may be physically located in one location, or it may convene electronically. In either case, integrated computer systems support the technical activities and sharing of information among the team, alerting members when data are available for their role in the process. This facilitates simultaneous execution of many tasks that would otherwise wait for a batch of information from the previous function before beginning to work. Engineering software and technical tools are integrated with (or accessible through) business information systems, providing full documentation and status of the project to all team members. This high level of integration provides synergy and discipline, which combine to prevent the costly and time-consuming design iterations that are common in more traditional and sequential environments. Without integrated companywide information systems supporting the process, little of this would be practical.

PROCESS DEFINITION AND CONTROL

Manufacturing process information is an integral part of product documentation, and its availability to those developing product designs is important. Process documentation allows the product designer to understand the current capabilities of the manufacturing plant, which aids the engineer in creating a design that can be produced in the existing facilities.

To ensure that reusability and manufacturability are supported, process documentation needs to be as complete and detailed as possible. Gone are the days when a manufacturing process briefly stated the major steps and work centers, referencing blueprints for dimensions and tolerances. Operation descriptions cannot say, "Machine per blueprint." Engineers must be able to display views of a manufactured item on their workstation and then display the manufacturing process steps in detail. This information aids the engineer in designing for manufacturability and provides a basis for costing similar designs to be derived from existing ones.

For these reasons, process documentation needs to include engineered time standards that have been validated by actual experience in production facilities. Test specifications and methods must also be included to constitute a complete manufacturing process. Finally, manufacturing processes need to be categorized to support reusability. Categorization may be by geometry, description, the manufacturing equipment the item is produced on, or other descriptors such as a family classification or item type coding scheme.

AN EXAMPLE OF PROGRESS AT PITNEY BOWES

In the spring of 1993, the Pitney Bowes Company began installation of a Unix-based client-server system that will be used primarily to manage engineering and manufacturing product data across multiple sites and departments. The servers will store engineering designs and documentation and will also include manufacturing process data. All users on the system will be able to access this data, no matter where they are physically located and without regard to which server the data being requested is from. A fiber optic network will link five geographically separate sites.

By the end of 1993, the system was fully implemented and used to replace a more traditional, paper-based method of product development. Pitney Bowes expects to cut product development time in half as a result of changes made possible and supported by the system. The system's database of product drawings and other documentation will facilitate improvements in product quality and time to market by providing a single consistent set of data that both engineering and manufacturing can use simultaneously, arising from the ability to view the data electronically.

It typically takes a number of weeks just to collect all the product information necessary to document a design, get the paper drawings to the necessary people, have them review it, and respond with changes and corrections. Now a designer can put a product concept together on the system, have all the interested parties view it electronically and make comments or corrections, and then download the product specifications to a model shop for creation of a prototype. Early results have reduced tooling development times from five or six weeks to two or three days.

Other benefits of the system include a reduction in the time manufacturing personnel spend chasing engineers for answers to questions on specific parts and elimination of mistakes made when engineering and manufacturing are working to different versions of a drawing. In the future, marketing will also be able to access the system and input data on customer demands, allowing products that correspond closely to current customer needs to be developed quickly.

Although the company is moving in the right direction with this product data-management system, their approach is typical of many companies that are doing much the same thing. These companies are developing islands of automation that are helpful but will not lift them past their competitors in terms of time-to-market. At best they will be able to maintain parity and not lose ground against the competition. What is needed is a greater effort to break the paradigm of the separation of engineering and manufacturing and design products with cross-functional teams. The product data-management system will move this company closer to adopting the new model of product development and therefore can be seen as an enabling technology. But management must still be the force that breaks the traditional organizational boundaries when it finally realizes the immense advantages inherent in the concept of multifunctional design teams.

RESOURCE IMPLICATIONS

In an engineering department without EDM systems, product documentation still relies on paper for the most part. CAD systems may be in use but are used for generation of paper drawings or microfilm. Implementation of links to business systems and the categorization of designs have not yet been achieved.

In companies that still rely on hard-copy drawings for the majority of their product development activity, many people are employed to manage the library of product documentation. Typically, there are numerous old drawings that were produced before CAD systems came into use, and these must be reproduced on the blueprint machine. CAD-produced drawings are still stored in hard-copy files and may be reproduced on copy machines or redrawn by the CAD system if the data files are available. Requesting a drawing in this type of environment is usually a process of submitting a request to the document-control function within the engineering department and waiting anywhere from a number of hours to a day or more for a copy of the requested document. It is labor intensive, and more important, it is very slow. In many companies, it is not uncommon to have a group of people employed full-time just to manage the documentation and to respond to the requests for copies of drawings that are required in the normal course of business.

In contrast, companies that have implemented EDM systems with graphic representation capabilities are enjoying a number of benefits. Product documentation is available in real time at any of the graphics-capable workstations throughout the company. There is no waiting other than the response time for the system to respond. Paper drawings can still be produced where necessary, but they do not require a staff of document librarians to maintain and produce them. Those who are unsure of which items they want to see can browse through the catalog of documentation by category (such as geometry) to identify items they want to view or use. Of course, somebody still has to enter and maintain the drawings and the catalog on the system, but this is done by the engineers themselves as designs are created or changed.

USE OF IMAGING

As technical progress continues to make large amounts of data storage less costly, imaging is becoming more popular as companies adapt it to replace paper records. Manufacturers are using imaging as a tool for routing drawings and other documentation between members of design teams. Typical time reductions in the processing of product drawings have been from days and weeks down to hours. Imaging is increasingly being seen as a method for improving document control and removing non–value-adding steps from the process.

A good example of the use of imaging was recently reported by the Boeing Company's commercial airplane group. An imaging system reduced the flow time of engineering changes by up to 90 percent. The amount of time engineers and others waited to see important data related to the process was also cut by 80 percent. This system shows how advanced technology that was not cost-effective ten years ago is now employed to advantage as hardware costs have fallen. The hardware storing the images uses more than 140 optical discs, includes more than 3 million graphic images, and has more than a terabyte of data storage.

The images on this graphic documentation system were created on

Boeing's CAD system and transferred electronically. In companies still operating in traditional environments with minimal EDM support, CAD images would have been transferred to microfilm and mounted on aperture cards. At Boeing, such lack of automated support used to require a staff of 100 people to maintain the aperture cards. Now technical drawings, schematics, and parts lists are electronically transmitted from the CAD system to the imaging system and company business systems. On-line access is avilable to more than 120,000 pages of drawings and other product documentation. Human resources are no longer required to maintain the manual aperture cards that have been made obsolete, and access to data has been improved exponentially. It isn't hard to estimate the cost saving potential of the imaging technology, not to mention the real benefits of reducing the time to process and release drawings by a reported 800 percent.

THE CURRENT STATE OF EDM USAGE

Despite the fact that computer support and automation is widely available and being implemented in numerous companies, most of the companies using computer automation are doing a poor job of applying it to the real problems of competition and time to market. Despite all the potential, information systems still play a minor role in most companies in speeding product development time. Computers are used to automate pieces of the design and manufacturing process, but the approach is fragmented at best.

The most frequent mistake that is made is to use computers and automation to perpetuate the old way of doing things. A primary example is the widespread use of CAD systems to create and store product designs. The CAD system is typically owned and operated by an engineering organization, with no integration to companywide information systems. Data stored in the CAD system are redundant with data stored in manufacturing and accounting systems. Access from areas outside of engineering is usually not possible or not allowed. Speed of access to product design documentation is generally slow.

Unfortunately, speed is more of a differentiating factor now than just a few years ago and continues to increase in importance. Xerox learned the hard way that product development time is crucial. Twenty years ago, Xerox owned the market for plain paper copiers; ten years later, their market share had plummeted to half of its former level, in large part because Japanese manufacturers had product development cycles that were less than half of Xerox's. The same situation exists in automobile manufacturing. Some U.S. car makers still take nearly five years to produce a new vehicle design, as compared to the three years it typically takes a Japanese manufacturer to produce a new car. Interestingly, Japanese electronics and automobile manufacturers employ less total technology than their U.S. counterparts but receive far greater benefit by avoiding the islands of automation common in the United States and investing in integrated systems.

Alarmingly, U.S. companies don't seem to be learning fast enough. Xerox, Chrysler, and others have recognized and corrected many of their mistakes, but the vast majority are ignoring integrated electronic support for product development as a way to reduce cycle time. A recent survey reported that only 20 percent of large U.S. companies will make significant investments in technology to support engineering and R&D. In the largest U.S. manufacturing firms, most are still manually entering product changes into production systems from CAD and other product development systems. This is very slow and has been proven to introduce errors. No wonder U.S. product development is slower than that of some of our foreign competitors. The saddest commentary on the situation is that we do not lack the technology, only the insight and the drive to organize for it and implement it.

ASSESSING DATA MANAGEMENT IN YOUR COMPANY

A useful engineering or product data-management system must be based on a clear understanding of how information *should* be used within the product development cycle, not how it may currently be used. The intention is not to duplicate the information flow that was used before the automated systems became available, as this will merely automate processes that are not efficient and ignore the integration requirements of the new development process.

To assess the current status of product data management in your company, it is necessary to investigate the way that engineering information is used by engineers, by the rest of the company, and by vendors. After this information is gathered, the systems that are in place to support EDM should be inventoried along with their current capabilities. It will also be useful to know how much product documentation is currently stored electronically and is accessible throughout the company. If there is a department or function dedicated to managing the clerical aspects of documentation maintenance, it will be useful to know how many people are engaged in these activities on a full-time basis. For a more detailed assessment that will indicate where improvement opportunities may lie, refer to the "Product Development" section of the checklist contained in Chapter 7.

ACCURACY IS ESSENTIAL

Although computerized data is universally recognized to be useless or even dangerous if it is inaccurate, many systems in use today have serious flaws in some of their data. The assumption is often made that because people are using the systems on a daily basis that the data accuracy must be sufficiently good. What is more often the case is that people are "working around" areas where they know of inaccurate or out-of-date information in the systems. Even worse, data accuracy is not formally measured or assessed in the majority of installations.

An example from recent experience illustrates inaccuracy and the sometimes costly extra work it spawns. At a generally well-managed food plant that is a division of a large, well-known company, a project was undertaken to reduce changeover time in a section of the plant where the products are cooked. The changeover required clean-out of the cooking vessels and associated piping when changing from one type of product to another. A documented manufacturing process existed for this part of the operation, explaining in detail how to perform the changeover.

As is customary in this type of project, a videotape of the process was made while one of the employees performed the procedure.

Additional employees who also performed the same job on different shifts were interviewed to discuss how they did the job and any suggestions they had for improvement. Each person's particular method of performing the changeover was documented and compared to the written procedure. Interestingly, none of the people doing this job was following the written procedure, which was deemed to be inaccurate. So there were at least three different methods of performing the clean-out, and none conformed to the formally documented manufacturing process. After further discussion and investigation, it was determined that *none* of the methods was the best way to do the job, and a new method that incorporated the best practices available was developed and implemented. The new method reduced the changeover time by half and identified additional areas with potential to further reduce cost.

Not only is process data accuracy important, but the data must be validated by checking documented methods against actual use and known best practices. Storing an incorrect process in the manufacturing system could lead new product development staff to make incorrect assumptions when developing a similar product in the future, which could generate unnecessary costs and cause delay of product introduction.

FORMAT STANDARDIZATION

Standardized formats for documentation may seem to be an obvious requirement to support data accuracy in product data management systems but are often ignored or circumvented in practice. Standard formats make it easier to pick out errors in data stored in the system and simplify the process of entering the data in the system in the first place. A standard format for documentation serves to ensure that all the necessary information gets developed and recorded quickly and accurately. It also reduces the effort to maintain documentation and helps to describe manufacturing operations more clearly, which can reduce the occurrence of errors on the shop floor.

Who Should Be Responsible for Data?

In an environment where there are many users of the data that is stored in the system, and a number of these people need to be able to change or otherwise modify what is stored in the system, there is almost always a question as to who is responsible for the completeness and accuracy of what has been entered. Generally, those responsible for creation of data entered into the system should be responsible for accuracy. They have a clear stake in accuracy and continued maintenance because they must use the data in their daily activities. If a number of people make transactions that can change data, it would be best to have the system log the transactions by the access code of the person making the transaction. If it is later found that errors have been introduced, a look at the transaction log will identify the culprit and subject the person responsible to sufficient embarrassment to help prevent future carelessness.

When design teams have been organized and given the responsibility to document their own output on the system, it may be preferable to designate one person on the team to be responsible for maintaining the information generated by the team. The team members still "own" their data and each has a stake in accuracy, but one person is clearly responsible. This reduces the number of opportunities to introduce errors by reducing the number of people who can make changes. In this case, there will be little or no need for transaction logging and investigations to determine the source of errors.

Clear responsibility equals quality of data. The general rule of thumb here is that where transaction capability is limited to a small number of people who are clearly designated as authorized to maintain specific types of documentation, errors will be rare and data will be highly accurate. This promotes confidence among all users of the system that the data is accurate and can be relied on. Less time will be wasted checking to see if system information is up to date and accurate or in correcting it and looking for causes of errors.

Accuracy is supported by continuous assessment of the completeness of data by users in their daily interaction with the system, by standardization of format, and by assignment of clear responsibility. All of these activities to support accuracy have the added benefit of reducing the time required to enter and maintain product documentation and allowing product development to proceed without delays caused by inaccuracy or lack of confidence in the data.

Procedures

Good procedures for creation and maintenance of data are invaluable in supporting data accuracy and minimizing the time actually spent maintaining documentation. Procedures help to ensure that standards are adhered to and that routine tasks are done the same way every time, with consistently high quality. Such things as coding and classification schemes are part of established design standards and can materially affect the time required to produce future designs if applied incorrectly. Procedures should therefore be embedded in system user interfaces wherever possible, to force adherence to standards and to minimize the reliance on paper procedures or the user's memory.

Embedded procedures normally include logic checks to validate that data being entered are correct or at least within predetermined ranges when there can be a number of correct choices. An example could be logic in a data-entry program to check that codes entered for classification purposes make sense. If we are producing bicycles and someone enters a material classification code for the handle bars indicating that the material is butyl rubber, the system should reject that entry as invalid based on other data in the system that will indicate that a part having this structure type must be made out of metal.

The user interface to the system should also be designed to require those persons who enter data to follow the prescribed sequence of events that is outlined in the procedure. In most cases, a procedure will prescribe a preferred sequence for performing a function, and too much flexibility in a data-entry program might allow undesirable results due to the sequence that data is entered in. In our previous example, entering the material type too soon, possibly before a part geometry or structure type code, could allow entry of an incorrect material type. The system would not have the information to determine that a butyl rubber material cannot be used to make handle bars. Other examples of systems that include procedural disciplines are all around us, but the primary thrust of all of them is the same: to ensure that data are accurate and complete and that standards (in this case, design standards) are adhered to.

Conclusion

In the 1980s, industry leaders reduced manufacturing time and costs, while increasing quality. In the 1990s all other companies are either following in the path of the leading companies or closing their doors. The massive level of corporate restructuring and cost reduction that has been taking place indicates that a large number of companies recognize that competition is impossible at previously acceptable levels of quality, lead time, and cost. The performance base line for world-class competition has been raised.

While those who failed to recognize and react to the changes taking place in the 1980s are now working to catch up, the present leaders have already chosen a new direction and they are executing a strategy that will preserve their leadership. Product development is already producing major competitive challenges in a number of industries and recognition is growing that this area will be the next competitive battleground. In some industries, the followers are already struggling to duplicate what the leaders are doing. Companies such as General Motors and Next Computer illustrate what can happen to those who do not recognize the challenge and respond quickly. Others, such as Hewlett-Packard and Toshiba, already understand the management issues, techniques, and technologies of the new competitive model, and are applying them at the expense of other companies' market share.

Product development capability is increasingly being utilized as part of a competitive strategy emphasizing greater understanding of customer desires and requirements, and achieving satisfaction of those requirements before competitors can do so. Companies who intend to lead and dominate markets in the coming years have already developed many of the capabilities we have identified in *Competing by Design*. They are actively working to continue to develop new capabilities and to refine those already in place.

What are the prospects for your company? If you intend to lead, you may already be late getting started. If you want to wait and see, you will be a follower. If you wait too long, you may be unable to stay in business. Recognizing that the bases of competition are shifting and that product development is playing an increasingly strategic role, it is time to take action.

Begin by assessing the opportunities for creating value and market advantage, listening to the voice of the customer. Make sure that the techniques and technologies we have discussed are well understood by executive management. Success will depend heavily on their vision and leadership. Take time to understand current capabilities, and establish performance metrics to measure progress. Establish cross-functional product development teams, and consider reorganization into product-line-oriented business units. Develop business strategies based on the voice of the customer. Recognizing the role of product development in supporting the business strategy, develop a vision for product development and plans to achieve that vision. Implement the plans using pilot programs to prove concepts, techniques, and technologies.

We have turned the corner into a new era of competition, one that is already driving change in the way we develop products. We have written about strategy, techniques, and technology, but our purpose in doing so has been solely to provide information that management can use in taking control of the product development process to compete more effectively. To accomplish this objective will require a clear vision, and active leadership. We have told you what has been proven to work in practice, and how to implement it. Now it is time to get started.

Index

ABB, 85
ABC, *see* Activity-based costing
Accounting, product life-cycle, 99, 132–33
  see also Traditional cost accounting
Activity-based costing (ABC), 98–99, 132, 155–56
Administration department, 65–66
Aerospace company, 15–18
Allied Signal, 85
Apple Computer, 5, 39
Appraisal costs, 131–32
Architectures, improvement project clarifying, 205
As-is situation, *see* Current situation
Ashton-Tate, 219
AT&T, 36
Auditors, 63
Automobile industry
  improvement in, 11–15, 145–47, 148, 150
  product development in, 22, 34, 268

Ballistic particle manufacturing, 250
Benchmarking, 131
  for awareness, 222
  future product development organization performance and, 97
  future product development organizations using, 99
  mechanical engineering corporation having, 9–10
  for product development process change, 226
BET (break-even time), 94
Black & Decker, 81
Boeing, 16, 100, 102, 266–67
Bottom-up model, 195–96

BPR, *see* Business-process reengineering
BUs, *see* Business units
Business benefits, improvement project clarifying, 202–4
Business objectives
  in future situation, 201–2, 205
  for improvement project, 223
Business-oriented approach, to improvement project, 194–95
Business process reengineering (BPR), 99
Business strategy, product development integrating, 33–36
Business units (BUs), 81–85, 87–88, 91, 92, 94, 185–86

CAD, *see* Computer-aided design
CAD/CAM, *see* Computer-aided design/computer-aided manufacture
CAD framework initiative (CFI), 44
CAE, *see* Computer-aided engineering
CALS, *see* Computer-aided acquisition and logistics support
CAM, *see* Computer-aided manufacturing
Cannondale bicycles, 22
Canon Ltd., 39
Capacity, of manufacturing and engineering, 156
CAPP, *see* Computer-aided process planning
CASE, *see* Computer-aided software engineering
CAT, *see* Computer-aided test
CFI, *see* CAD framework initiative
Change, *see under* Improvement
Chemical industry, 124
Children, in object-oriented programming, 253

About the Authors

Craig Erhorn

Craig Erhorn is a consultant working for the management consulting division of "big six" accounting firm Coopers & Lybrand in New York. He has more than twenty years' experience designing, implementing, and using manufacturing and engineering systems in a broad range of industries. He has assisted a number of former employers and clients with improvement and management of their product development process, and has hands-on experience developing and introducing new products in manufacturing industries.

Craig holds a B.A. degree from Ohio Wesleyan University, and an M.B.A. from the University of Connecticut. He has held management positions in manufacturing operations and information systems prior to becoming a consultant, and was responsible for controlling introduction of new products into manufacturing as well as working on new product development teams. Mr. Erhorn is a member of the American Production and Inventory Control Society (APICS) and is the author of a number of articles and book chapters dealing with manufacturing systems.

John Stark

John Stark is an independent management consultant based in Geneva, Switzerland. He has helped leading engineering and manufacturing companies in Europe, North America, and the Far East gain

competitive advantage by improving product development performance.

John holds B.Sc. and Ph.D. degrees from Imperial College, London,
England. He has worked in engineering and manufacturing environments for more than twenty years. Dr. Stark is a member of the
Institute of Directors (UK), AIAA, CASA/SME, and SAE (U.S.), and
the Swiss Computes Graphics Association. He is also the author of a
number of previous publications dealing with use of CAD and EDM,
and the improvement of engineering productivity. He is the editor of
the "Engineering Data Management Newsletter" and the "Effective
Engineering Management Newsletter."

Lightning Source UK Ltd.
Milton Keynes UK
UKOW031549020513

210114UK00001B/60/P